T0304575

Police Leadership as Practice

Police Leadership as Practice applies a leadership-as-practice approach (emphasising leader-employee relationships) to law enforcement. This book provides a progressive and collaborative leadership text for students of law enforcement, as well as insights into leadership dynamics in all organisations for students and researchers of business and management.

The police leadership-as-practice perspective provides a holistic understanding of leadership in the police, identifying factors that inhibit and promote learning. It refers to four main components as dynamic and continuously evolving processes:

- Strategies: social mission and organisation, along with strategies as practice
- Community: organisational and police culture, identity and belonging, community of practice and competencies
- Participation: sense-making and discretion; power and politics
- Activities: learning as practice, change and change management as practice

Practical and enriched with case studies, examples and best practice, the textbook is also rigorously research based. Authored by a professor of business and management with specialist knowledge in police leadership, it brings the cutting edge of leadership thinking to the practicalities of policing. It is essential reading for those engaged with policing, leadership roles, and management.

Cathrine Filstad is Professor at Kristiania University College, Department of Leadership and Organizational Behaviour, and at the Police University College, Department of Police Leadership Education, Norway. She received her PhD in Organizational Learning and Leadership in 2003 from Aarhus School of Business, Denmark.

"Unlike other contributions to the police leadership literature, which divorce the leader from the leadership they catalyse, Filstad's book embraces the whole in recognising police leadership *is* practice. Drawing on an extensive analysis and developing a framework to guide the reader, Filstad's book is both thoughtful and thought provoking. Those interested in better understanding the messy realities, paradoxes, and tensions in contemporary police leadership will find much in this book to enjoy."

Adjunct Professor Victoria Herrington, *Australian Institute of Police Management, Australia*

"*Police Leadership as Practice* represents an important contribution to the scholarship of police leadership. Practitioners and academics alike will find much value in this comprehensive, accessible and engaging account of the complex dynamics of contemporary police leadership. Its synthesis of literature and empirical data provides an excellent foundation for understanding police leadership as a collective rather than individual practice."

Dr Tom Cockcroft, *Leeds Beckett University, UK*

"This research-based and insightful book shows us why a practice perspective is vital for understanding the complexity of contemporary police leadership, as well as leadership as a collective effort. *Police Leadership as Practice* examines the how and why of police leaders' practice. Finally, Cathrine Filstad's important book is essential for challenging the individual leader perspective."

Professor Ulrika Haake, *Umeå Universitet, Sweden*

"From a leadership-as-practice perspective, Filstad skilfully identifies the complexity of leadership and the multiple factors that shape and determine its effectiveness. An accessible read for leaders and those who aspire to leadership."

Professor Jenny Fleming, *University of Southampton, UK*

Police Leadership as Practice

Cathrine Filstad

Routledge
Taylor & Francis Group

LONDON AND NEW YORK

Cover image: Getty Images

First published 2022
by Routledge
4 Park Square, Milton Park, Abingdon, Oxon OX14 4RN

and by Routledge
605 Third Avenue, New York, NY 10158

Routledge is an imprint of the Taylor & Francis Group, an informa business

British Library Cataloguing-in-Publication Data
A catalogue record for this book is available from the British Library

Library of Congress Cataloging-in-Publication Data
Names: Filstad, Cathrine, 1963- author.
Title: Police leadership as practice / Cathrine Filstad.
Description: 1 Edition. | New York, NY : Routledge, 2022. | Includes bibliographical references and index.
Identifiers: LCCN 2021041213 (print) | LCCN 2021041214 (ebook) |
ISBN 9781032123295 (hardback) | ISBN 9781032123288 (paperback) |
ISBN 9781003224105 (ebook)
Subjects: LCSH: Police. | Law enforcement. | Leadership. | Organizational learning.
Classification: LCC HV7921 .F495 2022 (print) | LCC HV7921 (ebook) |
DDC 363.2--dc23/eng/20211027
LC record available at https://lccn.loc.gov/2021041213
LC ebook record available at https://lccn.loc.gov/2021041214

ISBN: 978-1-032-12329-5 (hbk)
ISBN: 978-1-032-12328-8 (pbk)
ISBN: 978-1-003-22410-5 (ebk)

DOI: 10.4324/9781003224105

Typeset in Bembo
by Taylor & Francis Books

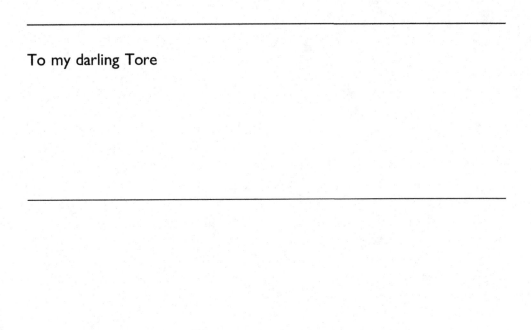

To my darling Tore

Contents

Illustrations

Figures

Tables

Introduction

This book is about police leadership as practice and approaches the topic from the leadership-as-practice perspective (Carroll, Levy & Richmond, 2008; Crevani & Endrissat, 2016; Raelin, 2016). This means understanding police leadership as a collective practice of relationships between leaders and their subordinates and eschewing the one-sided focus that the leadership literature often directs at the individual leader when describing leadership (Uhl-bien, Marion, & McKelvey, 2007; Mintzberg, 2009; Tengblad, 2012; Alvesson, 2016). The leadership-as-practice approach is concerned with what influences and shapes leadership practice(s), so it addresses both the bureaucratic-structural and the operational-cultural contexts of police leadership.

The book aims to demonstrate why a practice perspective is necessary for understanding the complexity of contemporary police leadership in a highly scrutinised ever-changing environment (Davis & Silvestri, 2020), and what promotes and inhibits police leaders from developing robust, knowledge-based leadership practices. This book contributes to the field of study by researching what police leaders do and how they exercise leadership, as well as by reflecting on and discussing why police leaders practise the way they do and the factors that shape their leadership practices.

This book is critical of many normative formulas for leadership, and the academic leadership models prescribing what leaders (and police leaders in particular) should do, and instead studies what they actually do.[1] The studies of what leaders do must include an explanation of why they do so. This is why police leadership practices should be considered within characteristic police culture(s), organisation-wide strategies and performance objectives, organisational structures and hierarchies, and political factors and the social mission.

Leadership as practice provides a perspective that, in my opinion, takes into consideration the complexity of leadership practices. This perspective argues that the conventional leadership literature does not accept that leadership cannot be limited to a leader's personality traits and leadership style, simply because leadership is not about the individual leader per se. Instead, it should be understood through the social relationships between the leader(s) and their subordinates and through the characteristic features of collective practice. The professions where leadership is exercised, the situational context (and hence the tasks to be performed), and the structural and cultural conditions that promote or inhibit leadership have all been given little attention in the traditional leadership literature.

Police Leadership as Practice examines what police leaders do, how they practise, why they practise the way they do, and what the characteristic features of leadership practice

DOI: 10.4324/9781003224105-1

are. The interaction between the leader and the participants, and the ways they continuously influence one another, are also equally important. Professional, relational, collective, dynamic, cultural, structural, and, last but not least, informal spheres (including informal leaders) are the domains in which the leadership-as-practice perspective provides greater knowledge about police leadership. This perspective does not apply only to police leadership but is relevant for all types of organisations. Allow me to briefly explain why the leadership-as-practice perspective contributes to a better understanding of leadership.

Leadership as practice is concerned with the gap between the theories prescribing what leaders should do and the things they actually do, as well as why leaders do not follow the formula for good leadership. Leadership as practice turns attention to leadership practices rather than focusing on an individual leader. Therefore, the leadership practices are what should be considered good, average or bad, not the leaders themselves. In other words, leaders are only as good (or bad) as the leadership practices they are responsible for. Leadership does not limit itself to what leaders do in practice but is also about what leaders and their subordinates think and how they act as a collective within the framework of leadership practices. This understanding of leadership integrates the relational and the collective, the formal and informal, and the dynamic and evolving factors of leadership practices. Leadership as practice directs attention to the dynamics where leadership includes all participants in its practices. The required competencies of the participants are adapted to various situations and work tasks that leadership practices are responsible for. This perspective does not provide instructions for completing the work tasks and therefore does not prescribe a particular form of leadership suitable for completing these tasks. This is why police leadership must not be limited to a unanimously accepted normative ideal but should instead be understood as a collection of leadership practices that also includes the knowledge of why police leaders act the way they do. For example, a police officer may still perform their duties well despite the leader, and vice versa. In any case, we need to study leadership practices to find possible reasons for the way police leaders act.

Leadership as practice includes both the features that characterise practices and the reasons why participants practise the way they do. Why can leadership, for example, be centred around the social mission, organisational culture and bureaucratic structure, and why is leadership exercised in a certain way locally, that is, in operations, geographical units, investigations and intelligence, crime prevention, administration, senior management, etc.? Both a particular police leader and police leadership as a whole could exercise police leadership differently or in the same way. There are also a number of factors that both promote and inhibit police leadership in practice and therefore give leadership practices different characteristic features.

This is a research-based book, which aims to discuss and reflect on police leadership as practice on the basis of research on police leadership and the Norwegian Community Policing Reform. There are in particular three studies I refer to throughout the book. The first one is a collection of interviews with and observations of 27 police leaders in 2016, which I refer to as "the 2016 study". The second includes two surveys conducted in the autumn of 2018; I call them "the 2018 survey". The third one consists of my own field studies that initially took two weeks in 2018, and then continued for four months in the autumn of 2019 in the same police district (and involving many of the same informants). These studies are referred to as "the 2019 field studies".[2] I have also included relevant data from several master theses on police research that I supervised during that period.

The aim is to invite the leader into the police leadership-as-practice perspective and prove that a police leader cannot be disconnected from the practice they are leading, which is often the case in police leadership literature, but also in leadership literature in general. Police leadership is less about ideal combinations of the leader's personality traits, personal style, leadership style and leadership models, and more about mastery, learning, experience, reflection, and even luck. When it comes to police leadership, the leader and their subordinates collectively influence practice, and at the same time police leadership is influenced *by* practice. Developing a practice is just as much about organisational structure(s), police culture(s), employees, work tasks, knowing, competencies, and resources, as it is about developing an individual police leader.

It does not come as a surprise for many police leaders that there is no perfect formula for police leadership, and they (along with the leaders in other organisations) have experienced this for a long time. Of course, this does not mean they do not see value in leadership education and training, or what many police leaders describe as professional skills upgrading. Such professional development can also be associated with a common language for leadership, safety, reflection, trust, mastery, etc. My intention is not to denigrate leadership courses, or the individual police leader for that matter. Instead, my purpose is to contribute to the idea that a clear understanding of how leadership theories can be applied in practice is necessary and that police leadership on the whole must be perceived as practice rather than as the individual actions of police leaders.

Police leaders emphasise that they learn leadership through practice. Through observations, interviews, and conversations, I identified many different and unique ways that police leaders exercise leadership. Police leaders themselves are the first ones to describe police leadership as something dynamic and situational that always needs to be adapted to the particular tasks to be completed, the people involved, and the way the participants collectively develop effective solutions together. Creating more knowledge on police leadership as practice therefore involves more effort and complexity. It requires the knowledge of leadership practices on the micro level involving local practices within, for instance, investigations, crime prevention, patrols, intelligence, white-collar crime, etc. Micro practices will, however, provide patterns, connections, and boundaries that need to be studied from the macro perspective and even on the national macro level (Nicolini, 2012; La Rocca, Hoholm, & Mørk, 2017; Pyrko, Dörfler, & Eden, 2019). Leadership as practice is therefore about zooming in and zooming out between the micro, meso, and macro levels where numerous leadership practices are interconnected as a whole (Carlile, 2004).

Accordingly, it is important to study police leadership based on the questions what, who, how, and why:

What: Activities where leadership is exercised and constitutes an integral part of practice. It involves identifying and describing what leaders and their subordinates do within this practice. It could be HR management, administration, operations, strategy, change, task completion, and problem solving. This also includes social and cultural activities within an organisation.

Who: The people who contribute to and are involved in police leadership, both on the individual and collective level, including formal and informal leaders. What role does the individual take on in completing work tasks? How do they contribute? What are the relationships between the leader and their subordinates? Who contributes to the group and in what way? How do they affect each other and other groupings within a practice? *How*: Processes and actions that in one way or another realise leadership, as well as reflect what people in organisations actually do and the way they take action. There are recurring patterns that shape group interaction, group actions, individual actions, and the way groups achieve collective results.

Why: Conditions that affect leadership as practice may include culture(s), structures and organisation, and bureaucracy, but also the social mission, and therefore goals and visions, in leadership practice.

The book is organised as follows. In Part 1, the focus is on discussing police leadership and how approaching it as practice contributes to a more comprehensive understanding of what police leadership is and may be. Accordingly, in Chapter 1, "Why a leadership-as-practice perspective?" I explain what leadership as practice is and why this approach is relevant for understanding police leadership. In Chapter 2, which focuses on what police leaders do, I analyse the activities police leaders are involved in, what these everyday activities look like, and what they spend time on doing. In Chapter 3, "When do police leaders lead?" the things police leaders do are contrasted against the dominating leadership literature, and I consider the factors that make police leaders lead. Chapter 4 is where I put together the ideas from the three preceding chapters to get a comprehensive view of police leadership as practice and give examples of police leadership practices.

The following chapters are organised around the topics of Strategy (Part 2), Community (Part 3), Participation (Part 4), and Activities (Part 5), all of which are important to understanding police leadership as practice. The topics are also integral parts of the whole. For instance, Community and Participation must be considered as interrelated rather than isolated topics. Similarly, knowing in practice, which I chose to place under Community, can also fall under Participation, learning can equally apply to both Participation and Activities, Community could have included sensemaking, and so on. This proves that leadership as practice must be viewed as a whole, consisting of integrated processes that underlie all topics in this book. Accordingly, the model below aims to help the reader follow the book's structure around police leadership as practice and explain why a particular chapter is concerned with a certain topic at any given time. The model demonstrates how integrated various factors and concepts are with one another. It is not a testable model, but instead a visualisation that is based on the topics and considerations that I believe to be crucial for a comprehensive understanding of police leadership as practice (please see the figure).

Part 2 deals with the specifics of particular organisations or industries. I have chosen to name this chapter "Strategy" because, in my opinion, profession-specific features can be understood from the organisation's strategies. In public organisations, strategies refer to the choices that are made to achieve the best possible value creation. For the police force, profession-specific value creation is associated with the social mission. As a public organisation, the police force is politically controlled and bureaucratically organised. I start by characterising the social mission of the police and the way the police force is organised in order to undertake that mission. Part 2 contains the chapters "Social mission, organisational structure, and goal management" and "Strategy as practice". Police leadership as practice needs to be considered in accordance with profession-specific features and the extent to which leadership practices are promoted and/or inhibited by them.

Figure PI.I Police leadership as practice model

Part 3 is concerned with community in a leadership practice. A community gathers around the members' collective actions and shared feelings or perception of reality. The members are the ones who give the community meaning. The "we" identity is created by mutual engagement and a collective feeling of being part of something bigger. How important the community is depends on how important it is for the identity of its individual members. It also depends on the conditions of full membership and consequently the opportunity to either gain access to or be excluded from the desired community. Power and politics are therefore part of the communities of practice, both formal and informal. Part 3 consists of Chapter 7, "Organisational culture and police culture", Chapter 8, "Identity and belonging in communities of practice", and Chapter 9, "Knowing in practice".

Part 4 deals with participation, which refers to how a community collectively makes sense of leadership practice. Leadership practice is shaped, developed, and established through participation and practice. Practice is developed when new participants replace the ones who leave. The experienced individuals often appear to be experts on practice because they have long participated in a practice that is composed of social, informal, relational, cultural, formal, and practical elements. The established practice is also related to power and politics that may or may not give membership and full participation. Knowing and competencies that is most relevant for police services provides for full membership through participation and practice. Work tasks are defined and meaning is created together with the leader and colleagues by means of formal participation. Participation includes such activities as learning and change (described in Part 5) and characteristic features of cultures in the form of norms, sanctions, negotiations, values, and interests (described in Part 3). Part 4 contains Chapter 10, "Sensemaking", Chapter 11, "Manoeuvring space", and Chapter 12, "Power and politics".

Part 5, "Activities", is focused on daily activities and daily practice. Activities refer to what happens, what is being done, what requires a lot of time, and what takes less time to accomplish. Activities do not necessarily lead to sensemaking and, on their own, do not necessarily mean that all subordinates are to be considered as full participants in leadership practice. The fact that police leaders take part in activities does not have to mean they are exercising leadership. However, activities are necessary for allowing room for learning and change in leadership practices. Learning and change in an organisation begin with the activities that are developed into participation and practising. This must be considered, facilitated for, and integrated into the activities within leadership practices. Part 5 comprises "Learning as practice" (Chapter 13) and "Change management as practice" (Chapter 14).

It is challenging to organise the book in accordance with the overview model, but I believe this contributes to creating a logical structure of leadership as practice and, consequently, to the logical organisation of this book. However, it is important to repeat that strategy, community, participation, and activities must not be considered in isolation, but instead must be understood as integrated into leadership practice. I would also like to emphasise the dynamic nature of the subject matter and the fact that some concepts may be understood as both activities and participation; for example, learning and change. In this sense, concepts can be moved around, and provided they had slightly different argumentation, they could also have been placed under a different category. In my view, it is not that important as long as the model does not provide for random placements, but instead serves its purpose as an illustrated complete overview of leadership as practice. What is crucial, however, is that leadership practices are to be understood as dynamic and evolving. Hence, leadership practices should be described by such verbs as, for example, *do, lead, produce, develop* (for example, manoeuvring space), *create* (for example, meaning), *learn, change, prioritise, negotiate, solve* (for example, dilemmas), *act, see, evaluate, motivate, involve, identify*.

Notes

1 Examples of leadership theories and models are many: transformational and transactional leadership (Bass, 1990), situational leadership (Hersey et al., 2008), distributed leadership (Gronn, 2002), cultural leadership (Alvesson, 2013), relational leadership (Uhl-Bien et al., 2007), trust-based leadership (Karp, 2019), value-based leadership (Kirkhaug, 2018), charismatic leadership (Bryman, 1993), ethical leadership (Burns, 1978); competent leadership (Filstad, 2016), etc. They are all characterised by limited knowledge and research that chooses one model over the other (Arnulf & Larsen, 2015), resulting in contradictory perspectives without any clear consensus about any of them (Rhodes & t' Hart, 2014).
2 The research consisted of 27 days of shadowing and interviewing, two focus groups, 115 interviews, a countless number of informal conversations, one four-month period of field studies and a total of 35 additional days of field studies, and a two-part survey.

References

Alvesson, M. (2013). *Understanding Organizational Culture* (2nd edn). London: Sage.

Alvesson, M. (2016). Studying leadership: taking meaning, relationality and ideology seriously. In J. Storey, J. Hartley, J.L. Denis, P.T. Hart & D. Ulrich (Eds.), *The Routledge Companion to Leadership* (pp. 67–88). New York: Routledge.

Arnulf, J.K. & Larsen, K.R. (2015). Overlapping semantics of leadership and heroism: expectations of omnipotence, identification with ideal leaders and disappointment in real managers. *Scandinavian Psychologist*, 2(e3), doi:10.15714/scandpsychol.2.e3.

Bass, B.M. (1990). From transactional to transformational leadership: learning to share the vision. *Organizational Dynamics*, 18(3), 19–31.

Burns, J.M. (1978). *Leadership*. New York: Harper Perennial.

Bryman, A. (1993). Research methods in the study of leadership. In A. Bryman, D. Collinson, K. Grint, B. Jackson, & M. Uhl-Bien (Eds.), *The Sage Handbook of Leadership* (pp. 269–285). London: Sage.

Carlile, P.R. (2004). Transferring, translation and transforming: an integrative framework for managing knowledge across boundaries. *Organizational Science*, 15(5), 555–568.

Carroll, B., Levy, L., & Richmond, D. (2008). Leadership as practice: challenging the competence paradigm. *Leadership*, 4(4), 363–379.

Crevani, L. & Endrissat, N. (2016). Mapping the leadership-as-practice terrain. In J.A. Raelin (Ed.), *Leadership-as-Practice: Theory and Application* (pp. 21–49). New York: Routledge.

Davis, C. & Silvestri, M. (2020). *Critical Perspectives on Police Leadership*. Bristol: Policy Press.

Filstad, C. (2016). *Organisasjonslæring – fra kunnskap til kompetanse* (2nd edn). Bergen: Fagbokforlaget.

Gronn, P. (2002). Distributed leadership as a unit of analysis. *The Leadership Quarterly*, 13, 423–451.

Hersey, P., Blanchard, K.H., & Johnson, D.E. (2008). *Management of Organizational Behavior* (9th edn). Hoboken, NJ: Prentice-Hall.

Karp, T. (2019). *God nok ledelse. Hva ledere gjør i praksis*. Oslo: Cappelen Damm Akademisk.

Kirkhaug, R. (2018). *Verdibasert ledelse* (2nd edn). Oslo: Universitetsforlaget.

La Rocca, A., Hoholm, T., & Mørk, B.E. (2017). Practice theory and the study of interaction in business relationships: some methodological implications. *Industrial Marketing Management*, 60, 187–195.

Mintzberg, H. (2009). *Managing*. San Francisco: Berrett-Koehler.

Nicolini, D. (2012). *Practice Theory, Work and Organization: An Introduction*. Oxford: Oxford University Press.

Pyrko, I., Dörfler, V., & Eden, C. (2019). Communities of practice in landscapes of practice. *Management Learning*, 50(4), 482–499.

Raelin, J.A. (Ed.) (2016). *Leadership-as-Practice: Theory and Application*. New York: Routledge.

Rhodes, R.A.W. & 't Hart, P. (2014). Puzzles of political leadership. In Rhodes, R.A.W. & 't Hart, P. (Eds.), *The Oxford Handbook of Political Leadership*. Oxford: Oxford University Press.

Tengblad, S. (2012). Conclusions and the way forward: towards a practice theory of management. In S. Tengblad (Ed.), *The Work of Managers: Towards a Practice Theory of Management* (pp. 337–356). Oxford: Oxford University Press.

Uhl-bien, M., Marion, R., & McKelvey, B. (2007). Complexity leadership theory: shifting leadership from industrial age to the knowledge era. *The Leadership Quarterly*, 18(4), 298–318.

Part I

Police leadership as practice

Chapter 1

Why a leadership-as-practice perspective?

This chapter discusses and argues for the importance of the leadership-as-practice approach to increase our knowledge of police leadership as relational and collective activities and performances. The chapter provides a critical view by providing a literature review on leadership perspectives and conventional leadership literature. Still, the leadership literature is dominated by normative leadership models on how the individual leaders must perform, independent of context. A practice perspective shifts focus to social and cultural relations and interactions between leaders and their subordinates, the collective, the negotiated, the sensemaking of participation in leadership practice.

Practice-based studies have made a profound impact in the fields of leadership, innovation, learning, knowing, and competencies in organisations since the early 2000s (Nicolini, Gherardi, & Yanow, 2003; Gherardi, 2006; Carroll, Levy, & Richmond, 2008; Crevani & Endrissat, 2016; Raelin, 2016; Christie, Hoholm, & Mørk, 2018). There are various approaches to practice within the field of practice-based research. For example, the *cultural approach* would focus on how the culture is produced and reproduced in collective and context-dependent practices. The *activity theory* points out that practices must be understood in relation to objects and artefacts. The *situated learning theory* considers learning and competence to be context-dependent and anchored in everyday practices (Gherardi, 2006; La Rocca, Hoholm, & Mørk, 2017). The situation- and context-dependent view of learning and knowledge previously introduced the notions of *situated learning* and *communities of practice* in 1991 (Lave & Wenger, 1991; Brown & Duguid, 1991). These notions represent an alternative approach to learning and knowledge, which used to be mainly seen as individual processes free from situations and practices.

The variety of approaches to practice-based studies still provides a common understanding of what the practice perspective entails. First of all, practice consists of continuous and dynamic processes and should therefore be described with the type of verbs listed in the introduction. Secondly, practice is a set of social, relational, cultural, and collective actions that are integrated and rooted in everyday practices. Thirdly, there may be several different practices competing, cooperating, or separated from each other by tight borders. Police leaders are going to participate in several practices, such as their own leadership practices and interdisciplinary leadership practices, but also various forms of professional practices, practices involving external partners, reform practices, and the like. This is illustrated by the notions of *landscapes of practice* and *networks of practice* (Pyrko, Dörfler, & Eden, 2019). Additionally, internally occurring phenomena within organisations also shape practice perspectives. This is why I will return to the topics of change

DOI: 10.4324/9781003224105-3

management as practice, strategy as practice, and learning as practice later. But first, what is practice, or what can it be?

What is practice?

In the academic world, the relation between theory and practice has attracted a lot of attention. The dualism between the two concepts is significant, and it is often reinforced through the idea that academics own and are experts in theory, while practitioners own and are experts in practice. This dualism is further reinforced by the fact that a phenomenon such as leadership is often either classified as purely theoretical or as practical rather than as a combination of both. Academia has developed theories, scientific "truths", and the "evidence basis", while practice has been kept separate but adjacent to these concepts. The distinction between theory and practice is claimed by many to be considerably larger and more pure now than before. Theories tend to be more often considered the "right thing", and practitioners who do not rely on theories enough are viewed as useless. This problematic development is not necessarily rooted in history, which I illustrate in the next paragraphs. The advocates for a different view, like Aristotle and Marx, did not distance knowledge from the practice it represents but instead built a bridge between viewing theories as pure knowledge and knowing a particular phenomenon, emphasising that academics and practitioners should be more interdependent.

Aristotle is still relevant for understanding knowledge, perhaps even more so because he was mostly concerned with practice. He distinguishes between *praxis, episteme* (thinking), and *poiesis* (creating) as the three forms of knowledge. *Praxis*, he argues, are actions that, together with *episteme* and *poiesis*, constitute basic human activities. Practice through actions constitutes the very goal of developing practical knowledge. What distinguishes good practice is that it serves the good of the people. Possessing practical wisdom (*fronesis*) is necessary for achieving good practice. To attain this kind of wisdom, the practitioner must have experience in and with practice. By emphasising the interdependence between theory and practice, where the prominence is given to practice, Aristotle shows that the distinction between theory and practice is artificial.

Similar ideas are also found in Karl Marx's philosophy. Not only do theory and practice presuppose each other, but they also mutually shape each other, he believes. In Marx's view, practice is the reciprocity that occurs when the subject and the object meet in a dialectical movement. The most challenging aspect of these examples of the earlier views on practice is understanding practice as the guiding force rather than completely detaching theory from practice – understanding what should be done rather than what could be done. The paradox can often occur when "others" are telling the practitioners what the characteristics of their practice are, without having studied that specific practice themselves.

By way of introduction, I have described how practice-based studies refer to practice as a common understanding of practical actions and experiences (Orlikowski, 2010). Reference is made to practice, relational and collective, as well as to formal and informal factors, which are described as dynamic and evolving processes between leaders and their subordinates, who are all participants in practice (Gherardi, 2009; Nicolini, 2012). Practice is described as a variety of activities, a nexus of what is being done and said (Levina & Orlikowski, 2009). The variety of activities is organised around: (1) an understanding of how things should be done, (2) rules, and (3) goals that give meaning and encourage the members to invest in practice (Schatzki, 1997: 3). Practice therefore consists of activities and dynamic processes (not stable entities) between participants that are orga-nised around a common understanding of "how things should be done" (Gherardi, 2009: 146). Accordingly, practice provides action resources, cognitive resources, procedural resources, and physical resources utilised and negotiated collectively by the participants in activities through social and cultural interactions (Whittington, 2006). This presents an alternative approach to leadership and to the perspectives on leadership that have largely dominated the literature. Leadership perspectives are considered in the next section.

Perspectives on leadership

Leadership literature looks like a large puzzle with pieces from different and sometimes contradictory perspectives and disciplines. Various forms of leadership are often claimed to be the perfect formula for good, effective, strategic, clear, and/or change-oriented leadership. But when, for instance, is leadership effective? What are the features that make it effective and who is it effective for? Is leadership effective when investigators process as many cases as possible in the shortest possible time and reduce the number of unresolved cases? Is it effective in terms of achieving goals? Effective for the investigator? Effective for those who are processing the case? The same applies to good leadership. Is it good because people agree to be led voluntarily? Does this form of good leadership provide equally good quality and competencies when completing work tasks? Is good leadership voluntary movement towards a goal based on the belief that leadership research has defined the "good" to be about how leaders can influence efficiency (Karp, 2019)?

What is good (or good enough) and what is effective are quite impossible to measure. When does, for instance, the investigator know it is time to finish the investigation? When is the collected evidence good enough for further proceedings? In my field studies from 2019, I found that many police leaders are concerned with being available for their team members. This applies to all leadership levels. They consider availability to be part of good leadership, but that is a subjective notion because what is perceived as good leadership and availability by one employee will not necessarily be the same for another. Besides, what makes a manager available? Seeing the manager twice a day, talking to them informally, or communicating via email? Or is it enough to simply know that the manager is around, possibly just a phone call away if you need them? Being a manager is demanding, complex, challenging, and sometimes quite trivial, and an increasing number of people even argue that managers are not more important than other workers and that belief in what managers are capable of accomplishing is greatly exaggerated (Alvesson, 2016). What is the best formula for relational leadership, situational leadership, value-based leadership, distributed leadership, value-based leadership, charismatic leadership, trust-based leadership, ethical leadership, cultural leadership, etc.? Some of these leader-ship perspectives deal with relations between leader and followers while others deal with leadership providing something special and that something happens when bringing people together. Other leadership perspectives are about the individual leader's accom-plishments. The complex puzzle of spanning between several academic disciplines leaves leadership as a conundrum.

The lack of consensus is problematic and needs to be acknowledged because distinc-tions between good and bad leadership are often made without consensus on what it means. The ideal of a heroic leader still exists in leadership literature (Antonakis, 2011; Arnulf & Larsen, 2015). Normative models of how the idealised leader should behave (Fleming, 2015; Karp 2019), undertaking performances across a variety of groups, organisational situations, and contexts (Zaccaro, Kemp, & Bader, 2004), as opposed to how leaders practice leadership, still dominate the leadership literature. Not acknowledging the situatedness and differences in social and cultural contexts makes it difficult to decide whether it is the leader, the leadership, or the context that is good or bad. Good leadership in the police, for instance, is based on the social mission where police managers shall: (1) set the direction and drive change, (2) motivate and develop staff, and (3) achieve results in cooperation with others (Police Directorate, 2017). Good leadership should be value-based, that is, based on the police values of respect, courage, commitment to the common good, and hands-on involvement. Is there a formula for this? Do certain personal traits and the leadership style of a police leader exemplify these qualities and therefore be characterised as good leadership across areas of responsibility, departments, and districts within the police? But how is good police leadership recognised in a police context where police leaders face somewhat incompatible sets of expectations from, on one hand, bureaucratic requirements, and on the other hand, risk-taking operative policing activities (Golding & Savage, 2011)? And can the leadership literature guide police leaders in their performances?

Leadership traits and leadership style

Outstanding leaders have traditionally been evaluated based on their personality capabilities (Arnulf, 2012), where contemporary theorists are preoccupied with traits and behavioural, situational, and transformational leadership styles (Davis & Silvestri, 2020). The kinds of traits these leaders had and the way they distinguished themselves from followers/colleagues formed the basis for trait theories in the leadership literature. It was important to identify which personal traits were essentially innate and therefore stable (as opposed to personal traits that may be developed), and which resulted in outstanding leaders (Martinsen, 2015). Personality was considered stable in the same way. An outstanding leader was supposed to be able to lead all types of organisations regardless of the industry, situations, participants, and so on. The personality traits of the leaders were their individual competencies, their "property". Trait-based leadership identify individuals' capacity for leadership, traits that are needed to succeed as effective leaders (Bass, 2008). They would not let circumstances affect them and could exercise great leadership in any situation. Also, traits are understood as stable and predictable for behaviours and leadership outcomes (Antonakis, 2011).

Trait theories of leadership did not prove to be very productive. Using the personal qualities of a leader as an explanation of good or bad leadership was too simplified. Also, the early studies lack validity and were not replicable (Zaccaro et al., 2004). Hence, the focus has been shifted to the interaction between leaders and subordinates in specific contexts, also known as the interactional perspective or behavioural perspective (Kaufmann & Kaufmann, 2015). Personal factors and personality traits are still important, but only to the extent that is required in different leadership situations. This way, personal *style* or leadership *style* was preferred over personality *traits* (Northouse, 2019). There is, however, no contradiction in the type of leadership literature where the trait and the behavioural approaches are considered to be closely related (Martinsen, 2015). The leader's behaviour is viewed as a function of their personality traits, but it may be easier to change behaviour than to change personality traits. The principle of trait theory has therefore been incredibly resilient (Davis & Silvestri, 2020).

The behavioural approach to leadership distinguishes between task-oriented behaviour and relationship-oriented behaviour, and leaders need to combine being relatively task- and relationship-oriented in order to adapt to their team's needs. Accordingly, leadership style theories refer to the behaviour of a particular leader where leadership is primarily seen as a function of a particular leader (Grint, 2005). Leadership is a question of who the leaders are, what they can do, and how they handle various situations and people (Hersey & Blanchard, 1988, 2008). More recent, leaders' personality is categorised by the Big Five traits, with extroversion as the strongest predictor of effective leadership (Judge et al., 2002). This relates to the fact that leadership research has been dominated by the positivist approach (about the rational human being) and has relied heavily on quantitative instruments such as questionnaires and the theory testing of large meta-studies across national borders and parts of the world, despite the fact that such quantitative instruments fail to take into account global, national, and cultural differences and contexts (Antonakis, Cianciolo, & Sternberg, 2004; Kroeck, Lowe, & Brown, 2004; Mumford et al., 2009).

Situational leadership considers the social context and the importance of different leadership styles required in different situations (Hersey et al., 2008). Still, the theoretical principles from trait and behavioural theories and the conceptualisation in terms of task and relation are incorporated (Davis & Silvestri, 2020). Conceptual ambiguity and a lack of rationale for proposed relationships between leadership style and the situated needs of the follower are criticised (Yukl, 2013).

Transformational leadership has been hailed for encouraging participation and collaboration and is currently the most utilised theory within leadership (Antonakis, 2011; Davis & Silvestri, 2020). Transformational leadership considers the role of emotions in the capacity of leaders to transform the value of attitudes of followers for collective commitment (Bass & Reggio, 2006). As opposed to transactional leadership as an exchange that relies on control and external motivation, transformational leadership is about leaders stimulating employee interest and creating visions of common goals, inspiring and creating the necessary awareness and acceptance of common goals, seeing the individual employee, and developing their instinctive motivation where the goals and interests of leader and follower become integrated (Burns, 1978; Bass, 1990).

Critics within the leadership research field argue that even today, a lot of leading research reproduces the leadership theorists' assumptions about who leaders are and how leaders should behave – assumptions which are often based on the idea of active leaders and passive followers – in addition to their assumptions about interactions between leaders and followers/subordinates, the context and situation in which leadership takes place (for example, a police executive versus a bank director), and the leadership level (a police commissioner versus an operational manager) (Pfeffer, 2015; Alvesson, 2016).

Tsoukas (1996) considers leadership research to be naive because the leader does not fully understand the organisation and its employees. He explains that the employees rely on their own subjective interpretations and sometimes ignore feedback from leaders on the decisions and actions they take. This is why it is naive of leadership research to set expectations for the ideal leader and then express disappointment over the actual leaders because leadership is often confused with heroism (Arnulf & Larsen, 2015). The general criticism is that many leadership studies reproduce the "feelgood" assumptions about how leaders should behave and the simplified ideologies about active leaders and passive subordinates, while also failing to address the relationships between leaders and sub-ordinates and, last but not least, among the subordinates themselves. As a result, little attention is given to the significance of creating a common meaning and conditions for the collective development of a common leadership practice (Haake, Rantatalo, & Lindberg, 2015). I am therefore returning to the idea that the leadership literature appears as a puzzle that, in my view, rather inhibits the practice field and those who exercise leadership out in the field. The danger in this is that it creates a dis-proportionately large gap between theorists who insist on what leaders should be like and what they should do and what leaders can be and are able to do in reality.

Police leadership

Action-oriented leadership received a lot of attention in the early police research (Adair, 1973), where the leader was responsible for first meeting the team members' demands and then for identifying and completing common tasks or working towards a common goal for the entire team. Later, and partly due to New Public Management, the police leadership literature moreover applied conventional leadership theories on effective lea-dership behaviours measuring the police leader's attitude, traits, capabilities, and leader-ship style (Davis & Silvestri, 2020). For instance, Hawkins and Dulewicz (2009) identified engaging leadership style as most common in the police. Schafer (2010) argues that integrity, work ethics, communication, and personal care are the most desirable leadership behaviours. Situated leadership theory has, according to these studies and other studies of police leadership styles, different responses to the need of followers and of the situation (Davis & Silvestri, 2020).

Reference is made to several studies where transformational leadership is regarded as the key to better police leadership (Fleming, 2015). The same applies to descriptions of a particular leadership style that would result in good police leadership. The common trait of all police leadership research is that it gives little evidence for the fact that transfor-mational leadership provides for better police leadership (Moggré, den Boer, & Fyfe, 2017). Still, some studies found that transformational police leadership was perceived as most effective (Dobby, Anscombe, & Tuffin, 2004; Sarver & Miller, 2014) and positive on job satisfaction (Swid, 2014). Other studies found that transformational leadership does not take into account the policing context or public sectors where the power to "transform" practices is problematic due to political and governmental pressure (Cock-croft, 2014; Davis & Silvestri, 2020).

Police leadership is often a question of rank and seniority. As a police executive, one must climb the steps of the career ladder internally, and the leadership levels within the areas of police responsibility are populated by police and law graduates. As a rule, police executives start their leadership careers by being picked as the "foremost among equals" and assigned to lead the team or department they were previously part of, which is regarded as action-oriented, hands-on leadership that is based on participation. Leader-ship and management, however, have not been considered as separate disciplines within the police (Karp, 2019). This is why little attention has been given to how police leaders operate and how a police leadership culture is shaped, developed, and distributed throughout the entire police force (Flynn & Herrington, 2015). However, the nature of power and the dynamics and conceptualisation of rank, command, and control, and the centralisation of decision making in police leadership is essential (Grint & Thornton, 2015; Davis 2019). Recognising police leadership as highly contextual, power-centric, and a task based on the efficiency of "getting the job done" is needed (Davies & Bailey, 2018; Davis & Silvestri, 2020).

Large parts of the national police forces in Western countries are undergoing reforms. To be able to handle the rapidly changing criminality patterns, police leadership is needed more than ever (Neyroud, 2011). Police researchers argue that the future criminal landscape presupposes a modern police organisation with leaders who facilitate and enable learning for change and competence rather than a bureaucratic organisation managed from the top down (Uhl-bien, Marion, & McKelvey, 2007). Leadership literature might be able to contribute more with sources for the development of unique, dynamic, and collective police leadership practices than with specific formulas for future police leadership. Of course, this does not mean police leaders do not need to possess certain competencies. Flynn and Herrington (2015), for instance, believe that the future police leader must have a combination of administrative competence (for organisation, budgeting, and HR administration), personal competence (for motivation and communication), and leadership competence (for analysis, strategy, and reflection). Similarly, police leadership research underlines the importance of problem solving, developing a shared vision, creating a feeling of belonging and commitment to the leadership community, and initiating and managing changes. Crucial, however, is that it is not possible to isolate leadership in the police from the multitude of external social, economic, or political factors of policing (Davis & Silvestri, 2020). The police leadership-as-practice perspective does not aim to mechanically list the competencies that the individual police leader must have. Police leadership cannot cover everything, just as police leaders and their teams cannot be or do everything all of the time. Police leadership as practice also depends on the leadership level of the leadership practice.

Leadership levels

The challenge of conventional leadership literature studying leadership as individualistic and context-free is that the context dependency of leadership levels is left out in the dark. The normative recipe of leadership gives very little insight into leadership levels, except for a few empirical studies of middle managers and first line managers where the same conventional leadership literature on trait and leadership styles are applied.

In the context of middle management (which can also constitute several levels in itself), middle managers are usually referred to as indispensable, balancing artists, flexible Jelly Babies, therapists, tightrope walkers, but with expectation of being agents of change and facilitators for strategies and common goals of the organisation. In the last decades, middle management has been given more attention. Leadership in the police is organised in a rank-based hierarchy (Silvestri, 2003; Herrington & Colvin, 2015), organised in accordance to strategic, operational, and tactical levels. The dynamics of rank and leadership practices as constructed, negotiated in relational and collaborative processes, therefore needs greater acknowledgement (Raelin, 2016; Davis, 2019; Filstad, 2020).

In 2010, De Church, with colleagues (2010), found that of all the leadership research articles published in 11 reputable journals over the past 25 years, only 7% were on middle management, 34% on senior management (often related to strategy), and 16% on first line management. Their biggest concern, however, was the fact that 24% of the research referred to leadership without identifying the leadership level at all. This underlines the point that leadership is to a large extent still considered regardless of its level, which can be said to be problematic at best.

Relevant studies of leadership in practice

So far, I have been critical of the lack of research into what leaders do in practice generally and what police leaders do in particular. This does not mean that no studies have been done at all, but the extent of leadership studies has been very limited. Here I would like to name a few studies that have been ground-breaking in many ways.

Sune Carlson's (1951) pioneering studies of ten senior managers in large Swedish companies show that senior management was hectic, fragmented, complex, disorganised, and was governed by habits and coincidence rather than by reflective and deliberate planning. Studies of middle managers show that the higher the pace of change in an organisation, the more time managers spend talking to each other, while middle managers use relatively little time to talk to subordinates. Since leadership is a relational and interactive process, personal relationships in leadership prevail over the hierarchies of authorities (Sayles, 1964; Burns, 1978). It is also important to mention that there are significant variations in middle management, which is why it could be misleading to talk about middle management in general terms (Stewart, 1967).

The famous organisational researcher Henry Mintzberg (1973) described what leaders "should do" and pointed out the great disconnect between what they are supposed to and want to do, and what they actually spend time on. In his later research, Mintzberg (2009) was critical of the distinction between leadership and management, pointing out that a leader has the generalist's ability to think, communicate, lead, and practise, but also the knowledge of the business they are leading. He emphasises that the relationship between leaders and their subordinates is mutually dependent and formulates an interactive approach where leadership is understood as a practice learnt primarily through experiences and embedded in context.

In his studies of three police leaders in Canada, Mintzberg (2009) found that they exercised normative control by being informed of, and giving permission to enact, police actions. He also found that police leaders are proud of their job and feel a strong commitment to the social mission. According to Fleming (2008), female police executives in Australia refer to unpredictable and uncertain internal and external circumstances that affect their leadership on a daily basis.

Relevant studies show that police leaders learn from leadership practices other than their own, which plays an important part in their development as leaders. Knowledge sharing between police leaders is also crucial to understanding one's own unique leadership practice (Gaston & King, 1995; Mead, 2002). It is emphasised that reflecting over one's own practice is essential for being able to learn from other police leaders (Schafer, 2009). This is confirmed in the studies of Dutch police leaders showing that the greatest value one can gain from their own development as a leader is getting feedback from colleagues under a high workload and challenging work tasks (Doornbos, Simons, & Denessen, 2008). Thus, police research overall underlines the significance of knowledge sharing between colleagues and other leaders in order to reflect on one's own leadership practice. Studies also show how external and internal conditions influence the opportunities to exercise the type of unique leadership that is most important to develop (Crank & Giacomazzi, 2009; Meaklim & Sims, 2011; Janssens et al., 2017).

Why leadership as practice?

As mentioned earlier, an increasing number of studies within the general leadership literature point out that leadership must be understood, researched, and recognised as practice (Alvesson, 2016; Mintzberg, 2009; Tengblad, 2012; Raelin, 2016). In leadership practices, an individual leader does not receive the most attention. Contrary to the dominating trend in leadership literature, an individual leader is considered much less significant than other factors in determining what happens in practice. What matters in practice is what individuals think, what competencies they have, what they are capable of doing, what they actually do, what experiences they have, and what the participants of the practice can achieve together as a collective. Accordingly, a leadership practice is not focused on an individual leader, but instead deals with the relationship between the participants, the community, and what the community can collectively achieve. The community is composed of formal and informal leaders depending on the situations and tasks to be completed. This is why *manoeuvring space* as socially constructed, negotiated, and relational between leader and employees (Filstad, Olsen, & Karp, 2020) is necessary for organising various work processes and tasks depending on what practice serves the purpose best (Raelin, 2016). This does not mean that an individual participant is not important, nor does it mean that the individual police leader is not that important for practice. Instead, this approach to leadership asserts that all practices that humans are part of constitute social phenomena and social constructions, so studying practice in this way is in fact not new.[1]

It is new, however, that a practice perspective applied to leadership helps to shift the focus away from the leader. Critics of the current leadership literature believe that an unconditional single focus has been placed on the extraordinary leader at the expense of both the participants and the characteristics of the practice that the leader is formally responsible for. This is why a practice perspective in many ways shifts the attention from the extraordinary individual or the heroic leader to what "ordinary" practitioners can achieve together when they are collectively engaged in a leadership practice (Crevani & Endrissat, 2016; Raelin, 2016). Leadership occurs and takes shape when people work together. Processes, coordinated efforts, cooperation, and interactions between subordinates and the leader are the key factors determining whether leadership is taking place or not. Whether or not leadership is actually exercised is indicated by the results of the conversations and discussions between the practitioners, as well as the thinking and behavioural patterns developed over time among those involved in the interactions. Leadership is therefore understood as a collective phenomenon that is not solely dependent on the ability of individuals to mobilise, motivate, manage, and guide others. Accordingly, leadership is shared and distributed to the same extent that it is relational, and it should be understood as a social and cultural phenomenon rather than associated with an individual person.

Leadership as practice means that a leader can never be considered apart from practice. The leader is part of practice, which is not solely dependent on one person's ability to mobilise others to act but instead mobilises as a process in a particular situation. Through social interaction between the participants in practice, various activities are distributed as a continuous process that has developed over time and through collective actions (Raelin, 2016; Sergi, 2016). This is why the emphasis is placed on interaction, relations, and ambiguity, while the role of hierarchies, power dynamics, and dyadic and vertical relationships in leadership is also recognised. Consequently, leadership as practice embodies a variety of themes, such as identity, skills, physical forms, material objects, routines, relational dynamics, power, knowledge, conversations, and incorporation, as well as the embeddedness and integration into the social and cultural context that practice represents.

Researching police leadership from the practice perspective involves shifting the focus from an individual police leader to the interaction between that leader and their subordinates, and consequently, the actions the leader is involved in. The distinguishing features of these actions, the way they occur, their results, the forms these actions can take, what the participants are doing, and the context in which the actions take place are also within the scope of the research (Crevani & Endrissat, 2016). By studying these things, we will uncover what leadership work is all about, how leadership is achieved, and where and how leadership is exercised. Accordingly, leadership as practice is based on a process perspective. This means that leadership is understood as a collection of ongoing processes, i.e. a leadership practice combines completing routine tasks and regularly achieving the goals that are set by the community of practice (Nicolini, 2012: 3). This is why all activity does not equal practice. A practice is instead a combination of actions that make sense for the participants within that practice and that represent a pattern (in this case, basic assumptions that are expressed through repetition). The knowledge within the practice is embedded in the participants' minds as something specific for this practice only, something that only insiders are aware of and understand. In this way, a practice represents this collectively shared knowledge.

The leadership-as-practice perspective shows that it is not the individual leader but the leadership as a whole that, through practice, is prepared to handle complex work tasks involving cooperation, crossing boundaries, and adaptation, which are the kinds of tasks that future police executives are facing (Heifetz, Grashow, & Linsky, 2009). I argue that we do not need more studies to discover the competencies that individual leaders must have when the research addresses something as complex, diverse, and interrelated as leadership, which has to be considered within the context and the culture, and in accordance with the mandate where leadership is exercised (Carroll et al., 2008).

Researching leadership as practice

First, studying leadership as practice means having to invest a lot of time into understanding the very context and conditions of leadership. This includes studying organisational structures, organisational culture(s), and the framework, guidelines, and implications of the social mission. Second, researchers are focused on the fact that leadership is formed through everyday actions and are concerned with what distinguishes practice. They are interested in leadership actions in and of themselves and in the fact that leadership can be exercised by individuals other than leaders in certain situations. They are less concerned with the formal position and specific qualities of a leader. Third, researchers are more focused on the realities of organisations, the challenging everyday situations that organisational groups and leaders face, and the day-to-day steps that are taken. Finally, the majority of practice-oriented researchers are not looking for universal truths or normative formulas for good leadership, and they believe that leaders have to find their own answers and develop their own leadership practice instead. They do not put themselves in the position to judge what good leadership entails but instead point to the kind of knowledge that is crucial for developing a good leadership practice.

In my own research, I have collected descriptive, inductive, and empirical data. This includes shadowing and observing police leaders and reflecting on and with them. I was present in informal arenas such as corridors, over the coffee machine, in the canteen, and in the break room. I had informal conversations, conducted interviews, and attended meetings. I have also accompanied them in the field – for example, on patrol, in court, and at meetings with external participants – and of course, I have read documents, reports, recommendations, and so on.

This allows me to describe both a leader's actions and the context in which they take place, and in turn relate them to what leaders and their subordinates themselves say about these actions. The context is crucial to understanding the process of exercising leadership, which is described as rather complex, chaotic, uncertain, and demanding, making leaders work with large volumes of varied and fragmented tasks that are often governed by coincidence. This is why I have also invested a lot of time into researching both police culture and organisational structure. Additionally, I have closely studied the Norwegian Community Policing Reform, which has greatly affected the context of my research since the reform was taking place during the four years when I was researching the police. Police leadership on all levels has an overall responsibility to lead the comprehensive and sometimes complex changes that this reform entails. Police leaders have been under a lot of pressure to establish and develop the new police organisation in accordance with goals, strategies, and expectations, along with carrying the extra workload of balancing the reform work with daily operations while also being part of internal political play, agendas, symbolic acts, legitimacy, and creating manoeuvring space in their own leadership practices. The next chapter will provide further information on what police leaders do.

Note

1 For instance, see Wittgenstein, 1958; Dreyfus, 1991; Taylor, 1911; Bourdieu, 1990; Giddens, 1984; Foucault, 1980; Lyotard, 1988.

References

Adair, J.E. (1973). *Action-Centered Leadership*. London and New York: McGraw-Hill.

Alvesson, M. (2016). Studying leadership: taking meaning, relationality and ideology seriously. In J. Storey, J. Hartley, J.L. Denis, P.T. Hart & D. Ulrich (Eds.), *The Routledge Companion to Leadership* (pp. 67–88). New York: Routledge.

Antonakis, J., Cianciolo, A.T. & Sternberg, R.J. (2004). Methods for studying leadership. In J. Antonakis, A.T. Cianciolo & R.J. Sternberg (Eds.), *The Nature of Leadership* (pp. 48–70). Thousand Oaks, CA: Sage.

Antonakis, J. (2011). Predictors of leadership: the usual suspects and the suspect trait. In A. Bryman, D. Collinson, K. Grint, B. Jackson, & M. Uhl-Bien (Eds). *The Sage Handbook of Leadership* (pp. 269–285). London: Sage.

Arnulf, J.K. (2012). Organizational change capacity and composition of management teams: a visualization of how personality traits may restrain team adaptability. *Team Performance Management*, 18(7/8), 433–454.

Arnulf, J.K. & Larsen, K.R. (2015). Overlapping semantics of leadership and heroism: expectations of omnipotence, identification with ideal leaders and disappointment in real managers. *Scandinavian Psychologist*, 2(e3), doi:10.15714/scandpsychol.2.e3.

Bass, B.M. (1990). From transactional to transformational leadership: learning to share the vision. *Organizational Dynamics*, 18(3), 19–31.

Bass, B.M. (2008). *The Bass Handbook of Leadership: Theory, Research and Managerial Applications* (4th edn). New York: NY Free Press.

Bass, B.M. & Reggio, R.E. (2006). *Transformational Leadership*. Mahwah, NJ: Lawrence Erlbaum.

Bourdieu, P. (1990). *The Logic of Practice*. Cambridge: Polity.

Brown, J.S. & Duguid, P. (1991). Organizational learning and communities of practice: towards a unified view of working, learning and innovating. *Organizational Science: A Journal of the Institute of Management Science*, 2(1), 40–57.

Burns, J.M. (1978). *Leadership*. New York: Harper Perennial.

Carlson, S. (1951). *Executive Behaviour*. Stockholm: Strömbergs.

Carroll, B., Levy, L., & Richmond, D. (2008). Leadership as practice: challenging the competence paradigm. *Leadership*, 4(4), 363–379.

Christie, W., Hoholm, T., & Mørk, B. (2018). Innovasjon og samhandling i helsevesenet. En praksisbasert tilnærming [Innovation and cooperation in healthcare. A practice-based approach]. *Praktisk økonomi & finans*, 34, 32–46.

Cockcroft, T. (2014). Police culture and transformational leadership: outlining the contours of a troubled relationship. *Policing*, 8(1), 5–13.

Crank, J.P. & Giacomazzi, A. (2009). A sheriff's office as a learning organization. *Police Quarterly*, 12(4), 351–369.

Crevani, L. & Endrissat, N. (2016). Mapping the leadership-as-practice terrain. In J.A. Raelin (Ed.), *Leadership-as-Practice: Theory and Application* (pp. 21–49). New York: Routledge.

Davies, C. & Bailey, D. (2018). Police leadership: the challenges for developing contemporary practice. *International Journal of Emergency Services*, 7(1), 13–23.

Davis, C. (2019). Police leadership and the authority of rank: a call for a critical perspective. In P. Ramshaw, M. Simpson, & M. Silvestri (Eds.), *Police Leadership: Changing Landscapes*. Basingstoke: Palgrave Macmillan.

Davis, C. & Silvestri, M. (2020). *Critical Perspectives on Police Leadership*. Bristol: Policy Press.

DeChurch, L.A., Hiller, N.J., Murase, T., Doty, D., & Salas, E. (2010). Leadership across levels: levels of leaders and their levels of impact. *The Leadership Quarterly*, 21, 1069–1085.

Dobby, J., Anscombe, J., & Tuffin, R. (2004). *Police Leadership: Expectations and Impact*. Home Office Online.

Doornbos, A.J., Simons, R.J., & Denessen, E. (2008). Relations between the characteristics of workplace practices and types of informal work-related learning: a survey study among Dutch police. *Human Resource Development Quarterly*, 19(2), 129–151.

Dreyfuss, H. (1991). *Being-in-the-World: A Commentary on Heidegger's Being and Time, Division One*. Cambridge, MA: MIT Press.

Filstad, C., Olsen, T.H., & Karp, T. (2020). Constructing managerial manoeuvring space in contradictory contexts. *European Management Journal*, 39(4), 467–475. https://doi.org/10.1016/j.emj.2020.10.003.

Filstad, C. (2020). *Politiledelse som praksis* [Police leadership as practice]. Bergen: Fagbokforlaget.

Fleming, J. (2008). Managing the diary: what does a police commissioner do? *Public Administration*, 86(3), 679–698.

Fleming, J. (2015). Experience as evidence: the learning of leadership. In J. Fleming (Ed.), *Police Leadership: Rising to the Top* (pp. 1–16). Oxford: Oxford University Press.

Flynn, E.A. & Herrington, V. (2015). *Towards a Profession of Police Leadership: New Perspectives in Policing Bulletin*. Washington: Department of Justice, National Institute of Justice (pp. 1–18).

Foucault, M. (1980). *Power/Knowledge: Selected Interviews and Other Writings 1972–1977*. New York: Pantheon.

Gaston, K. & King, L. (1995). Management development and training in the police. *A Survey of the Promotion Process*, 19(7), 20–25.

Gherardi, S. (2006). *Organizational Knowledge: The Texture of Workplace Learning*. Malden: Blackwell.

Gherardi, S. (2009). Knowing and learning in practice-based studies: an introduction. *The Learning Organization*, 16(5), 352–359.

Giddens, A. (1984). *The Constitution of Society*. California: University of California Press.

Golding, B. & Savage, S.P. (2011). Leadership and performance management. In T. Newburn (Ed.), *Handbook of Policing* (pp. 725–799) (2nd edn). Abingdon: Taylor & Francis.

Grint, K. (2005). Problems, problems, problems: the social construction of "leadership". *Human Relations*, 58(11), 1467–1494.

Grint, K. & Thornton, S. (2015). Leadership, management, and command in the police. In J. Fleming (Ed.), *Police Leadership: Rising to the Top* (pp. 95–109). Oxford: Oxford University Press.

Haake, U., Rantatalo, O., & Lindberg, O. (2015). Police leaders make poor change agents: leadership practice in the face of a major organisational reform. *Policing and Society: An International Journal of Research and Policy*, 27(7), 764–778.

Hawkins, J. & Dulewicz, V. (2009). Relationships between leadership style: the degree of change experienced, performance and follower commitment in policing. *Journal of Change Management*, 9(3), 251–270.

Heifetz, R., Grashow, A. & Linsky, M. (2009). *Leadership in a (Permanent) Crisis*. Boston: Harvard Business Press.

Herrington, V. & Colvin, A. (2015). Police leadership for complex times. *Policing*, 10(1), 7–16.

Hersey, P. & Blanchard, K.H. (1988). Situational leadership. In P. Hersey & K.H. Blanchard (Eds.), *Management of Organizational Behavior* (pp. 169–201) (5th edn). Englewood Cliffs: Prentice-Hall. https://ess220.files.wordpress.com/2008/02/hersey-blanchard-1988.pdf.

Hersey, P., Blanchard, K.H., & Johnson, D.E. (2008). *Management of Organizational Behavior* (9th edn). New Jersey, NJ: Prentice-Hall.

Janssens, L., Smet, K., Onghena, P. & Kyndt, E. (2017). The relationship between learning conditions in the workplace and informal learning outcomes: a study among police inspectors. *International Journal of Training and Development*, 21(2), 92–112.

Judge, T.A., Bono. J.E., Ilies, R., & Gerhardt, M.W. (2002). Personality and leadership: a qualitative and quantitative review. *Journal of Applied Psychology*, 87 (4), 765–780.

Karp, T. (2019). *God nok ledelse. Hva ledere gjør i praksis* [Good-enough leadership. What leaders do in practice]. Oslo: Cappelen Damm Akademisk.

Kaufmann, G. & Kaufmann, A. (2015). *Psykologi i organisasjon og ledelse* [Psychology in organisation and leadership]. Bergen: Fagbokforlaget.

Kroeck, G., Lowe, K., & Brown, K. (2004). The assessment of leadership. In J. Antonakis, A.T. Cianciolo & R.J. Sternberg (Eds.), *The Nature of Leadership* (pp. 71–95). Thousand Oaks, CA: Sage.

La Rocca, A., Hoholm, T., & Mørk, B.E. (2017). Practice theory and the study of interaction in business relationships: some methodological implications. *Industrial Marketing Management*, 60, 187–195.

Lave, J. & Wenger, E. (1991). *Situated Learning: Legitimate Peripheral Participation*. New York: Cambridge University Press.

Levina, N. & Orlikowski, W.J. (2009). Understanding shifting power relations within and across organizations: a critical genre analysis. *Academy of Management Journal*, 52(4), 672–703.

Lyotard, J.F. (1988). *Differend: Phrases in Dispute*, trans. G. van den Abbeele. Minneapolis: University of Minnesota Press.

Martinsen, Ø. (2015). Lederstil [Leadership style]. In Ø. Martinsen (Ed.), *Perspektiver på ledelse* (pp. 124–151) (4th edn). Oslo: Gyldendal Akademisk.

Mead, G. (2002). Developing ourselves as police leaders: how can we inquire collaboratively in hierarchical organization? *Systemic Practice and Action Research*, 13(3), 191–206.

Meaklim, T. & Sims, J. (2011). Leading powerful partnerships – a new model of public sectors leadership development. *The International Journal of Leadership in Public Services*, 7(1), 21–31.

Mintzberg, H. (1973). *The Nature of Managerial Work*. New York: Harper & Row.

Mintzberg, H. (2009). *Managing*. San Francisco: Berrett-Koehler Publishers.

Moggré, M., den Boer, M., & Fyfe, N.R. (2017). Police leadership in times of transition. *Policing*, 1–10. doi:10.1093/police/pax041.

Mumford, M., Friedrich, T., Caughron, J., & Antes, A. (2009). Leadership research: traditions, developments and current directions. In D. Buchanan & A. Bryman (Eds.), *The Sage Handbook of Organizational Research Methods* (pp. 111–127). London: Sage.

Neyroud, P. (2011). *Review of Police Leadership and Training*. London: Home Office.

Nicolini, D. (2012). *Practice Theory, Work and Organization: An Introduction*. Oxford: Oxford University Press.

Nicolini, D., Gherardi, S., & Yanow, D. (2003). Introduction: towards a practice-based view of knowing and learning in organizations. In D. Nicolini, D. Yanow, & S. Gherardi (Eds.), *Knowing in Organizations: A Practice-Based Approach*. Armonk: M.E. Sharpe.

Northouse, P.G. (2019). *Leadership: Theory and Practice* (8th edn). Kalamazoo: Western Michigan University.

Police Directorate [Politidirektoratet] (2017). *Politiet mot 2025. Politiets virksomhetsstrategi. POD-publikasjon 2017/08* [Towards 2025 – the police's organisational strategy. The National Police Directorate's publication 2017/18]. www.politiet.no/globalassets/05-om-oss/03-strategier-og-p laner/politiet-mot-2025—politiets-virksomhetsstrategi.pdf.

Orlikowski, W.J. (2010). The sociomateriality of organizational life: considering technology in management research. *Cambridge Journal of Economics*, 34, 125–141.

Pfeffer, J. (2015). *Leadership BS: Fixing Workplaces and Careers One Truth at a Time*. New York: HarperCollins.

Pyrko, I., Dörfler, V., & Eden, C. (2019). Communities of practice in landscapes of practice. *Management Learning*, 50(4), 482–499.

Raelin, J.A. (Ed.) (2016). *Leadership-as-Practice: Theory and Application*. New York: Routledge.

Sarver, M.B. & Miller, H. (2014). Police chief leadership: styles and effectiveness. *Policing: An International Journal of Police Strategies & Management*, 37(1), 126–143.

Sayles, L.R. (1964). *Managerial Behavior: Administration in Complex Organisations*. New York: McGraw-Hill.

Schafer, J. (2009). Developing effective leadership in policing: perils, pitfalls and paths forward. *Policing*, 32(2), 238–250.

Schafer, J. (2010). Effective leaders and leadership in policing: traits, assessments, development and expansion. *Policing: An International Journal of Police Strategies & Management*, 33(4), 644–663.

Schatzki, T.R. (1997). Practices and actions: a Wittgensteinian critique of Bourdieu and Giddens. *Philosophy of Social Sciences*, 27(3), 283–308.

Sergi, V. (2016). Materiality and leadership-as-practice. In J.A. Raelin (Ed.), *Leadership-as-Practice: Theory and Application* (pp. 110–131). New York: Routledge.

Silvestri, M. (2003). *Women in Change: Policing, Gender and Leadership*. London: Routledge.

Stewart, R. (1967). *Managers and Their Jobs*. London: Macmillan.

Swid, A. (2014). Police members' perception of their leaders' leadership style and its implications. *Policing: An International Journal of Police Strategies & Management*, 37(3), 579–595.

Taylor, F.W. (1911). *The Principles of Scientific Management*. New York: Harper.

Tengblad, S. (2012). Conclusions and the way forward: towards a practice theory of management. In S. Tengblad (Ed.), *The Work of Managers: Towards a Practice Theory of Management* (pp. 337–356). Oxford: Oxford University Press.

Tsoukas, H. (1996). The firm as a distributed knowledge system: a constructionist approach. *Strategic Management Journal*, 17, 11–25.

Uhl-bien, M., Marion, R., & McKelvey, B. (2007). Complexity leadership theory: shifting leadership from industrial age to the knowledge era. *The Leadership Quarterly*, 18(4), 298–318.

Wittgenstein, L. (1958). *Philosophical Investigations*, trans. G.E.M. Anscombe (3rd edn). Oxford: Blackwell.

Whittington, R. (2006). Completing the practice turn in strategy research. *Organization Science*, 27 (5), 613–634.

Yukl, G. (2013). *Leadership in Organizations* (8th edn). Boston: Pearson.

Zaccaro, S.J., Kemp, C. & Bader, P. (2004). Leader traits and attributes. In J. Antonakis, A.T. Cianciolo, & R.J. Sternberg (Eds.), *The Nature of Leadership* (pp. 101–124). Thousand Oaks, CA: Sage.

Chapter 2

What do police leaders do?

This chapter presents and discusses studies of police leaders' practice. The research is a combination of shadowing police leaders and observing how they perform and their priorities in their daily practice, interviews where they explain their use of time, and a survey testing out categories that we found in the qualitative data. The main categories of what police leaders do are about mastery and prioritising of what they perceive as limited resources. The coordination of resources and tasks dominates, and consequently much of their time is used on deciding priorities, informing, administration, reporting, and most importantly solving ad-hoc problems and issues.

There are few studies describing what police leaders do and what distinguishes Norwegian police leadership from other styles of police leadership, as demonstrated in Chapter 1. The Gjørv Report[1] was critical of police leaders' efforts on 22 July 2011, and so was the subsequent police analysis,[2] which concluded that there were bad attitudes and a bad leadership culture within the police. The empirical basis for both reports was extremely limited, which makes the research basis for this conclusion (attributed to one particular incident on 22 July) reprehensible. Whatever went wrong that day was not followed up on by the studies about why things went wrong and, accordingly, what failed the leadership culture in the police.

Concluding that something is wrong with the leadership culture in the police requires studying police leadership and cannot be narrowed down to one specific event. One has to take into account the everyday leadership practices and the reasons why leadership is exercised in a certain way because everyday leadership is what affects the way leadership is exercised on special occasions. Culture is a comprehensive phenomenon since it is value-based, symbolic, materialised through artefacts, and historical. It frequently involves subjective and often unconscious fundamental assumptions about what police leadership should be, which have usually been formed over a long period of time. Just as it takes a long time to establish leadership cultures, which in many ways represent a basic foundation, changing a leadership culture quickly would be very difficult, if not impossible. Knowledge about police leadership culture is a prerequisite since it would define the starting point and the result of such change. This was the background of the first research project carried out in early 2016.

The research coincided with the start of the Norwegian Community Policing Reform. According to the findings, there was nothing wrong with the leadership culture in the police, but similar to other organisations we have studied, there were good, average, and bad leaders in the police too (Filstad, Glomseth, & Karp, 2017). What we found was that little attention was given to leadership as a discipline, which, as we argued, is not equivalent to a bad leadership culture. Police leaders were often recruited

DOI: 10.4324/9781003224105-4

as "foremost among equals", and their professional development as leaders was not specifically facilitated or controlled. Any leadership education beyond taking the leadership programme at the Norwegian Police University College or another university was mostly self-initiated (Filstad, Karp, & Glomseth, 2018). Police leaders practise to become leaders, which they refer to as learning by doing. This means they feel more confident and cope with their role better after gaining experience as leaders over a long period of time. They explain that it is mostly about finding one's personal and unique path and one's own way to exercise leadership depending on what suits a particular police leader best. The development of their leadership practice is influenced by the dynamics of the actions that the police work represents, the nature of the work they are leading, the framework set by the interaction and cooperation with other leaders and employees, and their own expectations. A lot of attention is placed on what gives a leader the necessary legitimacy. Both nationally and internationally, police leaders typically move up the ranks (although this is about to change slightly), so the hiring process during the reform was dominated by the principle of rights and obligations and not necessarily by competence. Accordingly, legitimacy is often attained by being the first among equals, and the valuable experiences gained in the field are most often associated with policing tradecraft rather than leadership. The professional aspect of policing is of great value, and police leadership is more about being a leader within the policing profession and having certain expertise as a leader, rather than about leadership as a "profession" in itself. If you have been part of the emergency squad, you will always be "the one from the emergency squad", in the same way as you can be "the one who solved that case" or "the one who worked as an advocate for human rights in the Hague for many years". It can also have the opposite effect of preventing a leader from ever becoming more than a patrol officer, which could cause the leader to refuse to make unpopular decisions out of a desire to always "take care of their flock".

The importance of technical policing proficiency can be viewed in connection with the social mission. The overarching vision and mission in one, the social mission of the police is something that gives meaning and identity in policing. Doing something that "means something to people" is what motivates officers. This intrinsic motivation is of great importance, and it helps them cope with many inconveniences associated with the profession. Accordingly, police leaders emphasise the social mission and the fact that their identity and loyalty correspond to the importance of that social mission. Political control, bureaucracy, hierarchy, and loyalty distinguish the Norwegian police and hence the way Norwegian police leaders exercise leadership. The fact that police leaders are mostly recruited internally may also account for their loyalty locally. The hands-on involvement, the desire to be more available to their team than one can reasonably afford on a busy workday, being visible and informal, the sense of humour, and the occasionally light tone are the features police leaders retain as they move further up the leadership levels. Police leadership is largely about taking care of "your guys". We see this tendency on many leadership levels in the police, and it creates some challenges for the more senior leadership levels. The higher the level of leadership, the greater the expectation that the leader would be concerned with the whole, and the whole in the form of a matrix rather than a line is therefore a challenge. The more "silo mentality" there is, often well-meant and based on the desire to take care of "your guys", the more significant the consequences in terms of addressing all of the professional areas within the police. When resources are also limited and sometimes critical, which they proved to become locally as the result of the reform, a struggle for resources takes place. This struggle then causes rivalry rather than the necessary interdisciplinary cooperation within the management teams. Police leaders are well aware of these circumstances, the expectations they have of themselves and their team, and the way they perceive what is expected of them from their senior managers or political leaders. In the first study of 27 police leaders (2016) (Karp, Filstad, & Glomseth, 2019), we found that police leadership is largely focused around the following:

1   **Working towards mastering the leader role(s)**. These roles are influenced by expectations, leaders' own background/experience, professional values, management systems, leadership development, and the personal processes they go through in order to cope with the day-to-day experience of being a leader. To elaborate further, mastery of leadership roles may require that leaders themselves, based on expectations and feedback, take responsibility for defining their roles and improving themselves as they move along. A "role" in this context is a psychological construction that leaders may need in order to tackle the pressure, responsibility, and power (which has both an internal and an external aspect). Mastery is largely about dealing with busy workdays. This is why the notion of mastering leadership may be extended to dealing with the responsibility one has as a leader as well as one can. The conclusion is that police leaders manage responsibility through one or several leader roles, roles that are defined by themselves and by expectations from their senior managers and subordinates, and they are doing their best to cope with the demanding workdays as leaders.

2   **Dealing with organisational tasks**. By this, we mean responding to events that happen in an organisation, which also involves dealing with unplanned situations that have to be handled. It may involve unexpected problems or more trivial situations. This process takes place face-to-face or through digital media. It is a way of reacting that is most likely closely intertwined with police leaders' training/identity. The phenomenon may also be associated with structural conditions, but it seems to be emerging regardless of where the leaders are placed or where they work (with some exceptions). Dealing with tasks could, and should, also mean avoiding being "a spanner in the works" (that is, standing in the way of the course of events in the organisation) but at the same time pursuing the necessary quality assurance, exercising control, and creating legitimacy. For many police leaders, the process of "cleaning up" represents mastery and value, so dealing with organisational tasks can be something they unconsciously or consciously seek out in order to both confirm their identity as police leaders and to validate themselves. The findings above must be considered in view of the fact that we have studied medium and senior managers, especially in situations related to operations management.

3   **Operating the organisational unit they are responsible for**. This includes making meeting arrangements, financial management, planning, follow-up on personnel, and administrative tasks that are necessary to make the unit work over time. There seem to be different views on how important these tasks are and what their priority level should be. Nevertheless, they constitute a central part of the leader's responsibility, and it may be difficult to differentiate between "leading" (people) and "administering" (systems) in practice. Operating a unit presumably also gives leaders legitimacy and manoeuvring space while also sending out important signals about priorities and values, and it can therefore manifest a power basis.

4   **Making choices and setting priorities**. Leaders make choices and set priorities within the imposed framework. This is their responsibility, and they are expected to manage it. Many leaders say that the set of priorities they have to follow are often not in line with their own assessments, but instead imposed on them by, for example, the National Police Directorate. This concerns priorities that are universal in the sense that they will apply to the entire police regardless of the district or region. Leaders may not always be the obvious decision-makers that they think they are or that those around them expect them to be. This could be the case because they disagree with some of the decisions or do not build on their previous practice and do not use their previous experience of doing good police work. In certain cases, it seems that the best way to manage the decision-making responsibility is to run collective processes that lead to making decisions, setting priorities, and solving dilemmas (they often have to learn to live with dilemmas because they lack support for their own decisions or for the way those decisions should be implemented depending on a particular police district). This may ensure engagement, ownership, and better quality decisions, but it may also diffuse responsibility. This applies to collective processes that take place as part of daily operations within the unit a leader is responsible for. For assignment-based work, there are other processes that apply, and these are characterised by a greater degree of intensity and closer communication. The weakness of the existing data is that we have largely only observed daily operations and have not researched special operations. One could therefore argue that our findings may not be universally representative, especially in terms of the decision-making processes.

5   **Caring for and developing interpersonal relationships**. Leaders indicate that they are concerned with relationships, rely on values, and try to create a positive working environment that in turn creates good organisational culture. An alternative interpretation is that they are social architects who do their best to create the least dysfunctional social system possible. Leaders achieve this by talking to people and seeing them. They seek to "lubricate" the social system by making sure everything goes smoothly in the unit they are responsible for. This may be because many leaders are genuinely concerned about human relationships and are therefore relationship-oriented in their actions and behaviour. Alternatively, they might have a need to be liked, be unwilling to stand out as leaders, or be unwilling to create asymmetrical power relationships that would threaten the team spirit too much. The focus on interpersonal relationships can also be explained by the fact that they recognise the feeling of being ordered to prioritise something that they do not agree with and therefore know how this creates frustration, so they try their best to prevent this. The final interpretation is that police leaders engage in relationship management because this is expected nowadays (not least as the result of the Gjørv Report).

6   **Managing themselves**, more or less consciously and as well as they can, in order to make good choices when coping with the workload, stress, pressure, and responsibility they face on a daily basis. Day-to-day work may be demanding for many leaders, and they have to take care of themselves to handle the requirements and expectations they have to meet. However, some police leaders may be part of a public organisational culture where self-management is not widely discussed, and leaders are expected to take care of everything themselves. Complete the task, reach

the goals, and off you go. This means that there is barely room for self-care and little training in self-management. The workload pressure that many police leaders claim they have may also only be a construction they have built in order to make themselves more important as leaders than they really are. The majority of police leaders, however, most likely face the actual pressure, so there is a need to set boundaries and prioritise their time and capacity. They have to both define their role(s) and manage their own personal processes to be able to fulfil those role(s).

7   **Influencing the standard conditions** they work under. Not everyone is aware of it or talks about it, and one might ask whether there is any culture of addressing disagreement in the police at all. Those who do, however, are the people we would call practical and pragmatic strategists in everyday life: they see the big picture, choose their battles, exercise upward leadership, make allies, and take part in internal political discussions. In addition, they tend to be more positive towards change and development. There is apparently no strong tradition for such behaviour in the police, where the culture is more operational and assignment based. Working to create room for manoeuvring and leading changes are also the concepts that largely reflect the reform and the portion of the National Police Directorate's agenda that applies to police leaders. Change and development are often central to the discussion about so-called "modern police leadership". This defining authority might have influenced some of the informants who indicate a greater degree of positivity towards strategy and change than they might actually have otherwise. The category is somewhat unclear, but it is still central to what police leaders do or should do. Several informants also associate many of the concepts within this category with the reform, while we attempt to make the category and this analysis more general. It may also be defined so as to include different content. Still, the conclusion so far is that many police leaders are practice-oriented strategists who openly, or secretly, work to influence their strategic and operational manoeuvring space and want changes to happen. This is both because they are in the middle of a demanding reform and because they want to be able to operate in complex organisational systems where politics, conflicts of interest, and power struggles are also part of the process.

8   **Being committed to the social mission**. To accomplish the social mission in the best possible way, police leaders act and rely on identities and a set of values that reflect the mission they set out to complete. What makes police leadership special is that leaders exercise power on behalf of the authorities as well as tackle a number of demanding and very urgent tasks where clear leadership is a must. It regulates the need for both ethical considerations and clarity. There is little evidence in our data that the use of power affects the day-to-day exercise of organisational leadership – on the contrary, collectivity and loyalty to the team form a weak foundation for asymmetrical power relationships, and the use of power is not much discussed internally. This is also due to the fact that we were mostly observing daily operations and to a lesser extent participated in special operations. Therefore, our conclusion for now is that police leadership does not qualify as being so special/different in comparison to other types of leadership that it needs to be considered as a completely separate discipline. Nevertheless, police leadership is exercised in a context where the use of power and the demanding nature of operations define other conditions for parts of the mission completion and where leadership needs a different

form. Succeeding, however, is probably more about the kind of competence the police needs to have and develop, rather than about leadership forms and the exercise of leadership.

9   **Doing a job that is formed by a very specific leadership culture**, a culture that is both national and local. Particularly relevant are exercise of power, homogeneity, loyalty to the team, mission completion, and the fact that the value/ethics banner is held up high. The gap between the rhetoric and the reality is, however, difficult to analyse. (For example, are police leaders more ethical than other leaders?) Another important point is that police leaders are also co-creators of the culture that sets the framework for their leadership development, which is something that not all police leaders seem to be aware of. An alternative understanding and a possible conclusion is that police leadership is about being the "foremost among equals" and that being the foremost is often what gives legitimacy as a police leader, that is, a feeling of being "one of the guys" (which in turn creates the police leadership culture).

In accordance with the leadership-as-practice perspective, I do not distinguish between administration and leadership. This distinction is more theoretical in nature than based on practical studies of leadership. Administration and leadership are integrated as two sides of a coin when it comes to leadership (Mintzberg, 2009). Which is more significant partly depends on leadership level, especially when we consider the strategic, operational, and tactical levels of leadership. Police leaders administer, lead, and act in ways that may not always be identified as either administration or leadership but may constitute something else that could indirectly reflect these two concepts. Administration, leadership, and other activities leaders are involved in are instead integrated, combined, or separated. Accordingly, various types of administration and leadership that characterise a leadership practice are found in the integrated, sometimes combined, and sometimes also separated activities. What police leaders spend most of their time and capacity on will provide knowledge about what they do in practice and how they strive to achieve what Karp (2019) calls "good-enough leadership" on a daily basis. There is rarely anything heroic or perfectionist about leaders in general, nor does this apply to police leaders. The majority of police leaders are hard-working, engaged, and genuinely concerned with the social mission. They are not all the same. There is no homogeneous group of police leaders who follow a leadership formula; instead, they have different opportunities for exercising leadership that depend on the "what", "who", "how", and "why" described above. What police tasks they are going to complete, who has the competence to do so, how they will do so (given the resources at their disposal), and why they will do so (by making sense of the goals) are the kinds of priorities they have to set in order to complete the social mission. Police leaders are expected to exercise good and successful leadership and be strategic, effective, active, relationship-oriented, communicative, and good at decision-making, but at the same time they do not have enough time for their subordinates, need to solve dilemmas related to loyalty to senior managers versus loyalty to their subordinates based on the expected deliverables, compete for resources within their area of responsibility while being well aware of the fact that their silo mentality causes problems for other areas, and so on. My point is that the reason police leaders do not always manage to live up to the normative expectations of good leadership described earlier is that leadership is complex, uncertain, and difficult. It presents barriers related to the surroundings (the public, politicians), organisation (structures and cultures), and personality (aptitude and competence), as well as the expectations people have of leadership in general. For example, when police leaders say they do not have the opportunity to work strategically, which is expected at higher leadership levels, it is difficult to separate leadership from strategic leadership. Police leaders refer to strategic leadership as something separate from their day-to-day practice as leaders and something that requires time for stepping back and thinking the "big strategic thoughts". But what are the barriers that are preventing police leaders from working more strategically? Is it time, resources, culture, organisational structure and bureaucracy, manoeuvring space, or lack of strategic competence? To find the answer, we have to look closely at the police leaders' daily practice. Understanding practice is absolutely necessary in order to match this practice with the expectations people have for police leaders. This is what the leadership-as-practice perspective does, not least based on the idea, expressed by March (1991), that change, learning, and development of new competence are always about balancing between utilising already existing knowledge and exploring new knowledge on what future police services should be like. Just as leadership as practice represents a new approach to leadership, strategy as practice constitutes a new approach to the subject of strategy. This new approach views strategy as a stream of activities in a practice that are built up over time by actions and interactions that affect the strategy and are affected by it at the same time (Jarzabkowski, 2004). This is why practice, and the activities that occur in practice, enables the strategy and provides the tools and methods for the strategic work.

In our further studies (2018), we conducted a survey on what police leaders do and to what extent they recognise themselves in the description that, according to the other 27 police leaders, was characteristic of their leadership (Filstad & Karp, 2018):

Table 2.1 The results of a survey among police leaders on what they think they spend their time on (2,678 responses from police leaders)

What police leaders do	Agree	Neither/nor	Disagree
Coordinate resources and tasks	77	18	5
Inform and update subordinates	80	18	2
Make decisions	86	13	2
Prioritise	86	12	2
Administrate and report	62	26	12
Participate in meetings	61	27	11
Talk to people	67	28	5
Complete tasks with inadequate resources	70	24	6
Solve ad hoc issues	77	19	4
Cope with the uncertainty of the leader role	26	26	49
Look good – serve your own department	21	35	44
Deal with power and politics	22	32	46
Tackle pressure and expectations	71	26	3
Deal with changes of plans	60	34	6
Solve dilemmas and conflicts	43	41	17

We see that our findings from the qualitative interviews correspond with how police leaders describe their work life and with what the other employees say their leaders spend time on doing. Only police leaders with personnel responsibility took part in the 2016 study, and they represented leadership level 1 (four leaders), leadership level 2 (17 leaders), and leadership level 3 (six leaders). In the survey, both types of police leaders answer relatively similarly. The exception is that those without personnel responsibility say they use less time to talk to people, participate in meetings, inform, coordinate, solve dilemmas/conflicts, and tackle pressure and expectations. According to police leaders, they do not spend a lot of time coping with the uncertainty of the leader role or "looking good", so they do not see themselves as active participants in any kind of game of power and politics. This is an interesting finding given the fact that the police is a politically controlled organisation where leaders have to utilise contested resources as well as they can. (I will come back to this topic in Chapter 12, which is about power and politics, because it is crucial to understanding police leadership as practice.)

What police leaders are and what they spend time on doing can be summarised as follows: (1) Mastery of the leader role(s). "Mastery" means tackling hectic, chaotic, and complex workdays and issues. Mastery is also a matter of establishing themselves as legitimate leaders – which is often based on experience in operational work – and of being deeply aware of the social mission of the police. (2) Leading and dealing with organisational tasks in order not to be "a spanner in the works". (3) Operating and administering the organisational unit they are responsible for, which can give legitimacy and manoeuvring space but is mostly about the deliverables by which their performance is measured. (4) Choosing, prioritising, managing, and taking responsibility for decisions. These are often collective processes that take place as part of daily operations but can also be more direct and intense processes in terms of communications that relate to special operations. (5) Caring for and developing interpersonal relationships. Leaders achieve this by talking to people and seeing them. They seek to "lubricate" the social system by making sure everything goes smoothly in the unit they are responsible for. This is why they are particularly concerned with being available. (6) Managing themselves in order to cope with the workload, stress, pressure, and responsibility they face on a daily basis. There is no strong self-management tradition in the police. (7) Being practical and pragmatic strategists in their day-to-day work. They try to see the big picture, choose their battles, exercise upward leadership, make allies, and take part in internal political discussions. Their attempts to influence standard conditions and find local solutions are often part of daily operations. (8) Being committed to the social mission and trying to accomplish it the best way possible. They do this by acting and relying on identities and a set of values that reflect that social mission. (9) Exercising leadership within the framework of a police leadership culture that they co-create and that places a large focus on being "foremost among equals".

The practice perspective presupposes that leadership is more complex than the cause-and-effect relationship. The cause-and-effect relationship means that a specific action will always lead to the same result. For example, delegating responsibility should result in more autonomous and motivated team members. Is this always the case? Is it reliant upon how police leaders delegate this responsibility? Does it depend on the kind of co-responsibility an individual employee needs and what motivates that employee? Do the goals that are set in a particular department have any bearing? What about the tasks to be completed? The competence of the employee, leader, and colleagues? And so on. Isn't the answer that it depends? It is about learning as part of one's own leadership practice and, through experience, gaining more competence from the leadership style learnt from previous, current, and future colleagues and employees. Together with their subordinates, police leaders achieve mastery, adjust direction, and acquire new knowledge and apply it while developing their leadership practices. A leadership culture develops only by doing, by standing in the middle of something that will later turn into experience, and by establishing a leadership practice that takes its shape over time, which is a continuous learning process necessary for evolution. This is why making necessary changes to the leadership culture in accordance with the new challenges facing the police is about developing what police leaders already do, not presenting them with more normative models and leadership theories on what they should do. When the purpose is better leadership, police leaders must learn and develop their own leadership in practice. This should also be addressed by both the Norwegian Police University College and other leadership development programmes that are largely arranged locally by the police. Various police districts need to facilitate this development in practice. This requires practice to be developed parallel to the development of individual police leaders. This is where the potential for better police leadership is to be found.

But haven't police leaders always done that? Haven't they been developing a police leadership practice all this time? I am inclined to think so, but our research also shows that they have been doing that while leadership as a discipline was not necessarily the focus of the police. This does not only apply to the Norwegian police: I found that the same is true for other countries where the comparison to the Norwegian police would be relevant. Leadership as a discipline is therefore relatively new in the police.

To develop and change police leadership practice, and thus what police leaders do, we need to consider why they act the way they do and why the leadership practice has those particular distinguishing features. To do that, it is not enough to isolate an individual police leader and expect them to change. It is necessary to see the entirety and the potential for change, something that provides the necessary framework for developing good leadership practices in the police. The leadership culture in the police has not necessarily been bad, but leadership as a discipline has never been a focus. No one has come up with an adequate remedy either, other than arranging leadership courses, trainings, etc. This needs to be rooted in and developed by daily leadership practice, and it is important to know what could enable or prevent good leadership. I go more in-depth on this topic in the following chapters of this book, but in the next chapter, I first want to look at why leaders lead (or not) to begin with, what good leadership is, and for whom it is good. What is it that makes police leaders lead?

Notes

1 Official Norwegian Report (NOU) 2012: 14. Report from the 22/7–2011 terror attacks in Oslo/Utøya – the commission was led by A.B. Gjørv.
2 Official Norwegian Report (NOU) 2013: 9. One police force – equipped to meet future challenges (The Police Analysis from the Ministry of Justice and Public Security).

References

Filstad, C. & Karp, T. (2018). *Ledelsesimplementering, effekter og resultater av nærpolitireformen* [Leadership implementation, outcomes and results of the Norwegian Community Policing Reform]. Oslo: Politihøgskolen.
Filstad, C., Glomseth, R., & Karp, T. (2017). Er det noe galt med lederkulturen i politiet? Filstad, Glomseth og Karp [Is there something wrong with the police leadership culture? Filstad,

Glomseth, and Karp]. *Aftenposten.* www.aftenposten.no/meninger/kronikk/i/OMe3q/Er-det-noe-galt-med-lederkulturen-i-politiet-Filstad_-Glomseth-og-Karp.

Filstad, C., Karp, T., & Glomseth, R. (2018). How police leaders learn to lead. *Policing: A Journal of Policy and Practice.* https://academic.oup.com/policing/advance-article-abstract/doi/10.1093/police/pay043/5050176.

Jarzabkowski, P. (2004). Strategy as practice: recursiveness, adaptation, and practices-in-use. *Organization Studies,* 25(4), 529–560.

Karp, T. (2019). *God nok ledelse. Hva ledere gjør i praksis* [Good-enough leadership. What leaders do in practice]. Oslo: Cappelen Damm Akademisk.

Karp, T., Filstad, C., & Glomseth, R. (2019). 27 days of managerial work in the police service: being foremost among equals. *Police Practice and Research,* 20(5), 427–443.

March, J.G. (1991). Exploration and exploitation in organizational learning. *Organizational Science,* 2(1), 71–87.

Mintzberg, H. (2009). *Managing.* San Francisco, CA: Berrett-Koehler Publishers.

Chapter 3

When do police leaders lead?

This chapter outlines some commonly known and acknowledged statements in the leadership literature and discusses when police leaders lead. The common statements are that leaders lead when they influence others, when they have certain traits, skills, and/or knowledge, when they have moral authority, or when they create followership. The chapter argues that mastery needs to be acknowledged and that even though leaders influence or have certain skills and knowledge, they do not perform good leadership. Mastery will shift focus onto how leaders manage the collective co-creation process through the leader-subordinate and the employee-employee relationships in developing leadership practices.

A leadership practice is more than simply someone doing something. Practice is activity patterns that are professionalised, perfected, and automated over time. They are based on knowledge, skills, abilities, and any routines or habits that the practitioner acquires, as well as on who the leader is, what context they work in, and what tools are available. Therefore, research into practice emphasises the importance of culture, structure, organisation, context, and other conditions that affect a leadership practice, while taking into account that leadership practices also affect these conditions. As argued several times, there is no formula or recipe for police leadership, so is it still possible to determine when police leaders exercise leadership? I am initiating this discussion based on some statements in the leadership literature.

Police leaders lead when they influence others

According to leadership researcher Gary Yukl (1989), leadership is about influence. Many definitions of leadership describe it as processes aimed at influencing people and groups to reach a common goal. Yukl (2013) states further that leadership relates to the conscious influence that certain individuals exert over other people in order to guide, structure, and arrange activities and relationships in a group or an organisation. It is often added that the purpose of influencing is to achieve something, be it a goal, a result, or another ambition to be realised. Yukl's reasoning reflects prevalent assumptions about leadership. Some newer streams of research have additionally emphasised the significance of sensemaking (Arnulf, 2012).

The structure and culture in the police are hierarchical and order- and rank-based. The clearest form of influence we can observe here is when leaders give orders. Leadership is exercised in asymmetrical power relationships as those in the leader position have more power than other employees. There is a tradition of giving and receiving

DOI: 10.4324/9781003224105-5

orders in the police. The use of authority is perceived as legitimate. Given the police culture and its hierarchical structure, we see that employees accept this. As one of them explains: "My leader has to have the last word because it is his job, his position and function." This is further enhanced through the use of such symbols as a uniform, stars on the shoulder, titles, equipment, and education. We also observe that police leaders exert their influence by being role models in relation to certain actions, attitudes, and values. Many of them are hard-working – they maintain a high standard and in many ways appear to be the best among equals (Karp, 2019). One police leader says: "I am convinced that everything I say and do, just as everything I do not say and do not do, gets noticed. I am very conscious of my own behaviour and how I carry myself when I meet other people, what I place emphasis upon and what I might correct."

However, although we see that role models influence others, that does not mean they are exercising leadership. Leaders are not the only ones who influence other people within an organisation. Subordinates may be influenced by someone else's leaders, colleagues, cooperation partners, the public, politicians, and so on. This is why the idea of exerting influence does not explain leadership well enough. Influence may not always be traced back to leaders. For instance, does an order in the police result in all employees always working together for a common goal? No. An individual police leader can influence another employee by giving an order. The way that employee carries out the order, interacts with others, and then performs their duties, may vary significantly. Police officers do not passively let themselves be influenced; they are autonomous individuals with deep knowledge and experience in police work. They act as informal leaders in society, for other police officers, for the public, for criminals, etc. This is why it would be quite naïve to think that police officers will always collectively "move towards a common goal" because of the influence leaders have on them. So, we cannot claim that police leaders lead because they influence their subordinates.

Police leaders lead when they have certain qualities, traits, or knowledge

The leadership research has been concerned with the qualities, traits, or knowledge necessary to become a leader. It has been emphasised that leaders need to have special personality traits, charisma, specific skills, or social or emotional intelligence. According to Yukl (2013), leaders should have large working capacity and stamina, good stress resistance, a high degree of self-confidence, faith that they can influence their surroundings, emotional stability, willingness to have power, high integrity, and the need for high performance but little need for confirmation. Police researchers are especially concerned with police leaders having high ethical standards, having integrity and reliability, being role models, being good communicators and effective decision-makers, having critical/creative/strategic capacity, creating a shared vision, and taking care of their team.

We did not do a personality test. Nothing in our data indicates that the universal qualities, traits, or knowledge of certain individuals result in leaders exercising leadership. What we found, however, was that some typical qualities within particular groups may be crucial for leadership. Police leaders are expected to be relationship-oriented, be available, be good communicators, be action- and decision-oriented, be proficient in technical aspects of policing, and be committed to the social mission, and hence to serving the public. But, and this is a significant "but", employees prefer certain qualities or competencies in police leaders. They would rather the leader have particular qualities because they believe this will help them yield more for themselves and have better conditions at work. Is this good police leadership? Who is to decide what good police leadership is?

We observe that many police leaders are flexible and capable of adapting to situations and people. They try to form the big picture, which makes them both practical and pragmatic, among other things. However, the cause-and-effect link – according to which specific personal qualities lead to the right type of behaviour, which in its turn leads to a certain influence, which in its turn creates followership, and which ultimately results in many people working for a common goal – does not stand up to scrutiny. The fact that someone leads and others let themselves be led is more complex. A more likely explanation when it comes to personal qualities or skills is that a certain configuration of qualities, skills, and abilities, in a combination that is right for the person possessing them and adapted to the context that person operates in, is used for tackling relevant situations. This creates conditions for mutual interactions between lower-level employees, and between these employees and the leader. The sum of these interactions and their variations increases the likelihood of the group as a whole moving towards the goal they want to achieve. This is why we do not see much evidence that would suggest that specific universal qualities, traits, skills, and knowledge, when viewed regardless of situations, relationships, and context, would result in police leaders exercising leadership.

Police leaders lead as the result of moral authority

We would generally claim that a lot of modern leadership literature considers leadership to be a good thing. Leadership is used, at least unconsciously, as a hallelujah word. It would be great if this understanding of leadership reflected the reality, but it does not, which is problematic. First of all, other leadership perspectives may disappear in the large volume of the "feelgood" stories, reports, and leadership concepts. Second, the idea that leadership is always good reinforces itself and leads many people to look for facts that would confirm preconceived assumptions. Third, the pursuit of goodness creates unrealistic expectations of what leaders can achieve. And fourth, there are too many leaders who are not good or do not exercise good leadership to claim that leadership is universally good, not because leaders do not want it to be, but because there are too many barriers in the way of making it happen.

Police leaders lead when they create followership

Employees are expected to follow leaders because the job they get paid for implies taking a leader into account. They also follow leaders because leaders are given formal power over them. Leadership is an asymmetrical power relationship between a leader and those who are led, but let us first assume that the people this applies to, i.e. employees who follow leaders, largely have an ability to think independently, complete their work tasks the way they are supposed to, and are also generally self-sustained and self-motivated, which is mostly the case in the police. We can find some possible sources of followership. Leaders may create followership when they inspire hope or effectively manage especially challenging situations. The hope may be that the leader will contribute to creating a better future that the followers also believe in. A leader in the police is trusted in challenging situations and has the legitimacy to handle these situations due to experience, professional position, and professional integrity. The majority of employees in the police, with some exceptions, are fully capable of forming their own opinions and understanding what needs to be done. They are motivated and capable of taking care of themselves, so they cannot be considered passive followers. The employees as followers are instead the ones who create leaders, and thus create leadership as practice (Alvesson, 2016). This means co-creation rather than followership. First, members of a leadership practice act as intermediaries, sharing leadership in the process of implementing various tasks depending on, among other things, their knowledge, skills, experiences, abilities, and personality. The formal leader still has the responsibility, but different participants take on partial responsibility in various phases, processes, or situations. Second, followers create a framework for leadership. This framework defines what kind of leadership they want to have, when they want leadership to happen, and how they want to be led. This does not have to be explicitly stated, but it provides directions for the exercise of leadership and the way it is perceived. Third, we believe that leadership is a result of opportunities and constraints in a particular situation, which presupposes elements of co-creation. Therefore, it is co-creation rather than followership that makes police leaders lead.

Police leaders lead because they master the leadership work

Leaders in the police lead because they master the leadership work. They are good at what they do and capable of developing leadership practice. Within the leadership practice, they manage the collective co-creation process through the leader-subordinate and the employee-employee relationships. It is largely about their ability to cope with leadership tasks, which is the result of extensive practice and learning ability. However, we have not found a set of universal traits, abilities, qualities, or skills and knowledge that would guarantee success, since these vary from leader to leader, from employee to employee, and from context to context. From a conversation with a subordinate about a leader: "He is good at what he does." Another leader talks about their leader:

> He is a trendsetter in terms of always looking for new challenges. He gives free rein. He promotes autonomy. He used to be more concerned with taking care of "his guys", but now he is much more focused on the entirety/the big picture. A competent leader.

Another leader explains why he considers himself as a good leader:

> I have broad experience, and I'm still professionally strong. I keep track of the cases and have a good memory. I'm good at listening, I hear what is being said. I'm engaged, and I really pay attention to people.

And finally, a leader on what he thinks it takes to become a leader in the police:

> Presence. The ability to tell a story, to create stories. You have to be professionally competent, the police profession is a craft. Being conscious of the signals you send

out, of what you put on the agenda. Actions speak louder than words, what you do really means something. Being available. Being present and visible in important arenas. Influencing people through dialogue, police officers are knowledge workers. Leaders in the police have to be able to work with people. You must also rely on academic knowledge.

Leadership is formal responsibility. Organisation researcher Peter Drucker argues that leadership is not about rank, privileges, titles, or money, but about responsibility. Leaders must have, or take, responsibility, and this responsibility cannot be diffused. They must be held responsible for their actions, and it is therefore crucial to understand what this responsibility entails on different leadership levels in the police. Coping with this responsibility does not necessarily mean excellent leadership and expertise – it is instead something which is often the case in practice and which Karp (2019) calls "good-enough leadership". "Good-enough leadership" is when the job is done and all tasks and commitments are completed in a responsible and adequate manner, which helps the organisation achieve its goals.

Leadership is mastered through practice, and leaders achieve mastery through experiences. Mastery has received little attention in the leadership literature, but there are some insights on what factors are important for mastery. First, mastery is the result of experiences. Leadership development courses or a master's degree in leadership are not enough, although they can have an effect on what a leader does in practice. Policing as a profession requires many hours of hard work, exercise, training, and practice. The same is true for leadership. Mastery requires extensive training and long-term commitment, and one has to be focused on reflection, learning, and development (Haukedal, 2000).

The reasons why police leaders do not always exercise good leadership relate to the existing barriers and motivators for good leadership in the police. This is why I will reflect on possible barriers and motivators (most often viewed together, not separately) while looking closely at leadership culture, performance management, manoeuvring space, competence, leadership contexts such as structural and cultural logic, leadership of police services, and leadership levels in the police.

References

Alvesson, M. (2016). Studying leadership: taking meaning, relationality and ideology seriously. In J. Storey, J. Hartley, J.L. Denis, P.T. Hart & D. Ulrich (Eds.), *The Routledge Companion to Leadership* (pp. 67–88). New York: Routledge.

Arnulf, J.K. (2012). Organizational change capacity and composition of management teams: a visualization of how personality traits may restrain team adaptability. *Team Performance Management*, 18(7/8), 433–454.

Haukedal, W. (2000). Ledelse og kunnskapsarbeid: Motivering av autonome medarbeidere [Leadership and knowledge work: Motivating autonomous employees]. In S. Einarsen & A. Skogstad (Eds.), *Det gode arbeidsmiljø. Krav og utfordringer* (pp. 55–77). Bergen: Fagbokforlaget.

Karp, T. (2019). *God nok ledelse. Hva ledere gjør i praksis* [Good-enough leadership. What leaders do in practice]. Oslo: Cappelen Damm Akademisk.

Yukl, G. (1989). Managerial leadership: a review of theory and research. *Journal of Management*, 15, 251–289.

Yukl, G. (2013). *Leadership in Organizations* (8th edn). Boston: Pearson.

Chapter 4

Police leadership as practice

This chapter discusses what a police practice can be described as. What police leader practice can be is demonstrated by telling the stories of three leadership practices. A practice refers to what the practitioners do and a common understanding of why they do as they do. The social, relational, and collective activities and interactions develop common identities, negotiate power and authorities, values, norms, communication, sensemaking, and knowing. What characterises what a leadership practice might be needs to be described as a result of observations and the police leaders and their employees telling their stories about their practice. The stories provided in this chapter are examples of that.

What a police practice may be

In everyday language, we often refer to practising as an action. We practise by doing something, by creating something; for example, implementing a plan or testing out a theory in practice. "Practise" is a verb that refers to doing something, an action. A practice reflects where we act, that is, where we practise. Overall, we can view the police as a landscape of practice where police employees practise their social mission. We can find the formal police practices in the organisational charts. An example could be investigation practices that have their own sections or a section that is combined with intelligence services at the 12 police districts, in addition to the special units of the police.

Many police leaders and other employees say they are surprised by the differences in the way they work with the same police tasks in various districts, which has become evident in the process of merging geographical units as part of the reform. The same is true for the police leaders who manage the same tasks but exercise leadership in significantly different ways, and their subordinates are satisfied with the leadership. Emphasising the dynamic and evolving nature of practising, which is considered as a verb related to the actions and the people who perform them, provides a common understanding of which actions should be done, when they should be done, and how they should be led. Practice dynamics could involve producing, creating meaning, negotiating, interpreting, cooperating, participating, reflecting, communicating, and so on. Practice dynamics overall refer to the distinguishing features of a leadership practice, but also to the differences between various leadership practices in the police. One leadership practice within investigations may be different from another. The differences occur in spite of the same national goals, political control and administration, requirements for priorities and deliverables, and the like. The police is not a homogeneous group of

DOI: 10.4324/9781003224105-6

leaders and employees, and dividing them into those with police training, lawyers, and civilian employees would be a generalisation. What about the differences associated with areas of expertise such as intelligence, operations, investigation, or crime prevention? Or how about the difference between the districts and geographical units, or between the residents of Oslo, Northern Norway, and Western Norway, for that matter? It is not surprising that there are differences coming from the original districts, units, and departments when geographical units merge into one. The police is, after all, a complex organisation consisting of countless practices, and police leadership has to be studied with this in mind.

A practice shows what the practitioners do within a community where the participants share a common understanding of "why". There are some basic phenomena that are attributed to the social, relationship-oriented, and active individuals, and these phenomena are maintained and expressed in organisational practices.

1 *Identity*: perception of who you are in a practice, and who you are in relation to others. Perception of identity, sense, and structure is therefore crucial to understanding the culture and practice.
2 *Power and authority*: relations that are always present in practice. Human actions, be they strategic, planning-oriented, rational, or intuitive actions, are evaluated in the light of acknowledgement, validation, loyalty, submission, and dominance in a practice.
3 *Moral and ethics*: the idea of right and wrong. The evaluation of one's own actions, norms, values, and constraints, and those of others.
4 *Communication*: this is how meaning occurs when people express themselves in relation to each other and themselves.

A practice is often characterised by the competence or the behaviours it represents. However, organisations are not reserved for formal practices only. To understand police leadership as practice, one has to study both formal and informal practices. In Chapter 8, I will return to informal practices, which are described as communities of practice. To conclude this part of the book on police leadership as practice, I will give some examples of police practices.

Examples of police leadership practices

The following descriptions are from two leadership practices at a police patrol unit in a large Norwegian city. They are followed by a leadership practice example of the managers at a major police station. The purpose of these examples is to identify the characteristics of leadership practices and describe how leadership as practice can be studied through observations of and conversations with those involved. These examples are therefore an important beginning, which is then extended by studying the factors that influence community, participation, activities, and strategies in accordance with the overview model of police leadership as a practice.

Leadership practice – example I

John greets me in the control room and says the dust has finally settled. Things have been crazy since 06.00. He looks a little stressed, or rather busy, but emphasises that sure, he has time, I can come in. On the way up to the guard room, he says that he has already had someone sobbing in his office. While walking from the guard room to the briefing room, he points at the officers who are relaxing in the day room. They were on night duty this weekend, he explains. He waves to the officers in the day room and in the briefing room before he sits down behind the computer and connects the presentation. He praises his team and says they are good at following up. They have been criticised for not being present enough at Q (he names the place) at the weekend, he says, and he makes it clear that he disagrees with that. His people have patrolled the agreed-upon permanent places. John also goes through a report and says the staffing at Q was good this weekend. He talks about Olga, who is bipolar and is becoming a problem for the police. He says they must be careful and share information with each other about what happens. It is important that the others know what to expect. He is still sitting behind the computer, and he quickly answers a phone call.

People in his unit giggle and comment about crazy women, hinting at Olga. John smiles along, reads from the screen, looks up and asks if anyone knows any good people that they should hire. He says they do not know yet how many people they will be allowed to hire to replace those who have quit, but they will listen to suggestions. Social skills are important, he emphasises. He informs his team about the free weekend rules and says they have no flexibility on this issue. Everyone has to show understanding. The discussion about the time for duty shifts is now over, he informs them; the decision is made. That's it, then! All unit managers agree with this, he explains – it has to be the same for everyone! (The change of duty schedule was met with a lot of resistance. John has passed this on to his manager but did not receive support.) One of the team members says something. John says he thinks a reorganisation is highly unlikely now, so soon after the previous one, but he explains that it may be necessary since some of the departments are taking damage. He asks if anyone has any questions. Nobody responds. They are more in the middle in terms of staffing, he says, while two of the other departments are spread thin. He also informs them about a collective project in the criminal intelligence register, Indicia. None of them have uploaded any information yet. John says they have been reprimanded for not using the register. They need to bring in a trainer for a few hours, he insists. He will follow up on this. He shows the team how to upload the information. It should be used for important information when they do not have the opportunity to attend a briefing and have to jump straight into the car. They have to enter a status, numbers, and so on, he explains. It is important for him and it is important for them as well! Important for knowledge and information sharing. There is no clear explanation as to what information must be entered. They have to decide what they think is relevant to enter. John: What do you think about Indicia? Are you doing all right? There is no specific response, only some informal chatting and a bit of laughter. John delegates further training on Indicia to Jane, a member of the team. He emphasises that it is important for them to listen carefully, wishes everyone a good shift, leaves the briefing room, and returns to the guard room.

John's leadership practice

John has over 20 years of experience in this position. He is often out on patrol together with his team. He says that the amount of paperwork is constantly growing, which is why he has to spend a lot of time behind the scenes making the necessary arrangements so that his team can do their best work. I do not feel like John is "one of the gang". He is instead a role model, a mentor, someone who sets the direction, and someone who is respected and trusted by the team. He does not appear to be a dominant person. Instead, embodying the role of a guide or a facilitator is important for the way he practises leadership. He says there are many personal issues, conflicts that have to be resolved, complaints from the public, and the like. He tries to protect his team from these issues as well as he can. He is also very concerned with the social environment and says there are always some alpha males who he needs to settle down a little. He is now working with a complaint about one of the team members who did not behave himself in public this weekend. It is important to him that everyone contribute based on their competence, which is why he gave Jane an opportunity to do just that at the meeting. He is concerned with truly listening to each one of them in their day-to-day work life.

The people in his unit talk about an unwieldy system. There are some people higher in the ranks who make decisions, and it is challenging when such decisions trickle down to their level, they explain. They also say that John is concerned about who is going to be in the car together and that not all of the units do that. There is a nice atmosphere in the lunch corner. A little light teasing, a lot of laughter, and talks about sport and nutrition. When out on patrol, they praise John and say that everyone wants to be in his department. He keeps control of the situations that arise, and he really listens to everyone, they explain. He always has time for everyone. He has shared a plan all the way up to August and took into account everyone's holiday plans. They disagree with the new regulations on duty shifts – this is decided by the management, they say. John has not been able to change this, they say, although they know he agrees with them that the old duty shift regulations were better. They are sure that John argues their case but has not found support among the "higher-ups".

Leadership practice – example 2

Chris has chosen to use the sofa corner instead of the briefing room for this evening shift. The sofas are arranged into a square shape so that everyone can see each other. Along with me, Chris's manager, Paul, and an intern are present. There is a lot of joking and laughter going on, and the team gradually take their seats; several people are eating. Chris says to his department that it is important to use the time they have to talk to each other this way. Especially now when they are so few, which often results in interrupted briefings, or no briefings at all, because they have to dash right away. He takes his turn and gives everyone an opportunity to speak. The topics are a combination of work and private life. It is clear that they know each other very well, and that Chris knows them well. They also express their frustration about having too little staff and the shift schedule that makes them think they will never have a weekend free again. Chris says that as a result, it has also been almost impossible to arrange any social gatherings. He makes it clear that they must do something about it. The team also clearly state that they miss socialising together. It is an absolute crisis in terms of staffing at the moment, he says. Paul also explains how they are working on the issue but says he cannot promise anything. They still do not know how many people they will be allowed to hire. Chris follows up by saying he is going to fight for them and that something must be done. It is a crisis now, he says.

Chris's leadership practice

Chris is very visible physically, and he is also visible in terms of his leadership. He is a natural centre of attention and appears to be "one of the gang". He has almost 20 years of experience in the police behind him and says that his job as a leader is to be out in the field with his team. The team ask the higher-ups to allow Chris to always be out in the field with them so that he can always have their backs. They tell me he has a great vision for their department. Chris expresses very clearly that they should strive for the best and that their job is to be out in the field. His team fully trust that he acts in their best interests when communicating with management. They say he is concerned with building up a culture, and the experienced members of the team are consciously used as culture bearers when new people join their unit. Working environment trumps everything, they explain, even though there are talks about old or lacking equipment and some decisions that they do not understand. Chris and the team say that taking care of each other and being social is what makes the police so special. They get to know each other very well, and this is a tough job that involves many powerful experiences. They feel they are allowed a lot of freedom in their work, and Chris encourages this: "It is up to you what you do in your job, what you choose to engage in and what not to; you have to make such decisions every single day." They say they can always count on Chris's support, but at the same time, he makes it very clear when things need to be improved.

Brief summary – John and Chris

John and Chris are very different as leaders since they have quite different personalities. John is more analytical and quiet (the facilitator) while Chris appears to be more out-going, loud, and noisy (the participant). They are both good at adapting their communication and dialogue to their team, even if they do it differently. In many ways, they represent the same set of values and the same perception of right and wrong, and they never lose focus on the importance of the social mission. This is evident from the way they motivate their teams – they underline the significance of being there for the people and making a difference. This means they are proactive and constantly prepared to fight for their team, and they are both very confident about what constitutes good police work. Both are praised by their teams as very good leaders. If they do not find support further up the chain of command, their team members attribute it to either the top management or "the system", instead of blaming it on John or Chris's leadership.

Leadership practice – example 3

There is some laughter, joking, and a generally casual atmosphere before everyone in the management team sits down. Two managers come in later, and the meeting starts when all ten of them are present. Bill, chief of the police station, is sitting at the end of the table. The topic today is the budget, Bill says, and he refers to the documents from the financial manager that they were supposed to read in advance. Some people flip through the documents, others use a computer, and the financial manager takes the floor and explains the guidelines they have received.

Bill jokingly says that they have to do all the work by themselves, as usual, and that they only got some general guidelines from the Police Directorate. Someone says they have not got enough money to implement something they have previously been promised more funding for. Another person follows up by saying there is growing frustration in her department because they do not know what to expect in the future. Several people nod to her suggestion that they must decide what to do. They cannot wait any longer. The three people who have spoken and expressed their frustration are now primarily engaged in the dialogues. The others are mostly quiet. The financial manager breaks in a little and says that the way forward would be communicating this further, but he does not believe they would be met with support now. Another district is prioritised at the moment, and they have been granted funding because they need it more. Bill says he understands that this district needs funding, but it does not make the situation better for them. He says he has discussed this with the chief of police but received no promises, so they have to wait and see. They should now prioritise delivering the numbers they have been asked about. He explains that to get the necessary support, it is all the more important that their budget is in balance – the others do not have that.

The team are taking part in the discussion with their areas of responsibility in mind, but Bill says they must try to see the big picture in order to stay ahead. He also says it means they are stealing from each other, and the police as a whole is losing out as a result. Bill makes it clear that they have to overcome the situation and therefore have to find local solutions. The discussions go on for a long time, and eventually, only two or three people out of those who expressed their frustration at the start of the meeting are very active. Bill is not one of them. Some people appear to have withdrawn themselves from the discussion. Bill ends the discussion a little later than planned by saying that the financial manager will take into account their comments and review the new draft before sending it to everyone before the next management meeting.

Brief summary

The leaders in this management team appear to be very different. The atmosphere is light and informal, but not everyone shares this light mood. Some people become very dominant in the discussion, and a couple of managers look clearly annoyed with each other at times. This is why on several occasions Bill has to make some comments to stop it. It is also obvious that the managers are fighting for their own responsibility areas, so Bill has to repeat several times that they have to consider the interests of the entire organisation. In many ways, they look more like a group of managers rather than a management team. As part of the Norwegian Community Policing Reform, several new management teams have been established on all levels, and they are facing some of the same challenges that I observed here. Establishing new management teams takes time. (There will be more on this topic in Chapter 14, "Change management as practice", where I also discuss change processes in the establishment of new management as part of the reform.) The discussion goes off on a bit of a tangent, so it becomes difficult for the team to focus and arrive at any conclusions. The issue is put off until the next meeting.

I have several examples indicating that it is challenging to make decisions, not least strategic decisions, at management meetings in the police. In the next part of this book, I will give more examples of factors that can affect strategic leadership in the police.

Part 2

Strategy

I have chosen to refer to profession-specific features in a leadership practice as "strategy". Strategies are based on choices and priorities that serve a comprehensive, overarching, and long-term plan of achieving the organisation's goals (Mintzberg, 1991). In public organisations, strategy refers to the choices made in relation to the use of public funds for best possible value creation associated with the social mission (Johnsen, 2014). Accordingly, the social mission is associated with the specific features of being a police leader compared to being a leader in other types of organisations. Other organisations will have other overall goals and strategies, structures and cultures, and different types of competencies based on what products and services they provide.

§ 1 of the Police Act describes the social mission of the police force as follows: "The police force shall, by means of prevention, enforcement, and supporting activities, be part of society's collective efforts to promote and strengthen the citizens' legal security, safety, and general welfare." The social mission is essential to the police force, and the level of commitment to it is high among both police leaders and police officers. According to the employee survey (2020), police officers' identification with the social mission scores 4.6 points on a Likert scale from 1 to 5. The social mission *is* an important concept and has to be subject to interpretation and prioritisation. After all, according to many police employees, there are no limits for what the police force can do – they will never run out of work. At the same time, they point to the importance of not losing the focus on who they are there for.

As of 2018, there were just over 16,700 employees in the Norwegian police force, of which just over 10,000 represented police person-years, just under 900 were legal person-years, and just under 6,000 were administrative person-years (Police Directorate, 2018). Most of the police employees are educated in policing. A large number of professionals within the police force are also legal professionals who either work as lawyers or as police leaders. Those who work in administrative positions represent various professions, such as economists, psychologists, sociologists, IT (information technology) specialists, HR specialists, and the like.

To find out how they can make the social mission operational, the police spend a lot of time and resources understanding the various contexts they operate in. This means collecting signals from politicians, the local community, the business community, and society at large, and then adapting them for the development of their own police practice. The government's policy in relation to the police, and the Police Directorate's administration of this policy, defines the choices and priorities to be made in order to accomplish the social mission. Strategies require strategic leadership that is capable of

DOI: 10.4324/9781003224105-7

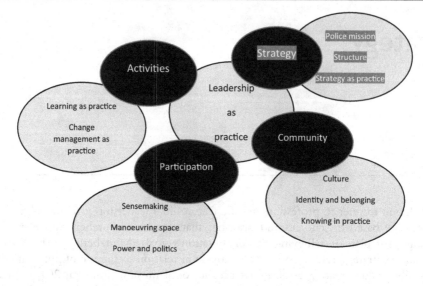

Figure P2.1 Police leadership as practice model: strategy

developing and following up on binding priorities, in addition to daily operations and crisis management. Strategies involve all leadership levels where the organisational structure in the police force affects the way strategies are transformed into strategic knowledge in a leadership practice. This means strategies are a way in which a leadership practice can work strategically while adapting to the particular leadership level in the organisational structure. Performance management in the police force has to be adjusted in accordance with the strategic choices of direction and the priorities that are set.

References

Johnsen, Å. (2014). Strategi i offentlig sektor [Strategy in the public sector]. In Å. Johnsen (Ed.), *En strategisk offentlig sektor* (pp. 269–291). Bergen: Fagbokforlaget.

Mintzberg, H. (1991). Learning 1, planning 0: reply to Igor Ansoff. *Strategic Management Journal, 12* (6), 463–466.

Police Directorate [Politidirektoratet] (2018). *Ressursanalyse for 2018. Utgifter og bemanning i politiet* [Resource analysis for 2018. Costs and staffing in the police force]. www.politiet.no/globala ssets/04-aktuelt-tall-og-fakta/bemanning-ressurser-og-dekningsgrad/ressursanalyser/ressursana lysen-2018.pdf.

Chapter 5

Social mission, organisational structure, and goal management

This chapter gives a brief introduction to the police as a quasi-military organisation and describes it as a hierarchical, bureaucratic, controlled, and order-based organisation. The context dependence of the political and structural ways of organising the police set the scene for understanding police culture. The political and structural logics dominate goal management, which is discussed in this chapter. Goal management is reduced to figures and numbers and not quality and knowledge goals of police services, all of which will influence how leadership practices are constructed as context dependent.

The topic of Chapter 7 is police culture. In this chapter, I focus on the organisational structure of the police. It is important to emphasise that culture and structure should not be confused, they are the topics of two different chapters. Organisational structure is explicit and systematic − it is the very organisation of the police as presented in the organisational charts (Jacobsen & Thorsvik, 2013). Organisational culture is complex, often not visible, integrated in actions, as basic assumptions, sets of values, norms, and constructions of reality (Bang, 2011; Charman, 2017; Cockcroft, 2020).

In many ways, the police is a quasi-military organisation (Filstad & Karp, 2020). Police leaders themselves describe it as a hierarchical, bureaucratic, controlled, and order-based organisation characterised by a strong loyalty to the line of duty. This is also evident from the language of the police culture and its artefacts. The police wear a uniform, they have equipment that symbolises authority, and they can use power in peacetime. They refer to themselves as police service officers, and they join the ranks of the police. They use a common language, such as "duty assignment", "a takedown", "loyalty", "rights and obligations", "copy that", "understood", "assistance", and the like. The language reinforces the strong sense of loyalty to the line of duty and the fact that they are subject to a hierarchical and bureaucratic logic that errs more on the side of control than leadership. Balancing between these two types of logic, that is balancing between control and leadership, is a major feature of the everyday work life of police leaders. I have considered in detail the two types of logic and the conflicting dilemmas they may often entail in Chapter 11 on police leaders' manoeuvring space. In the next section, I focus on how the controlling and structural logic dominates goal management in the police and what consequences goal management has for the development of competence in the leadership practices.

The police is a knowledge-based organisation. Its competence is characterised by a high degree of complexity, which is why it is difficult to measure its contribution and competence. When has the police done a good job? Who has the defining power to say what good police work entails? According to Finstad (2018), the decline in crime, safety,

DOI: 10.4324/9781003224105-8

and justice may clarify the notion of good police work. Finstad warns, however, that these concepts can be mutually exclusive, and whether they are effective measurements depends on the angle of the observer. She explains it by the fact that the police that fights and prevents crime is now stronger in Norway than ever before. However, she poses the question of whether it is the police's responsibility to prevent crime by means of punishment and threats, or whether there is a common social responsibility to facilitate the research that contributes more knowledge on the possible reasons for law obedience.

Goal management in the police

Goal management in the police largely involves explicit objectives in the form of the number of police reports, new cases, unresolved cases, emergency response times, deadlines and number of interrogations, deadlines for investigation, number of arrests, and so on. I do not have the entire overview of all police objectives. I know that some of them are politically determined, required by law, and therefore mandatory. According to police leaders, goal management has very little to do with the quality of police services. They refer to the New Public Management and say that goal management is reduced to figures and numbers. They also explain that the reform introduced very few changes to it. Police leaders feel like the objectives are largely the same as before. One police leader makes it clear: "We have the same target numbers we had before the reforms. What kind of leaders are we if we keep quiet about this?" Police employees say they no longer operate with clearance rates and that staffing plans are put on hold in some places. I do not intend to focus on this here. Instead, I would like to discuss how goal management affects the development of competence in the police.

Goal management sets the direction and priorities for competence development. When the emphasis is on performance targets rather than what competence is required in order to achieve the goals, this is problematic for competence development in the police. Much of this competence is tacit knowledge which cannot be explicitly stated, measured, or counted. For example, how can we measure crime prevention? Is the number of police reports a good indicator of prevention? In a knowledge-based organisation such as the police, a large part of the employees' competence cannot be measured. A level 1 leader explains: "The important thing is what lies behind the numbers. Are we using our competence correctly, and do the numbers show what we are actually good at? Is it the quality or the deliverables that we are good at?" Many leaders express a similar idea – that goal management does not measure quality. My finding is therefore that police leaders have little trust in goal management. This has not changed as part of the reform. In 2016, police leaders said they were loyal to what they described as "deliverables" (performance objectives), but they did not associate these deliverables with developing good police service.

Police leaders are primarily responsible for competence within the leadership practice. Of course, this involves more than the things that can be measured by performance objectives, including tacit knowledge. One of the questions asked in the survey conducted by the Work Research Institute (Wathne, Talberg, & Gundhus, 2019) was intended to help determine to what extent leaders break down goal management so that it makes sense to the other employees. Just over 43% of responders answered that they completely agree or somewhat agree that leaders do this.

To enable the development of the police into a knowledge-based and learning-oriented organisation, competence objectives that are to a greater extent both quantitative and qualitative are a prerequisite. Activities that promote interdisciplinary cooperation can hardly be measured by quantity. The same is true of meeting points for reflecting over events and knowledge sharing. Competence objectives are therefore more dynamic in form, and they involve goal management in that these objectives are discussed and interpreted. This will result in competence objectives that are continuously evaluated, reflected over, and assessed based on what will be important for the future of the police. Competence objectives typically have the highest value when they are dynamic and include such aspects as self-determination in the workplace, perception of feedback at work, and perception of responsibility. All criteria that are important for work performance have to be considered, including self-determination, control, and manoeuvring space. Evaluating and adapting the objectives is absolutely necessary since the increased reporting requirements and the pressure of being measured can be very damaging for the employees' performance. In fact, a number of studies show that such measurements can be perceived as excessive control, surveillance, and restriction of work conditions.

Goal management in the police is delivered to districts, geographical units, common units, departments, etc. Given my description of police culture, goal management also tends to result in silo mentality. It often causes competition that is intensified by the goal management. There may be a combination of humour and friendly bickering depending on where one ends up in terms of statistics. However, this primarily happens internally when the green numbers are presented and reference is made to those who did not achieve them. Someone may consider it unfair that a large number of cases did not result in equally large staffing, and so on. Placing the focus on target numbers and not on the way cases should be opened and investigated may, in the worst-case scenario, result in a culture of blame.

In terms of goal management in relation to unresolved cases, for instance, employees demonstrate their creativity and enormous effort aimed at reducing the number of unresolved cases and reaching the common goal in this type of project has a positive effect overall. At the same time, many leaders underscore the fact that they have to rely on short-term solutions rather than long-term ones because goal management favours the short-term perspective. This is intensified through budgeting, which, according to many leaders, is associated with a great deal of uncertainty and conflicting signals, thus making it difficult to use it as a management tool.

The police workforce is largely driven by intrinsic motivation associated with work responsibilities and the social mission rather than by external factors such as, for example, salary. Performance targets may lead to unethical behaviour and even cheating with numbers, but this is less of a problem among employees with intrinsic motivation (Kuvaas & Dysvik, 2012). However, when objectives that cannot be adjusted or departed from lead to stress, lack of coping ability, and employee turnover, these performance targets could still affect even the intrinsically motivated employees.

References

Bang, H. (2011). *Organisasjonskultur* [Organisational Culture] (4th edn). Oslo: Universitetsforlaget.
Charman, S. (2017). *Police Socialisation, Identity and Culture: Becoming Blue*. Portsmouth: Palgrave Macmillan.
Cockcroft, T. (2020). *Police Occupational Culture: Research and Practice*. Bristol: Policy Press.

Filstad, C. & Karp, T. (2020). Police leadership as a professional practice. *Policing and Society. An International Journal of Research and Policy.* www.tandfonline.com/doi/full/10.1080/10439463. 2020.1777996.

Finstad, L. (2018). *Hva er POLITI* [What is POLICE]. Oslo: Universitetsforlaget.

Jacobsen, D.I. & Thorsvik, J. (2013). *Hvordan organisasjoner fungerer. Innføring i organisasjon og ledelse* [How organisations work. Introduction to organisation and leadership]. Bergen: Fagbokforlaget.

Kuvaas, B. & Dysvik, A. (2012). *Lønnsomhet gjennom menneskelige ressurser. Evidensbasert HRM* [Profitability through human resources. Evidence-based HRM] (2nd edn). Bergen: Fagbokforlaget.

Wathne, C.T., Talberg, N., & Gundhus, H. (2019). *Nærpolitireformen og politiets relasjon til publikum* [The Norwegian Community Policing Reform and the police's relationship to the public]. Report 2019: 01. Oslo: Arbeidsforskningsinstituttet, OsloMet – storbyuniversitetet.

Chapter 6

Strategy as practice

This chapter argues that strategy cannot be considered as something a leadership practice *has*. Instead, strategy as practice acknowledges strategy as integrated and socially constructed components of leadership practices, as something a leadership practice *is*. Strategies and strategic knowledge are created in leadership practices. The chapter also discusses the extent to which police leaders can be strategic. What are police leaders' possibilities for transforming practice or making decisions on long-term visions of good policing in a public organisation constrained by political and governmental pressure and control? The chapter includes a number of quotes from top management in the police and their perceived understanding of the possibilities of strategic leadership.

Strategic leadership is achieving binding priorities that extend into the future, so it is not about daily operations and crisis management (Klausen, 2014). Depending on the leadership level, and the organisational and hierarchical placement of the leadership practice, there are different forms of leadership in policing. As part of the Norwegian police reform, four leadership levels have been defined. Level 1 leaders are chiefs of police, level 2 leaders are heads of units (which includes the heads of geographical operating units), level 3 are heads of sections, and level 4 are heads of departments. Leadership at levels 3 and 4 is in accordance with a particular area of expertise, and heads of departments at level 4 are first-line managers within that area.

Leadership levels in organisations have the following distinguishing features:

1   The institutional and strategic leadership level responsible for the overall goals, strategies, long-term planning, and budgeting. This is where we find senior leaders.
2   The administrative level with an overall responsibility for certain areas of the organisation's activity. Leaders at this level will typically set goals and organise, administer, and integrate the decisions made at the senior leadership level. Middle managers, who are a crucial link between senior leadership and operational management, are found at this level.
3   The operational level is responsible for day-to-day practice and the implementation of core activities in an organisation. This involves guidance, facilitation, coordination, and development of the tasks that the operational department is responsible for.

Strategic, tactical, and operational are well-known leadership classifications that indicate what kind of leadership is expected at each level. Research on senior leaders, however, shows that their strategic decisions are formulated intuitively, strategies are often not followed by a review and analysis of potential problems, there is a lack of subsequent

DOI: 10.4324/9781003224105-9

discussions, and the consequences of achieving the goals are not analysed (Jacobsen & Thorsvik, 2013).

Leadership needs to have a strategic direction and cater to organisational development and the development of the skills and competencies that enable the organisation to reach its strategic goals. Strategic leadership is about the choice of direction, which is usually required for making the highest level decisions. Senior leaders have the overall responsibility for setting the strategic standard and using the different leadership levels for sensemaking and implementation in all parts of the organisation (Fedor et al., 2003). This is why strategic leadership should combine the strategic and visionary aspects with the administrative aspects (Rowe, 2006; Rowe & Macauley, 2018), but this combination is challenging. According to the studies of what police leaders do that were referenced in Chapter 1, the amount of work that can be described as strategic is limited. Many police leaders admit they do not always have time to work strategically, and it is also unclear *how* they are supposed to work strategically. Instead, many police leaders are busy with what can be described as micro-leadership. For example, shift and annual leave schedules are often processed by heads of sections and sometimes even by heads of units/chiefs of police. The same may apply to employment matters and monitoring various measures taken and decisions made. This is why police leaders often say they have too much of a "finger in the pie", which is a frequently used expression. Some leaders may also be seeking control or not taking advantage of what other leadership levels can offer in terms of workload. I will return to this topic later and reflect on where strategic police leadership can take place.

Strategic leadership is described in the literature as having an overview, a combination of looking inwards and forwards. It is about overseeing, seeing through, and seeing ahead (Klausen, 2014). The strategic outlook is where the opportunity to shape the future is to be found. The extent to which leaders are capable of departing from the complexity of chaos in order to form an overview – and by doing this, distinguish between what is important and what is less important – may vary. It is, however, possible to learn strategic leadership by creating a space for strategic reflection where knowledge could be shared and a common understanding of what strategic leadership is could be formed.

Leadership is being good at seeing the demand for change and acting on it, while administration is being good at handling the complexity those changes entail and implementing them within the organisation. Blom and Alvesson (2014) argue that, first of all, requirements for leadership influence the way leaders' initiatives are perceived and make sense. Second, when relationships between the leader and their subordinates are good, it could be unclear to what extent leadership or cooperation are exercised by either the leader or the subordinates in a practical work situation. In other words, the leader might act as a subordinate and the subordinate might act as a leader. In many ways, this established leader-subordinate relationship is needed for successful strategic leadership. It is important to have a strategic direction that is anchored in the organisation's vision and overall objectives. Strategic processes must be integrated into all leadership practices at all levels within the police. To make a leadership practice work strategically, the defining strategies at the senior leadership level have to be translatable. Translatability and sensemaking at different levels provide for the effective use of the available leadership levels when strategy is to be implemented in leadership practices.

Strategic leadership in a public sector organisation such as the police is based on a social mission. Compared to the private sector, public sector organisations do not compete with each other, and the knowledge and experience they gain is not proprietary. Public sector institutions are commissioned to work on behalf of the citizens. This means that the formulation of this social mission and strategic leadership in public sector organisations generally, as well as in policing in particular, need a different approach compared to leadership in the business sector. The police does not intend to earn money or compete with other service providers in the market. This makes many of the available analytical tools and models for strategic leadership relatively useless for the development of strategic leadership in policing. The police force is not designed by powerful leaders in order to realise their predefined strategies (Johannessen, 2015a).

In policing, the notion of strategy is primarily applied to managing and developing the police, special agencies, or police districts, and it is understood as a method for preventing, fighting, and controlling crime. Wegner (2007) describes how systematic strategic thinking and planning can help the police be more effective in fighting crime and providing public safety.

The police is largely governed by regulations. Many of the work assignments in policing require a legal basis, and criminal proceedings have to be defined by regulations. These requirements imply that the police will largely be governed by the rule of law in the future too.

The Ministry of Justice and Public Security has to provide appropriate clarifications and restrictions so that the police force's social mission can be translated into strategies and addressed through strategic leadership (Meyer & Norman, 2019). These are comprehensive goals which entail few priority-setting opportunities and choices of direction for a particular police leader/chief of police. The way police leaders create opportunities for strategic leadership and strategic work in their leadership practices can be explained by manoeuvring space (Filstad, Olsen, & Karp, 2020). The notion of manoeuvring space refers to how a leadership practice accomplishes the social mission.

Strategy researcher Kurt Klaudi Klausen (2014) makes a distinction between three important factors for strategic leadership. The first one is to *extrapolate*. This involves reacting to the conditions and trends in the outside world and analysing how they can define the future of the organisation. The second factor is to *envisage* and, in doing so, try to anticipate what is going to happen without being able to see into the future. The third one is to *imagine*, meaning to create a vision of what the future will be like. We are not talking about a high degree of authority or certainty here either. These three factors represent strategic processes and have to form the backbone for developing strategies in policing. The first factor involves analysing where the police is today and discussing the problems it faces based on the current state of criminal activities. To envisage and to anticipate means to extend the analysis by looking at history and prior experience, other countries and their experiences, warning signs, changes in the criminal landscape as perceived by those on the front line, the development of society in general, and so on. Thorough strategic work around the two first factors will ensure better opportunities for forming visions of the future, being able to imagine various future scenarios, developing creative ideas, and the like.

Strategic leadership as practice

A practical perspective on strategy in organisations is denoted as *strategy as practice* (Chia & MacKay, 2007; Jarzabkowski & Whittington, 2008; Vaara & Whittington, 2012; de la

Ville & Mounoud, 2018). The advantage of this perspective is that it explains how social practices (including leadership practices) either enable or constrain strategies by extending the notion of strategy and encompassing the roles and identities of the practitioners (Vaara & Whittington, 2012). Similar to leadership as practice, strategy as practice is based on the assumption that strategy must not be considered as something an organisation *has*. Instead, strategies should be understood as integrated and socially constructed components of social practices, as something a leadership practice *is*. Strategy research needs to consider the strategist's engagement in strategy processes as participation in practice (Whittington, 2003). A practical approach to strategy can contribute to the connection between strategy and politics, structure and culture, relationships and collectivity, sensemaking, identity, etc. This means extending the research to include cultural aspects that, often unconsciously, are interpreted through and embedded in leadership practices, and to include tacit and informal aspects (Whittington, 2011; de la Ville & Mounoud, 2018). These connections have long been missing, and power and politics have never been addressed in the literature on strategy as practice (Carter, Clegg, & Kornberger, 2008; Clegg et al., 2011). It is argued that the literature focuses more on the explicit aspects of strategy as practice, which are just the tip of the iceberg (Jarzabkowski & Whittington, 2008). A practice perspective on strategy does not mean only studying the particular events and actions of individuals in a practice and connecting them to the overall results and senior leadership; instead, it is more about shifting the focus from the individual strategist to the historical and cultural social practices that strategies are "translated" into (Chia & MacKay, 2007). Leadership practices are where strategies emerge, make sense (or not) for the participants, and, in doing so, influence what the participants do and what they choose not to do. This way, leadership practices provide the participants with the resources to interpret roles and initiate identity-shaping and strategic activities (Chia & Holt, 2006).

The way leadership practices influence strategies in policing, what methods they use, and to what extent they can be identified with strategies all have to be considered in connection with the distinguishing features of leadership practice. These mechanisms can explain organisational connections between, for example, strategic and operational leadership in the police. This is because hierarchies, formal responsibilities, and levels that are controllable and predictable can nevertheless develop into something unpredictable because strategy is a cultural and interpersonal phenomenon that is embedded in day-to-day practice.

Strategies and strategic knowledge are created in a leadership practice. This is why differentiating between the formulation and implementation of strategies and phases in strategy processes is problematic, argues Johannessen (2015b). We should instead consider differences in practices because the strategies would change as they were adapted to a particular leadership practice. Therefore, in policing, strategic leadership as bureaucratic practice would be very different from strategic leadership as operational practice.

Strategic leadership as leadership practice

In accordance with the Norwegian national emergency preparedness plan, chiefs of police are placed at the tactical leadership level (the strategic level is occupied by the ministries), while within police districts, they are on the strategic level. There are four leadership levels in police districts and, consequently, in day-to-day policing.

Level 1 is occupied by the chiefs of police, followed by two middle management levels, and then the first-line managers at level 4. The lowest two levels, where we find heads of departments and sections, respectively, are organised according to specific areas of expertise. Heads of geographical operating units and common units at level 2 and chiefs of police at level 1 deal with multiple areas of expertise. This is why the chief of police is expected to exercise leadership practice at the strategic level. However, my studies have shown that the extent to which the police chief's leadership practice can be described as strategic is sometimes unclear. I have found that the overarching strategic decisions and documentation are largely provided by the National Police Directorate. Chiefs of police are part of the national management team, which is led by the National Police Commissioner, but they report having different experiences in terms of their involvement in the strategic work. National management teams are not decision-making bodies either, but chiefs of police say they discuss strategies and have an opportunity to come up with suggestions. This could increase the distance between strategy as bureaucratic practice and strategy as operational practice, which chiefs of police have to balance in their own respective leadership practices. They report, however, having management discussions with the National Police Directorate that they consider important for the strategic work in their police districts. However, this could only refer to "translating" strategies into the operational activities of a police district and clarifying the manoeuvring space of a particular chief of police.

I would like to finish this chapter on strategic leadership with quotes by senior police leaders – that is, level 1 leaders – about their own strategic leadership. They express somewhat different ideas that can all be used for reflecting on what strategic leadership is or could be in policing.

> Yes, but I don't think we should make too many people in the organisation think strategically. They don't have time for this. And if you are busy with your day-to-day routine tasks, there is almost no use in switching to being strategic once a year. There are few who can switch between different modes so fast. I've always thought that if we manage to make the management team work effectively, then it can help to be strategic to a greater extent... help me to be strategic... So we had a management discussion with the operating units and I said I don't want to talk about finances, I don't want to talk about results, I only want to talk about the strategic priorities.

> I'm quite humble. I can admit it when I've made a mistake, and I think it's important to be open about our weaknesses. Our job is too important to be hiding our weaknesses. In the police force, there is a tendency to go over the edge all the time really, and you cannot build a developing and learning organisation if you don't dare to look into the problems and see that you are doing this so that... what is good and what is bad, but as a police organisation, you might not always be good at thinking strategically long-term since you are so used to leaping into action, and this is what makes the day worth living. Right? And then all that stuff about strategy is kind of a bit boring.

> You have to find that balance. If you are going to work strategically long-term, you need to know what you are doing, to understand the starting point and how to

move forward. But I have... we have focused on the content of leadership, requirements for leadership, focused on operational training, content of operational training, its benefits. We have focused on the social mission, our role, how we should appear in front of the public, and we have focused a lot on strategic intelligence. More on understanding the society around us and forming a proper decision-making basis in order to conduct intelligence processes. In a small police district like ours, it helps to be one step ahead.

Yes... it is the overall police strategy we've got up to 2023 and now to 2025. It's the big picture, the long-term picture. The reform documentation is also about the long-term pictures. And of course it's from one year to the other. We've now got an agreement on performance targets... so it's a bit like this, how is the management process going? Well, the teams are reassured when they see that leadership is working on their problems, things that are most important to the teams, that we are not only concerned with some general issues imposed from above that we think are important... Because this is also a strategy... I'm working very consciously to test my manoeuvring space and ensure I have as much of it as possible, but it could also be a different strategy where I would just be under control and my manoeuvring space would be very small. And then it's just hopeless if you are also going to sit down and work on a shift schedule at a police station. You need the skills to pull it all together at the strategic level.

The Ministry of Justice is working on developing a long-term plan for the police, which I think is very... it's a good thing. It has become a lot more strategic than it used to be, I can say. The strategic development of the police organisation, the strategic development of the judicial sector – in a way, that's where we want to be... at the senior level. Also, more defining power for the subordinate levels, but that's... and I think we are taking some steps... you find your way as you go.

When it comes to new directives on strategies that are part of the reform, some of them are like... we will have something better or more... and then I think it's a dangerous way to introduce strategies because it means we should explain that the way it used to be was bad. Really bad dynamics, bad mechanism... not a good way to unite forces, which has been extremely beneficial for the police in years. So some of the strategies, I think, are mature enough to be considered again, and I can see the willingness to do so among the new senior leadership in the police directorate... In other words, how are these strategies reflected in the way we have split the budget... is it based on tradition and the way we've always done it, or is there a thought behind it? When you give directions about what the organisation is supposed to look like... because changes in an organisation can also show that we are strengthening some areas... we're closing something down, we're setting something up, we're joining something together, we are strengthening things. Things like that are implicit in communicating what the strategies are further down.

Strategic leadership is about long-term commitment and seeing the big picture, which is a challenge in policing. Many leaders claim there is greater focus on strategic leadership in policing now, and the purpose of the senior management teams is making strategic decisions Others experience that the Norwegian police reform may lead to more micromanagement and scarcity of resources. Besides, and this is the case for public sector organisations, year-to-year budgeting makes strategic leadership especially difficult, and the more tactical case-by-case approach is often taken at the expense of seeing the big picture and long-term commitment. At the same time, the quotes above reflect how senior leaders in the police connect strategic leadership to manoeuvring space. Accordingly, Cockcroft (2020) argues that many of the tensions we can identity in the police reforms is that of discretion where the reforms seek to limit, control, or make transparent operational discretion. Many of them feel like they have some room to manoeuvre at their level, but management by objectives and results restricts their opportunities to exercise strategic leadership. This creates a number of strategic dilemmas, and many leaders feel the need for a clearer common arena for strategic leadership. This challenge of what strategic leadership actually is what Reiner and O'Connor (2015) call the terrible twins of political policing, instead of true effective reform seeking to build consent in policy and policing. Strategy as practice rests on police leaders' possibilities of transforming practice or making decisions on long-time visions of good policing in a public organisation constrained by political and governmental pressure and control (Cockcroft, 2014; Davis & Silvestri, 2020).

Police leadership has to be considered in accordance with its levels, where leadership practices move between strategic, tactical, and operative aspects. Still, leadership practices need to preferably belong somewhere. Many police leaders, for instance, say there are too many "fingers in the pie". They are used to controlling several leadership levels with the same cases, which is why it may be problematic when the same cases largely tend to have almost identical content at several leadership levels. It must be considered whether the use of time and resources is necessary and desirable. This is important in the development of leadership practices and the community that they represent. The need of a shift from the universalised conception of police leadership to consider its distinctive feature is argued for (Davis & Silvestri, 2020). Police reform that moreover outlines the important of effective and strategic leadership needs to acknowledge the need for a shift from generic skills and elaborate what is necessary to perform leadership at the strategic level of policing (Caless & Tong, 2015). Although strategic decisions are made in senior leadership practices, strategies will be interpreted and integrated as practice in the communities that leadership practices represent at various levels. This is why the distinguishing features of the communities, with special attention to culture, identity, and competence, are considered in the next part of this book.

References

Blom, M. & Alvesson, M. (2014). Leadership on demand: followers as initiators and inhibitors of managerial leadership. *Scandinavian Journal of Management*, 30(3), 322–357.

Caless, B. & Tong, S. (2015). *Leading Policing in Europe*. Bristol: Policy Press.

Carter, C., Clegg, S.R., & Kornberger, M. (2008). Strategy as practice? *Strategic Organization*, 6(1), 83–99.

Chia, R. & Holt, R. (2006). Strategy as practical coping: a Heideggerian perspective. *Organisation Studies*, 27(5), 635–655.

Chia, R. & MacKay, B. (2007). Post-processual challenges for the emerging strategy-as-practice perspective: discovering strategy in the logic of practice. *Human Relations*, 60(1), 217–242.

Clegg, S., Carter, C., Kornberger, M., & Schweitzer, J. (2011). *Strategy: Theory and Practice*. London: Sage.

Cockcroft, T. (2014). Police culture and transformational leadership: outlining the contours of a troubled relationship. *Policing*, 8(1), 5–13.

Cockcroft, T. (2020). *Police Occupational Culture. Research and Practice*. Bristol: Policy Press.

Davis, C. & Silvestri, M. (2020). *Critical Perspectives on Police Leadership*. Bristol: Policy Press.

de la Ville, V.-I. & Mounoud, E. (2018). A narrative to approach to strategy as practice: strategy making from texts and narratives. In D. Golsorkhi, L. Rouleau, D. Seidl, & E. Vaara (Eds.), *Cambridge Handbook of Strategy as Practice* (pp. 249–264). Cambridge: Cambridge University Press. https://halshs.archives-ouvertes.fr/halshs-01390100/document.

Fedor, D.B., Ghosh, S., Caldwell, S.D., Maurer, T.J., & Singhal, V.R. (2003). The effects of knowledge management on team members' ratings of project success and impact. *Decision Science*, 34(3) 513–539.

Filstad, C., Olsen, T.H., & Karp, T. (2020). Constructing managerial manoeuvring space in contradictory contexts. *European Management Journal*, 39(4), 467–475. https://doi.org/10.1016/j.emj.2020.10.003.

Jacobsen, D.I. & Thorsvik, J. (2013). *Hvordan organisasjoner fungerer. Innføring i organisasjon og ledelse* [How organisations work. Introduction to organisation and leadership]. Bergen: Fagbokforlaget.

Jarzabkowski, P. & Whittington, R. (2008). A strategy-as-practice approach to strategy research and education. *Journal of Management Inquiry*, 17(4), 282–286.

Johannessen, S.O. (2015a). Å forstå politiet som organisasjons- og ledelsespraksiser [Understanding the police as organisational and leadership practices]. In S.O. Johannessen & R. Glomseth (Eds.), *Politiledelse* (pp. 22–41). Oslo: Gyldendal Akademisk.

Johannessen, S.O. (2015b). Beslutningstaking og organisasjonsdynamikk i operative nettverk [Decision-making and organisational dynamics in operational networks]. In S.O. Johannessen & R. Glomseth (Eds.), *Politiledelse* (pp. 250–270). Oslo: Gyldendal Akademisk.

Klausen, K.K. (2014). *Strategisk ledelse i det offentlige* [Strategic leadership in the public sector]. København: Gyldendal.

Meyer, C. & Norman, V. (2019). *Ikke for å konkurrere. Strategi for fellesskapets tjenere* [Not for competing. Strategy for the servants of the society]. Bergen: Fagbokforlaget.

Reiner, R. & O'Connor, D. (2015). Politics and policing: the terrible twin. In Fleming, J. (Ed.), *Police Leadership: Rising to the Top* (42–70). Oxford: Oxford University Press.

Rowe, M. (2006). Following the leader: front-line narratives on police leadership. *Policing: An International Journal of Police Strategies and Management*, 29(4), 757–767.

Rowe, M. & Macauley, M. (2018). Giving voice to the victims of sexual assault: the role of police leadership in organisational change. *Policing: An International Journal of Policy and Practice*, 42(3), 394–407.

Vaara, E. & Whittington, R. (2012). Strategy-as-practice: taking social practices seriously. *The Academy of Management Annals*, 6(1), 285–336. doi:10.1080/19416520.2012.672039.

Wegner, R.B. (2007). *Politistrategi* [Policing strategy]. Oslo: Universitetsforlaget.

Whittington, R. (2003). The work of strategizing and organizing: from a practice perspective. *Strategic Organization*, 1(1), 119–127.

Whittington, R. (2011), The practice turn in organization research: towards a disciplined transdisciplinarity. *Accounting, Organizations and Society*, 36, 183–186.

Part 3

Community

A community can be understood as a group of people who are united by common actions and have a shared feeling/perception of what the community is (Wenger, 1998,2003). The "we" identity is created by mutual engagement and a collective feeling of being part of something bigger. "We" often refers to common resources, competencies, language, routines, activities, history, stories, etc., that define who the participants are and what the community represents. It also refers to the individual member identity, which is strongly connected with the identity of the entire community and to the way the community wants to be perceived from the outside. How important the community is depends on how important it is for the identity of an individual member and whether the things this community represents agree with who that member wants to be.

People are part of many communities, including various communities in the workplace. Participation in a community is not just a characteristic of formal organisations; informal communities of practice are just as widespread and greatly influence leadership practices (Brown & Duguid, 1991; Wenger, 1998). A community of practice has to be

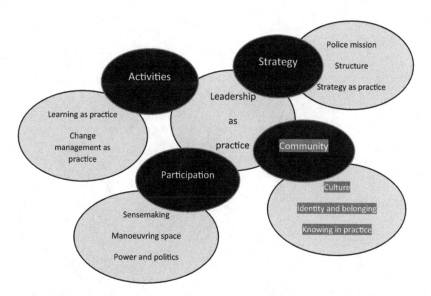

Figure P3.1 Police leadership as practice model: community

DOI: 10.4324/9781003224105-10

understood based on identity and belonging, what the community wants to represent in terms of competence, and what distinguishes its culture. This is why the following chapters deal with organisational culture and police culture (Chapter 7), identity and belonging (Chapter 8), and competence (Chapter 9).

References

Brown, J.S. & Duguid, P. (1991). Organizational learning and communities of practice: towards a unified view of working, learning and innovating. *Organizational Science: A Journal of the Institute of Management Science*, 2(1), 40–57.

Wenger, E. (1998). *Communities of Practice: Learning, Meaning and Identity*. New York: Cambridge University Press.

Wenger, E. (2003). Communities of practice and social learning systems. In D. Nicolini, D. Yanow, & S. Gherardi (Eds.), *Knowing in Organizations: A Practice-based Approach* (pp. 76–99). London: Routledge.

Chapter 7

Organisational culture and police culture

Organisational culture is viewed as something leadership practices are and not as something they have. Also, police culture is affected by being a public and politically controlled organisation, where the bureaucratic hierarchy provides the structural logic that needs to be balanced with the cultural and practical logics of policing. The lack of addressing police culture in a meaningful manner and the close relationships between police leadership and police culture is discussed. So are the possibilities of police culture (s) having innovative responses to changes, and why.

Organisational culture

Organisational culture is a complex phenomenon that embraces all that is known but often not visible or explicitly expressed in an organisation (Charman, 2017). An organisational culture is a construction of reality, a shared taken-for-granted understanding of reality. It could be a shared view of what constitutes good police work or good judgement in policing decisions. It makes sense for the participants but can rarely be expressed explicitly. Understanding a culture means considering everything that is not specific, explicit, or tangible, and that is taken for granted. Organisational culture is integrated in organisational practices and relationships between leaders and colleagues, their actions, as well as in decision making, routines, and the characteristics of political and strategic considerations (Schraeder, Tears, & Jordan, 2005: 493).

A leadership practice is only one of many practices that constitute an overarching culture. A culture can be defined as sets of values, norms, and perceptions of reality that develop in an organisation as the members interact with each other and their environment (Bang, 2011: 23).

Geert Hofstede, Edgar Schein, Mary Jo Hatch, and Johanne Martin all have important contributions to organisational culture literature. Hofstede considers values to be the core of organisational culture, Schein considers basic underlying assumptions to be the most important cultural component, cultural dynamics as symbolic values matter the most to Hatch, and Martin proposes three perspectives on culture, as integration, differentiation, and fragmentation, and how they are combined. Schein illustrates the three levels of culture components and the relationship between them as shown in Figure 7.1 (Schein, 2010).

The basic assumptions result from beliefs and values that have been accepted and considered valid. Basic assumptions are based on experiences that have developed into something that is no longer called into question or reflected upon. Instead, they become a common perception of reality which is tacit and integrated into the culture, and which

DOI: 10.4324/9781003224105-11

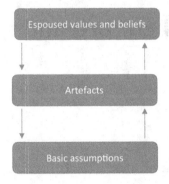

Figure 7.1 Schein's three important cultural components in organisations

gradually becomes less and less tangible (Charman, 2017). Culture is difficult to change because everything that can be observed and communicated in the form of values and artefacts is governed by the basic assumptions. It is these basic assumptions that give meaning to the actions which are possible to observe. This shared understanding of reality is therefore what needs to be changed in order to change cultures.

Culture as sensemaking

A shared perception of reality is the result of negotiations about meaning between the participants. It does not mean that everyone always agrees. It means that the cultural community makes sense of shared competence and what it means to be a full member. Sensemaking is reinforced through values, symbols, and rituals. In policing, it could be uniform and equipment that vary depending on the type of task. The number of stars on the shoulder or a symbolic mark on the bulletproof vest may represent a united community that has formed as the result of merging two large patrolling sections (cultures) as part of the police reform. The latter is an example of what can be done to promote the development of a new common culture.

Culture is therefore defined through observable artefacts, symbols, and rituals that form certain patterns based on the fundamental assumptions and shared values that make sense to the group's participants. Solving problems or performing actions as a result of internal and external conditions and adjustments makes sense. This sensemaking represented by artefacts, symbols, etc. is what can be observed from the outside and what often identifies the police to the rest of society.

What makes an organisational culture complex is all that is taken for granted, the unconscious, and the feelings that are associated with stability and meaning. I have heard many leaders talking about culture as "the way we do it here". This approach to culture is problematic at best because culture as meaning is narrowed down to what is being done and the way it is done, to the correct way of perceiving, thinking, and feeling in a police practice. The "why", which as I mentioned before is crucial to understanding police leadership as practice, is missing again. Culture is where we often find the answer to this "why".

Culture is created by people, so it cannot be changed if people do not change (Hennestad, 2015). This, however, requires knowledge of why people act the way they do and, accordingly, reflection on and change of the learned understanding of reality.

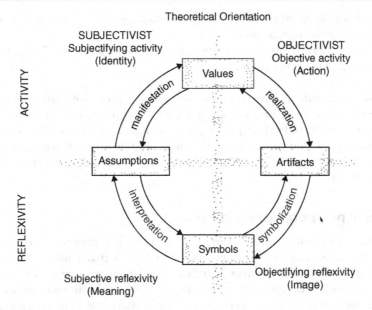

Figure 7.2 The dynamics of organisational culture

Cultural dynamics

Hatch emphasises cultural dynamics as the symbolic, interpretative, and sensemaking components of culture. These dynamics link cultural conditions, basic assumptions, values, and artefacts together, and show that they are integrated rather than hierarchical in relation to one another. Hatch emphasises the symbolic-interpretive perspective on understanding of reality and the added meanings that exist within a culture (Hatch, 2001: 394):

An organisational culture is composed of the cultural dynamics between artefacts and common sensemaking. Accordingly, opportunities for cultural development can be found in this dynamic sensemaking. Hatch interconnects Schein's levels of culture and directs more attention at the symbolic aspect, which is understood as an integrated process of (1) *manifestation*, when specific values for an action occur as the result of cognitive or emotional interpretations and sensemaking, (2) *realisation*, when sensemaking emerges through results and actions as a consequence of manifestation, (3) *symbolisation*, when cultural processes connect artefacts and sensemaking with personal, social, and collective values, which are then reflected in motivations, feelings, thoughts, and shared identity, and (4) *interpretation*, which provides for further sensemaking when experiences, symbols, assumptions, and shared stories reinforce the community within a culture.

Three different approaches to culture

Martin (1992) describes three approaches to culture and stresses that they are complementary:

1   The integration perspective studies culture as a community characterised by consensus. This means that all the members in the organisation have a shared understanding of reality, and research explores all that is shared.

2   The differentiation perspective focuses on studying culture as the sum of various subcultures in the organisation.
3   The fragmentation perspective studies culture as a "spider's web" that is complex, diverse, and constantly evolving.

The combination of these three perspectives is what matters. Integration of shared elements, differentiation of various cultural groupings, and fragmentation through dividing the whole into small individual pieces are all crucial to understanding organisational culture. Focusing only on consensus has the effect of hiding the differences, diversity, and conflicts, as well as the fact that there will always be several cultures within an organisation (Bang, 2011).

Two major perspectives on culture

The literature on organisational culture also distinguishes between two more fundamental perspectives about how organisational culture is maintained, changed, developed, and even unlearned. Unlike Martin's complementary perspectives on culture, these two are either/or approaches that are fundamentally distinct: an instrumental perspective and an institutional perspective. An instrumental perspective views organisational culture as something an organisation *has*, while an institutional perspective approaches organisational culture as something an organisation *is* (Høyer, Madsbu, & Tranøy, 2018).

The Norwegian police reform is a good example that demonstrates the differences between the two. The reform is primarily based on the instrumental perspective on police culture(s). According to this perspective, police culture can be changed and unlearned because it is something the organisation *has* and thus can be manipulated. From the instrumental perspective, changing the culture is the responsibility of the leader, hence it is a top-down responsibility. Accordingly, the instrumental perspective considers organisational culture to be normative, police culture to be strong or weak, leadership culture to be good or bad, and the culture of change to be large or small. A perspective that views culture as something the police organisation possesses represents a challenge because it assumes that organisational structure will ensure necessary changes in the organisational culture. This is because, according to this perspective, it is possible to change culture from the top down.

An institutional approach, by contrast, considers cultural change to be considerably more demanding, and sometimes impossible. Schein (2010: 6) explains:

> When we say that something is "cultural," we imply that it is not only shared, but also stable, because it defines the group. Culture is hard to change because group members value stability in that it provides meaning and predictability.

An institutional perspective is an evolving perspective in which culture *is*. Police culture has to be understood as a social phenomenon, and hence cultural changes need to be facilitated. This means that police culture has to be influenced more indirectly than directly in order to enable changes to happen. Cultural changes must occur from the bottom up because the individuals in established practices shaped the culture, so they are also the ones who must change and develop it.

When senior leadership decides that leadership culture in the police must be changed, there will always be tensions between culture and management/control. It is challenging to alternative approaches to leadership practices in a hierarchical command-oriented environment as the police (Davies & Bailey, 2018). Instead of letting these tensions control the processes, senior leadership has to base the changes on the evolving institutional perspective, according to which culture is developed over a long time without being planned and defines who the practising police leaders *are*.

Police culture

Police culture includes collectively shared values, internalised assumptions, and more symbolic aspects which are found in myths, stories, and rituals of policing. Police culture is stable, durable, and often rooted in policing actions (Charman, 2017). It therefore represents a form of security and predictability for those who are part of the culture. Occupational culture, as opposed to organisational culture, refers to people identifying more strongly with the values of their particular occupation than with the organisation (Cockcroft, 2020). Police occupational culture is affected by being a public and politically controlled organisation, while at the same time it influences the public and political control. Accordingly, police culture generally refers to an organisation characterised by bureaucracy, hierarchy, size, function, goals, professions, politics, and nationality (Johnson, Scholes, & Whittington, 2009). The police is strongly influenced by the military as task oriented and command-based (Grint & Thornton, 2015; Filstad, 2020). Davies and Bailey (2018) argue about the paradox of policing being more complex and the need for innovations and relational orientation in developing police culture to ensure contemporary practice.

Different areas of responsibility may have different cultures, so leadership practices within, for instance, prosecution, investigation, patrolling, or crime prevention will vary. Leadership cultures can vary depending on leadership levels, or they can be interdisciplinary across multiple areas of responsibility. Culture can be based on geography or special competence, such as the emergency squad or dog patrol. A leadership practice culture may also be a combination of, for instance, geographical factors, area(s) of expertise, and the competence of the leader and their subordinates. The point is that leadership practices are characterised by an integrated culture that contains common values, symbols, understanding of reality, norms, and the like, which also results in differences. (In the next chapter on identity and belonging, I will demonstrate possible differences and similarities based on what creates a sense of shared identity and belonging in a leadership practice.)

There is plenty of literature on police culture worldwide. A lot of it is dominated by criminologists who have approached police culture as an explanation of negative behaviour in policing (Waddington, Kleinig, & Wright, 2013). Many studies refer to a police culture that is characterised by the internal solidarity of its members, which results in tolerance of corruption, racism, breach of law, and resistance to change and reforms (Chan, 1997; Waddington et al., 2013; Cockcroft, 2013, 2020). The literature is primarily oriented towards an earlier time in policing culture. It gives little attention to the policing transformation that has been caused by significant changes in the criminal landscape. Additionally, the bulk of literature on police culture narrows analysis down to patrolling only (Loftus, 2010). It refers to street-level resistance that is characterised by learning through experience and the use of professional discretion. Researchers suggest that the manoeuvring space in policing is too big and not research- and knowledge-based enough (Gundhus, 2017). The studies point out an "inward orientation" which can develop into a suspicious and cynical predisposition based on the idea that the police is isolated from the rest of the world (Loftus, 2010; Reiner, 2017).

Peter Anthony James Waddington (1947–2018) was a key policing researcher who was critical of the criminologists' approach to police culture. He believed that blaming police culture is a simplified way of explaining policing actions, where the focus is primarily placed on negative actions (Waddington et al., 2013). He saw a pattern that always attributed negative policing actions to the police culture and believed that pattern needed to be changed. The notion of police culture often becomes negatively charged from the onset. He explained:

> The fundamentals of policing cannot easily be changed, if at all. What point is there in a police officer who does not "read between the lines" and act on suspicion? The task then is to help police to confront the realities of their work and construct a professional culture that enables them to cope with those realities. This means identifying the cultural challenges found, not in the canteen or the personnel carrier, but on the street and in dealing with sometimes difficult people in ambiguous and threatening conditions. (2013: 6)

The literature on police culture fails to explain actions that are part of practical policing work and active individual contributions to cultural knowledge. Additionally, little consideration is given to the relationship between the police and the police environment – police culture cannot be understood without taking national differences into account. The Norwegian police is adapted to the expectations the public, the politicians, and the police itself have for the accomplishment of the social mission in Norway. There are significant differences between nations and thus corresponding differences in police cultures between, for example, the USA, Great Britain, Italy, and Denmark. Police cultures will also vary from place to place within different countries. Accordingly, the literature on police culture cannot operate in a vacuum and disregard the various contexts that affect practical policing.

This idea is developed further by police culture researcher Tom Cockcroft (2013). He has also found that research on policing makes little distinction between actions and police culture. He explains:

> Whilst we often fail to appropriately articulate the complexity of the relationship that links culture and behavior we still tend to invoke culture as a key causal factor. In other words, we stubbornly cling to the concept of police culture but fail to articulate how, for example, it might differ from, say, police socialization. At the same time, organizational cultures need to be understood in respect of other variables that are particular to that individual profession. Therefore, whilst we need to analyse, for example, the role of police discretion at the cultural and symbolic level, we tend not to take into account the essentially legal dimensions of the discretion in the police role. In part, these tendencies may be a result of much police research focusing upon ways of managing rather than understanding police culture. The symbolic world of policing is as important as the operational world for those exploring police culture. (2013: 148)

To ensure the accomplishment of the social mission, the police is expected to change its services in accordance with societal changes. Political authorities allocate resources that are administered by the Norwegian Police Directorate and distributed among the police districts and special agencies. The establishment and development of police culture in these districts and special agencies is affected by political control, the Police Directorate's administration, and the decisions of the Ministry of Justice and Public Security in accordance with political guidelines. These forms of control in relation to the social mission are where police cultures have developed. Police cultures have developed within practical police work and leadership, based on the working methods and solutions that are appropriate for good policing. Police culture is a common understanding of reality within policing which provides action patterns learned over time, and which is maintained by being transferred to new members as the correct way of acting, perceiving, thinking, and feeling (Loftus, 2010; Cockcroft, 2013).

The Norwegian police is characterised by a bureaucratic and controlling logic from political authorities, the Ministry of Justice and Public Security, and the National Police Directorate on the one hand, and by an operational and cultural logic of practical police work on the other hand. These two logics are mutually independent, while at the same time they strongly influence each other and police culture(s).

New structures and initiatives for change are often based on bureaucratic logic in policing. The change initiatives meet with an operational logic where they are going to be implemented and thus change the established practice. The bureaucratic logic represents the instrumental approach to culture described above. According to this approach, the police has a culture which can be manipulated so as to be changed, which can be clearly seen in the reports made after 22 July. These reports concluded that the distribution of resources had not been properly coordinated and that the things that went wrong that day pertain to leadership culture and attitudes in the police. These conclusions illustrate what several police culture researchers have warned against: the actions that police leaders performed that day are attributed to bad leadership culture and attitudes in the police. The initiated police reform includes a number of measures that entail more control and micromanagement of the police. The purpose of the police reform is to change leadership culture, which also requires changes in police culture. Thus, police culture and actions get confused and are perceived to be the same (Waddington et al., 2013). The reasoning here is that negative behaviour in the police is attributed to the police culture, and the police culture must be changed.

Some researchers believe that the literature on police culture relies on a traditional and sometimes even orthodox approach (Loftus, 2010). They call for more field studies in order to understand various factors associated with policing, and in doing so, identify police culture over time and place. Loftus (2010) considers the ideas that police culture is supposed to be timeless, that the police are suspicious, and that police officers are living in social isolation and stand in absolute solidarity with their colleagues to be old-fashioned and a cliché. She argues that this approach to police culture is problematic because as a result (1) police culture exercises significant influence over police work, often for the worse, and (2) the sensibilities that comprise the police's identity can undermine reform endeavours (Loftus, 2010: 1).

The police identity and the importance of forming identity are the topics of the next chapter. Identity as a concept is apparently more outward-looking, while culture is more inward-looking. It is interesting that organisational identity, identity work, social identity, and the importance of forming identity are also given more attention within the police culture literature, not least because the police are now working in a more out-ward-oriented fashion with other social actors. *Community policing* has become a trending topic, especially in England, Scotland, and Wales. Norwegian police leaders say they are using increasingly more time on external meetings arranged by security guard services, child welfare services, various organisations that have access to vulnerable social groups, municipalities, religious communities, etc. This is how police culture and organisational identity can provide a complimentary understanding of the police. Several police leaders admit that they have become less inward-oriented in their police services. This means that through a shared feeling of identity among employees, identity and culture can positively influence and strengthen a shared culture and shared sense of responsibility with regards to other professions.

Police cultures are shaped through practice, from the bottom up – this is in accordance with an operational and institutional logic that understands police culture as something that *is*, and that therefore must be developed or changed within operational practice (Johannessen, 2013). (The institutional approach to culture is described previously.) Just as policing work is complex and most policing competence is tacit, police cultures are also the result of complex and dynamic learning and organisational processes (practices). The organisational processes are repeated, and learning changes the way tasks are per-formed and shapes the day-to-day action patterns over time. Changing a leadership cul-ture is therefore not something one can simply decide to do. A leadership culture is not tangible or explicit, and it cannot be changed by directing police leaders to exercise leadership in new ways. Police leadership is found in formal organisational patterns, in the informal aspects of various leadership practices, in operational practice, in bureau-cratic practice, in trade union practice, in academic practice, and so on. Police leadership is integrated into day-to-day thinking patterns, perception of reality, attitudes, and actions. These phenomena are sometimes hard to observe because they are largely taken for granted, they partially conflict with one another, and they represent frustrations, dilemmas, and opportunities for police leadership.

Which components of a police culture are long-lasting and which provide opportu-nities for cultural development are questions with no definitive answer. A police culture is created by people through the relationships that members of a community build with each other. It is therefore collective and characterised by a common inner identity that is reflected in what members want to present to the outside world. There is no formula for good policing. Still, various police cultures swear by the formulas they believe in. During the reform, many were surprised to discover so many differences in how various districts and units work with the same policing tasks. Merging police districts and units revealed many such examples. On the one hand, there are leaders who stress the importance of being "out there"; they are physically present and exercise management by walking around. Work tasks get completed with delegated responsibility, and leaders prefer a lot of room for manoeuvring. On the other hand, there are leaders who are more focused on budget compliance, performance targets, loyalty, and analysis instead of always being out in the field. These interesting differences are all the more noticeable when two dif-ferent police cultures are merged into one, like, for example, Grønland and Sentrum, two police stations which have largely competed with each other, often fighting for resources. The same applies to Stovner and Manglerud, or Drammen and Tønsberg. Nicknames like "the others", "cowboys", "bestfold",[1] etc., and phrases like "they are spending money like drunken sailors" are used about each other. This can reinforce the original police culture and the notion of "us" vs. "them".

The fact that police culture has many facets is emphasised in more recent research. It can be imagined as an onion with multiple layers of varying size (Hofstede et al., 1990). By moving between the skins of the onion, we find that the deeper we get, the more unconscious, intangible, and hard to observe the culture becomes. Getting through the various layers and reaching the core is essential, especially when seemingly different police cultures are merged into one. The employees' perception of their own roles is also part of the police culture, and changes mean that this perception has to be renegotiated, has to be given new meaning and developed into a new common perception and thus a common police culture.

The recent literature referred to earlier in this chapter on police culture raises the question of the police culture's longevity in the light of an increasingly complex criminal landscape, new forms of crime, terror, expanding globalisation, internet crime, and the like. It is claimed that a police organisation that is undergoing change/innovation has an increased chance of changing the police culture overall. However, this requires: (1) that the police culture have an innovative response to changes, and (2) that the changes pose a significant threat to the established police culture and hence the need for it to develop (Loftus, 2010). The essentially negative and singular view suggests the lack of addressing police culture in a meaningful manner and not acknowledging the close relationships between police leadership and police culture in a wider context of policing, politics, and resource restrictions (Cockcroft, 2020; Filstad, 2021).

Working climate and culture

Developing culture is a demanding task and is not something that is done at one's own or another's discretion. Culture is unconscious, long-lasting, and embedded in what the police does, and how all the small and large factors form what it does as a whole; therefore, culture cannot be given as part of the police reform (Hennestad, 2015). The formal organisational patterns in policing, operational practice, bureaucratic practice, trade union practice, academic practice, and so on all become intertwined as integrated components of the police culture.

The fact that police officers get along in their new departments is not evidence of changes in the culture. It is instead an example of establishing a good working climate, which is important to differentiate from culture. Working climate is superficial and primarily short-term, and it applies to the very individuals who work together and the particular police leaders within a leadership practice. Working climate refers to particular situations and the way the participants think, feel, and act based on what a situation requires. It is not stable, underlying, predictable, and established, and it does not last long-term. Working climate also does not have to be based on shared sensemaking or understanding of reality, which we have found to be crucial to cultures (Alvesson, 2013). It refers to the employees' emotions, involvement, obligations, and so on, in contrast to culture, which is the "hard stuff" (Schein, 2010) involving structures, strategies, values, artefacts, and all that is taken for granted. This is why a working climate is easier to achieve and change. For example, a management team may have a positive working climate. The atmosphere of the management meetings may be good and filled with humour, everyone may participate in the discussion, they may have developed trust-based relationships and share their frustrations, which are met with openness and support in finding solutions. This good working climate is reserved just for those particular leaders who participate and who have developed the environment based on openness, competence, comfort, conflict resolution, and helpfulness. This working climate, however, does not change the leadership culture in the police. Many management teams with such good working climates are needed in order to exercise good police leadership. A good working climate is necessary for more than just management meetings, and it cannot be attributed to these particular police leaders only. Leadership culture has to be based on the unconscious – a shared idea of what good police leadership is – and it should last over time. Good police leadership in all relevant arenas and effective leadership practices that work long-term and do not depend on particular individuals are both essential. These practices *may* lead to the development of the leadership culture in policing long-term. In the short-term perspective, it can result in a good working climate for police leadership.

Leadership culture in the police

I have previously described what police leaders do. How they learn leadership will be considered later. Why police leaders exercise leadership a certain way relates to both culture and structure, which is a recurring topic throughout this book. The following are my reflections on the possible characteristic features of the leadership culture in policing. The development of a leader in policing is primarily a question of experiences. Leadership experience can be seen in connection with background, such as previous experiences, formal education, and other activities which are not directly associated with leadership practice. Personal qualities, motives, attitude, abilities, and skills are also part of it. This influences leadership development toward gaining knowledge and competence when the focus is primarily on learning by doing and knowing how leadership tasks are to be performed in practice (competence). Leadership development through practical exercise of leadership can be observed within an action-oriented culture. The police must be "on the ball", prepared for the unpredictable and the unknown, and ready to perform operational tasks that occur. Leadership development in policing is therefore characterised by the culture(s) the particular leaders operate within. Accordingly, the context that the culture represents influences both the expectations the leader has for themselves and what the leader expects from their subordinates, as well as what expectations the system has for that particular leader. Leadership development therefore largely involves clarifying expectations, meeting and acting according to expectations, and finding a way to perform the leader role based on one's own expectations.

This is a continuous process for leaders, and it occurs in practical work that involves the tasks to be completed and the results to be delivered (which also measure the leaders' performance) and is based on their idea of how to accomplish the social mission in the best possible way. Expectations should be largely considered in the context of mastery to help understand leadership development. This is due to the fact that expectations are also associated with dilemmas and paradoxes related to the deliverables, the solutions leaders consider to be good, and, last but not least, the resources they have at their disposal. While the police are in the midst of a profound process of change, leaders are also supposed to manage day-to-day practice. This is why leadership development must be understood in the context of expectations and mastery, a context which constitutes a continuous process that is taking place under constantly changing conditions, new requirements to leadership and, not least, new expectations the public has for the police in the complex and unpredictable future.

Accordingly, leadership implies continuous development through trial and error, willingness to learn, and willingness to change. We believe that to the extent leadership development results in leader identity – an identity based on the leader's own role awareness and reflection on what the leader role(s) should entail – the leader identity also undergoes continuous development. Our studies show that this happens when leaders use other leaders as role models and learn from them throughout their entire careers, and they are aware of other leader's importance for their own leadership development. We have also found that leader identity can be linked to legitimacy. Legitimacy is largely based on (1) the fact that leaders have an operational background, i.e. they are police officers and have "been there, done that" themselves, and (2) the fact that they have formal leadership training. Our conclusion is therefore that leadership development is learning. Learning implies continuous processes in practice and has to be considered in connection with concrete actions. Learning also takes place through formal training and leadership courses, but the knowledge acquired this way has to be put into practice and is also linked to legitimacy.

To sum up: leadership development is a continuous learning process in practice that involves clarifying expectations, establishing relationships with other leaders and employees, becoming aware of roles and mastery, finding one's identity and legitimacy as a leader, meeting day-to-day challenges, and influencing dilemmas and decisions within the framework of a police culture. Police culture is action-oriented and involves loyalty and following orders, but also offers manoeuvring space and room for local solutions, which is where local identity and belonging become important. The topic of the next chapter is therefore identity and belonging in communities of practice.

Note

1 Translator's note: a wordplay based on the words "best" and "Vestfold", a region in Eastern Norway.

References

Alvesson, M. (2013). *Understanding Organizational Culture* (2nd edn). London: Sage.

Bang, H. (2011). *Organisasjonskultur* [Organisational Culture] (4th edn). Oslo: Universitetsforlaget.

Chan, J. (1997). *Changing Police Culture*. Cambridge: Cambridge University Press.

Charman, S. (2017). *Police Socialisation, Identity and Culture: Becoming Blue*. Portsmouth: Palgrave Macmillan.

Cockcroft, T. (2013). *Police Culture, Themes and Concepts*. London: Routledge.

Cockcroft, T. (2020). *Police Occupational Culture: Research and Practice*. Bristol: Policy Press.

Davies, C. & Bailey, D. (2018). Police leadership: the challenges for developing contemporary practice. *International Journal of Emergency Services*, 7(1), 13–23.

Filstad, C. (2020). *Politiledelse og ledelse av nærpolitiformen – forskning, diskusjoner og refleksjoner* [Police leadership and leadership of the Norwegian Community Policing Reform – research, discussions, and reflections]. PHS Forskning rapport 2020: 2. Oslo: Politihøgskolen.

Filstad, C. (2021). The power and politics of reforming leadership practices. *Policing: A Journal of Policy and Practice*. In press.

Grint, K. & Thornton, S. (2015). Leadership, management, and command in the police. In Fleming, J. (Ed.), *Police Leadership: Rising to the Top* (pp. 95–109). Oxford: Oxford University Press.

Gundhus, H.O.I. (2017). Discretion as an obstacle: police culture, change, and governance in a Norwegian context. *Policing*, 11(3), 258–272.

Hatch, M.J. (2001). *Organisasjonsteori: moderne, symbolske og postmoderne perspektiver* [Organisation theory: Modern, symbolic, and postmodern perspectives]. Oslo: Abstrakt forlag.

Hennestad, B.W. (2015). *Kulturbevisst ledelse. Fra ord til handling* [Management with cultural awareness. From words to actions]. Oslo: Universitetsforlaget.

Hofstede, G., Neuijen, B., Ohayv, D.D., & Sanders, G. (1990). Measuring organizational cultures: a qualitative and quantitative study across 20 cases. *Administrative Science Quarterly*, 35(2), 286–316. doi:10.2307/2393392.

Høyer, H.C., Madsbu, J.P., & Tranøy, B.S. (2018). *Kultur som problem og reformobjekt i norsk politi. Innganger til forståelse av kultur i politiet* [Culture as a problem and an object of the Norwegian police reform. Ways of understanding police culture]. Elverum: Høgskolen i Innlandet.

Johannessen, S.O. (2013). *Politikultur. Identitet, makt og forandring i politiet* [Police culture. Identity, power, and change in the police]. Trondheim: Akademika Forlag.

Johnson, G., Scholes, K., & Whittington, R. (2009). *Exploring Corporate Strategy* (8th edn). Essex: Prentice Hall.

Loftus, B. (2010). Police occupational culture: classical themes, altered times. *Policing & Society*, 20 (1), 1–20.

Martin, J. (1992). *Cultures in Organizations: Three Perspectives*. New York: Oxford University Press.

Reiner, R. (2017). Is police culture cultural? *Policing*, 11(3), 236–241.

Schein, E.H. (2010). *Organizational Culture and Leadership*. San Francisco, CA: Jossey-Bass.

Schraeder, M., Tears, R., & Jordan, M. (2005). Organizational culture in public sector organizations: promoting change through training and leading by example. *Leadership & Organization Development Journal*, 26, 492–502. doi:10.1108/01437730510617681.

Waddington, P.A.J., Kleinig, J., & Wright, M. (Eds.) (2013). *Professional Police Practice: Scenarios and Dilemmas*. Oxford: Oxford University Press.

Chapter 8

Identity and belonging in communities of practice

This chapter demonstrates the importance of social identity and belonging in leadership practices as being part of the collective sense of us. The basic needs of belonging and social identity in the literature are provided, followed by empirical studies where police leaders provide images and text of their perception of belonging in the police. Next, the chapter acknowledges the importance of informal groups at work by using the concept of communities of practice. The mutual engagement in communities of practice as a sense of belonging and identifying is in addition to mutual engagement about joint enterprise and shared repertoires informally "organised" around knowledge of the community of practice.

Studies on police culture have argued that the police sense of mission strongly influences police identities (Chan, 1997; Loftus, 2009; Cockcroft, 2020), and that identity plays an important role in policing (Van Maanen, 1978; Hoggett et al., 2014, 2019). The argument that police culture develops "bottom-up" from operative practice (Waddington, Kleinig, & Wright, 2013) might indicate belonging (or not belonging) as embedded in what constitutes practices and how police identities are developed (Filstad, 2021).

The need to answer the question of who a person is and wants to be underlies the person's identity. The question of who one wants to be is reinforced in relationships with others and within different cultures, where the focus is on who the person is in the eyes of the others. A common understanding of reality is created in relationships with others and within the society one belongs to, for instance the police community. Social identity is relational because it focuses on who a person wants to be in relation to others and in meeting the expectations of others. Accordingly, people make sense of what is expected from them by their environment and of how they are supposed to behave in relationships with others. Social identity is developed in communities and groupings that are of great value to an individual. This is why social identity is not limited to who a person is but is also concerned with who a person is together with others.

Theories on social identity focus on the relationship between the individual and the specific group, and on the expectations, and hence the distinguishing features, of the community members. Social identity is also associated with the value and the emotional connection that one has to the community. Is one proud to be a member of the community the police represent? Is being there for the people and making a difference an intrinsic part of the values? Theories on social identity are concerned with all aspects of groupings and collective actions. The key is to characterise the relationships between people and identify the features of a community and the values it stands for, rather than to understand a community as a collection of isolated individual actions (Charman, 2017).

DOI: 10.4324/9781003224105-12

These theories can therefore contribute to the existing knowledge on various communities in the workplace. To better understand the police officers' personal definition of who they are and who they want to be, we need to consider the communities, both formal and informal, that they belong to within the police organisation. A police officer develops their social identity in various situations and through various activities. It is developed through relationships with other police officers and/or people they cooperate and practise with. Common social identity and identifying oneself with the characteristic features of a leadership practice are essential for allowing the members to feel they are part of the community.

By developing a shared sense of belonging, the collective and representative for "us" (Haslam et al., 2001; Platow & van Knippenberg, 2001), leaders are more likely to stimulate followers through embodiment of what the collective is and who's involved (Ellemers, de Gilder, & Haslam, 2004; Haslam, Reicher, & Platow, 2011; Steffens, Haslam, & Reicher, 2014). The importance of identification is evident, as followers regard leaders as more trustworthy, fair, and charismatic to the extent that they are seen to represent, understand, and advance the interests of a common in-group in a way that followers identify with (Haslam et al., 2001; Platow et al., 2003). For instance, frontline officers place great value on being led by senior officers who have considerable direct experience of street level police work (Rowe, 2006), leaders they strongly identify with and their hard-learned and hard-earned knowledge (Caless, 2011) they respect, trust, and consequently follow (Hoggett et al., 2019).

There are two important factors to understanding how identity formation shapes a community and what distinguishes the members of that community. The first factor is *categorisation*. Members of a community are motivated by the way they categorise themselves within that community as they identify with the group values, and by feeling that they have a voice within the group. That motivation is strengthened by supporting the group leader and the values they stand for. They identify with the role they have been assigned within the community and feel a sense of belonging (Bradford, Murphy, & Jackson, 2014). As a result of this categorisation, the members attach significance to the actions, values, and beliefs which they perceive to be fundamental to the community and which correspond to the overall perception of the community by its other members. Thus, categorisation involves finding one's role as part of a whole within the community. Examples of roles within a work community are the shaper, the evaluator, the coordinator, the team player, the implementer, the completer, the specialist, the jokester, etc. The members' roles can be associated with the differences in their personal qualities, knowledge, skills, and competence. A leadership practice is more than just expertise. It is characterised by who the members are, how expertise develops into competence in various situations, and how the members demonstrate their competence in various ways. Leadership adapts to the members, the work tasks to be completed, and the completion schedule, and is therefore exercised in different ways. The characteristic features of the leadership practice create a common inward identity, and the perception of what the members believe in forms an outward identity.

The other factor of identity formation is *comparison*. A community is not isolated. The members' perceptions of similarities are often reinforced by comparison with other practices. The purpose of differentiating from others is to emphasise the value of the community and strengthen the internal sense of belonging, which then reinforces the group's sense of shared meaning. The establishment of a community around shared knowledge and experiences will guide future activity within the community (Charman, 2017). This is why examining the social identities of police officers has become essential to understanding leadership practices.

Social identity in leadership practices

In addition to their social identities as police officers, the police have many other social identities, for example, those connected with nationality, ethnicity, gender, religion, age, education, place of residence, lifestyle and family, or work and profession. Social identities are associated with status, position, professional membership, and ownership. They also involve values, attitudes, activities, or roles such as son, wife, patient, family member, leader, and so on. In many ways, the formation of social identities may be understood as socialisation processes. We socialise within a society through family, preschool, school, and workplaces. We are met by the expectations of being good citizens, but we also have expectations of society (Filstad, 2017). We socialise within educational institutions, and we socialise within professions and organisations. Organisational socialisation therefore involves individual, social, and cultural learning processes aimed at acquiring skills and knowledge that are necessary for a full membership in a new organisation (Filstad, 2017). The purpose of policing education is to socialise students into a professional culture in order to develop a common professional identity as police officers. The context of education is very different from the work context, and the big challenge is to build a bridge between education and the exercise of practice. Students attach significantly more value to organisational socialisation in practical policing work compared to the value of education across most of the areas of expertise they focus on in their studies (Bäck, 2020).

Knowledge as knowing is situation-dependent. Being knowledgeable refers to how the knowledge acquired through education finds its way into practical work. (I focus on this topic in the next chapter on knowledge and knowing.) The police officer identity starts to form at the Norwegian Police University College (NPUC), but according to the study I referred to above, what matters most for the students is practical police work.

Police students quickly become part of the "we" identity at NPUC. They wear uniforms and take part in physical training activities together, which strengthens their we-feeling. The curriculum places much emphasis on communication, so they learn to complete policing tasks that require cooperation early on, and tasks are often solved based on collective efforts.

Most people prefer developing social relationships with the people they identify with, consider similar, and therefore recognise themselves in (Wilson & Elman, 1990). Not all social identities are equally important. Whether our social identity is important or not depends on situations and contexts.

The police is not the only organisation where people of the same profession identify with each other. Within other types of organisations, communication specialists, IT specialists, engineers, doctors, lawyers, or auditors are just some examples of the employees who identify with each other more than with other colleagues. This identification has an effect on sensemaking and defines a community which may, for instance, consist of lawyers, and accordingly, the belonging of an individual to the lawyers' practice. Of all the identities that influence the sense of belonging to informal communities of practice at work, profession has proven to be the most important (Filstad, 2014a). (More on informal communities of practice later in this chapter.)

Our individual social identities as citizens can illustrate why we have to understand social identity as situation- and context-dependent. When is social identity important? On meeting with other nationalities, one often becomes more aware of one's own identity as a citizen of the country. Naturally, this does not happen when interacting with the citizens of one's own country. Uniformed police officers will be more aware of their social identity as part of the police in encounters with the public than at the police station. Female police leaders may be more aware of their gender identity in situations dominated by male police leaders, perhaps even more so in situations where gender is relevant to the case. Interviews with female police leaders from 2019 show that some of them are conscious of not behaving "like a girl" and that within the police, they meet other women who are more like themselves. A female police leader explains: "The kind of women I meet here are not the ones I met at the upper secondary school. They have more, hmm, masculine hormones. I mean they are more independent, outgoing, and they really want to do the job."

It seems that identifying as a female leader does not give high status in the police. At the same time, the studies demonstrate that female police leaders support each other more than female leaders in other organisations. A female police leader explains: "Women can be mean to each other, and they often envy each other. But I have never experienced that with the police. Of course, there are women like that, but they are very few."

We have also found that women tend to be more supportive towards each other when there are many women in a department compared to when there are only a few. The cases when they experience little support from other women involve leadership levels. A female police leader explains:

> When I became a leader, I felt that other women reacted like: "Right, it's okay that you have reached this level, but it's not okay if you go further up. We don't support you anymore." It was sort of enough for them. But I have had a lot of support from male leaders in my management team. Male leaders are the ones who have supported me up to this point. I don't think female leaders support other female leaders.

Social identity is associated with, among other things, age, gender, geographical factors, lifestyle, position, education, and, not least, profession. These are examples of identity variables that create a sense of belonging. They are also example of where one consciously searches for a community. However, as demonstrated in the previous example, women or people coming from minority backgrounds are not willing to join potential communities. There may be situations where one does not want to be identified as a woman, police officer from a minority background, northerner, newcomer, and the like because one finds other social identities to be more important. A person wants to belong to a community if it is based on a social identity that is important for that person.

Social identity and role models

Police leaders are concerned with serving as role models for their subordinates. For them, being a role model in terms of the social mission is as much inward-oriented as it is oriented towards the public. They are seen as role models because they are considerate, knowledgeable, intelligent, and trustworthy. They are the ones others look up to and want to learn from (Lockwood & Kunda, 2000; Filstad, 2017). Accordingly, the notion of a role model is part of a further notion of identification (Moriearty & Robbins-Carter, 1985).

Police officers have chosen their education based on the desire to undertake a social mission. Many of them say they are motivated by the opportunity "to make a difference for people", which is how they often explain why they chose to join the police. A police leader says:

> I think being a role model really matters in policing. Ethics is important, and we emphasise this when hiring. You are still a police officer even when you are not at work. It's not off when you are living your private life either. We have a public profile, and that's very important to remember. It's actually similar to other public sector organisations.

Being a good role model and acting in a fair and ethical manner is a recurring topic in policing, which is communicated to police students and new hires with particular emphasis. Role models are people who, through their actions, personal style, and/or special qualities, are essential for social identity within the police. In the previous chapter on police culture, police leaders talked about the importance of taking care of each other as part of being a role model. A police leader explains:

> We all have families, so we try to take care of each other in both the good and the bad times. It's important to care for each other. It's not something you just say, it's something you do. I'm trying, constantly trying to be mindful of it.

People learn more from role models that they perceive to be more like themselves. They can more easily identify with certain aspects of the role model's attitudes, behaviour, and values because this is where they recognise themselves (Gibson & Cordova, 1990). People with high self-esteem are often positively influenced by role models since they feel they can achieve the same results as their role model. It can be the opposite for people with low self-esteem, who might be negatively influenced by role models because they think they are not capable of achieving what their role model has (Lockwood & Kunda, 2000).

Police leaders do not consider themselves good role models all the time. There is one area in particular where they are especially critical of their own leadership, and that is being more assertive and coming into conflicts more often. Many suggest that this has become easier as a result of long experience, but they still see the potential for becoming more assertive when it comes to difficult cases. Two police leaders explain:

> I think I'm a good role model, but at the same time it's hard to say for sure because the question is, are you assertive enough for your department? Are you assertive enough for the goals that are set? Are you assertive enough for producing good police work for the public? That's what it is all about, and it's probably something you can struggle with the most. Otherwise, I think I'm in good control of everything that's going on, both in my department and in terms of the results we deliver to the public. These are the things I follow very closely.

For me it's easier to be more direct now. It took me many years to learn to come directly into conflicts and take the battles before they developed into something bigger. Dare to speak out and stand by it. It is demanding but absolutely necessary for a leader at this level.

Leaders are not the only ones who can be role models. Within a leadership practice, subordinates can also be role models for each other. There are two aspects that are rarely considered when attempting to understand the importance of role models for identification and as sources of knowledge in, for instance, a leadership practice (Filstad, 2017). The first one is that there are hardly absolute role models. People learn from several role models who might have different qualities or activities that are unique to them. In other words, through observation, shared practice, conversations, and the like, a person is influenced by role models and uses them partially and piece by piece in order to put them together and adapt to their own leadership practice. The other aspect is that we can also have negative role models. One observes what a role model does and chooses not to act this way, either because this is far beyond what one can achieve or because they consider the observed behaviour to be negative. One might also think that the price to pay as a consequence of an action is too high. An example of the latter can be when a police leader gives an interview in an attempt to be heard in connection with the consequences of the police reform and expresses frustration at the fact that there have never been fewer patrolling police officers in Oslo. Because of the reaction of the Police Directorate and the fuss about the lack of loyalty from other employees, one may consider the consequences of such an action to be too big, and it does not lead to increased staffing either. From the observational learning perspective, the process of assessing the actions of other people and their consequences is referred to as vicarious experience (Bandura, 1986). The observed action becomes role modelling. One considers whether one has the capabilities to act in the same way and is motivated enough to take the consequences, that is how important the case is for that person. And finally, one assesses the fairness. Will the consequences for oneself be the same as for the role model, i.e. will everyone be treated fairly? If the consequences of the police leader's interview are positive, they receive much positive feedback internally, and they are promised more resources for their department, one will consider if one can successfully complete the same task.

The social identity of the police is related to how the public perceive them and how they want to appear in the eyes of the public – what does the public want the police to be? Police officers are role models in terms of the social mission and, in many ways, symbols of the desired future of the society. The debate over armed police is an example of this. Other examples include the police's participation and presence in the local community and in Oslo Pride. The police are often seen in the media, and they act as spokespersons for how to overcome various social problems. Their social identities as employees in the police organisation are therefore influenced by this social participation, by the uniformity, and by the symbolic meaning of belonging to a group, a police force. In the police internally, there are several social identities in play which affect different leadership practices in various ways.

Social identity based on a profession, such as a police officer, lawyer, psychologist, sociologist, and so on, is important. To construct a common social identity within a leadership practice, several identities may be important for the participants. All police person-years do not involve the same type of work. Where an individual police employee wants to work can be seen in connection with their desired identity within the police. When the members' identities correspond to what a leadership practice wants to stand for, this influences the motivation to work for the best of that leadership practice. It also gives the desired sense of belonging. The importance of one's social identity therefore depends on belonging to the community's identity. Is it important to be identified as a member of the emergency squad, the National Criminal Investigation Service (Kripos), the Norwegian Police Security Service (PST), the National Authority for Investigation and Prosecution of Economic and Environmental Crime (Økokrim), the National Mobile Police Service (UP), or work with, for example, crime prevention, general investigations, special investigations, or operational work? Is the identity associated with *where* one works, be it a special investigator in Troms Police District, a crime prevention specialist in Oslo East, or operational specialist in Eastern Police District? What a police employee wants to represent by working in a particular place and with particular types of tasks within the police indicates the close connection between social identity and belonging in a leadership practice. It is also associated with positioning within the community. Social identity is a question of positioning, belonging, and negotiating within a leadership practice.

Social identity as negotiating and positioning

Social identities develop in a leadership practice through the investment of the leader and the other employees. These investments provide for various forms of belonging in a community and influence the negotiation of desired meaning. The question is to what extent the members' investments will lead to the desired sense of belonging. This means that social identity formation is not only about who an individual identifies with within the community of practice. Social identity formation is a two-sided process: on the one hand, it is a question of who an individual identifies with, and on the other hand, which is just as important, whether that individual wants to invest in a leadership practice in order to develop a common social identity. This involves negotiating the desired positioning and, if it is worth the effort, whether one is motivated to put the required effort in. Hence, social identity formation is twofold – it comprises positioning and belonging. The sense of belonging to a community is reinforced when the result of positioning and negotiating leads to the development of a social identity that agrees with who one wants to be in a leadership practice. This creates similarity within the leadership practice and distinguishes it from other leadership practices. It is characterised by the dynamics of social relationships that encourage and strengthen the sense of belonging through the individual's social identity (Child & Rodrigues, 2011).

Belonging in leadership practices

By developing a shared sense of belonging, the collective and representative for "us" (Haslam et al., 2001; Platow & van Knippenberg, 2001), leaders are more likely to stimulate followers through embodiment of what the collective is and who's involved (Ellemers et al., 2004; Haslam et al., 2011; Steffens et al., 2014). The importance of identification is evident, as followers regard leaders as more trustworthy, fair, and charismatic to the extent that they are seen to represent, understand, and advance the interests of a common in-group in a way that followers identify with (Haslam et al., 2001; Platow et al., 2003). For instance, frontline officers place great value on being led by senior officers who have considerable direct experience of street level police work (Rowe, 2006), leaders they strongly identify with and their hard-learned and hard-earned knowledge (Caless, 2011) they respect, trust, and consequently follow (Hoggett et al., 2019).

Similar to social identity, belonging refers to a human need for, and the importance of, feeling valued and being part of something bigger. This is why belonging is a social and relational phenomenon which influences people's cognition, emotions, and behaviour (Hagerty et al., 1992; Malone, Pillow, & Osman, 2012). A sense of belonging, whether formal or informal, is essential for social identity when it comes to people, practices, groups, or an organisation, and, accordingly, also essential for whether one identifies with those people, practices, groups, and organisations. Belonging is embedded in processes that are aimed at identifying with the social, relational, and material surroundings one wants to be part of (May, 2011: 368). However, the sense of belonging is subjective. It reflects one's subjective feeling of whether one belongs to a community, and therefore one's own perception of reality. It revolves around a perceived sense of belonging to something unique (Pickett, Silver, & Brewer, 2002).

The sense of belonging to a practice is reinforced when it reflects who the person wants to be (Child & Rodrigues, 2011). This can be illustrated by the way the person accomplishes the social mission of the police. The social role of the police is to contribute to and be useful for providing public safety. According to police leaders, their work involves a great degree of flexibility, and they are ready to go the extra length in order to deliver a great result. This is the core of the police organisation. Two police leaders explain:

> I do care about the society we work in, about the mission we undertake as police. I feel engaged, I really care, and I think it is interesting.

> We have focused on the social mission, our role, what the public view of the police will be. We have to understand the society around us and form a proper decision-making basis in order to conduct intelligence processes. It's an engaging process.

Police identity is important. One of the informants goes so far as to say: "If I am not a police officer, then what am I?" After completing police education, lawyers are the largest professional group in the police, and they are allowed to wear police uniforms. There is a great deal of joking, but also frustration, about lawyers who have not learned to wear the uniform the right way. There are many civilian employees in the police organisation who cannot wear the uniform, with some exceptions for when they are police leaders, for example, a rector at NPUC. In the same way the police uniform *creates* the sense of belonging, the lack of uniform can result in not feeling a sense of belonging. Civilian personnel often say they feel excluded or that their identity is, for example, an educator, a psychologist, a social worker, a journalist, an economist, or an analyst who is employed by the police.

To investigate belonging in organisations, I have used a research method called "snaplog" (Filstad, Traavik, & Gorli, 2019). The snaplog method asks the participants to take a photo that illustrates their sense of belonging to the organisation. They also write a short text explaining why they think this photo illustrates belonging. Other than that, no guidelines and definitions or other information explaining what belonging or identity can refer to are provided to the participants. The purpose is to avoid influencing the informants in any way in order to find out how an individual understands belonging.

Belonging is often about the "here and now", collectively completing tasks, having a common goal, and achieving something together. It is important that everyone contributes and is valued for who they are regardless of their place in the organisational hierarchy. There are no descriptions or photos of leaders in our original study based on 51 informants. They were included in photos only as "equals" rather than leaders. The informants referred to feeling themselves unique and being part of a community, often emphasising informal communities. Among the 23 police leader informants, there was one who chose to submit a photo of their leader to illustrate belonging.

Belonging gives a feeling of pride, and it revolves around shared values, taking care of each other, and the positive aspects of hard work aimed at achieving common goals. The photos and texts below are examples of what police leaders (who participated in the leadership programme organised by NPUC in the autumn of 2018) think is important for belonging to the police organisation.

State visit   Locker room   Pride of lions

Figure 8.1 Images of belonging

a: State visit
Although this is not the unit I mainly work for, this photo represents belonging for me. It is taken in connection with an official state visit and convoy management. As a leader, you have to get the best out of a group who need to work together to complete the task. We are no stronger than our weakest link, so it is up to every individual person to encourage and support each other. The photo represents what it means to be part of something bigger and to have the opportunity to lead a group who want to perform and are motivated by mastering the task. This gives a sense of joy, belonging, and makes me proud of being part of such a group.

b: Locker room
The photo shows my personal locker. It is one of the first and last things you see at the start of the day and before you leave work. In addition to framing the everyday at work, the locker for me is also an illustration of equality and flat structure – one locker for everyone regardless of your level or function. I work in a uniformed organisation. When I put on my uniform, the transition from private life to being a police officer becomes even more evident. I think this photo represents an arena where organisational belonging is reinforced as a result of this role change. Stability and solidarity are what distinguishes my workplace. The start of a career and "entry" into the unit are usually described as "getting assigned a locker". Similarly, "emptying the locker" means the end of a career. For me, this metaphor amplifies the intuitive relevance of this photo to the concept of belonging.

c: Pride of lions
The pride of lions symbolises belonging for me. We are social individuals who rely on being part of a community where we are looked out for and accepted. The pride of lions moves in the same direction, they have the same goals, and are dependent on each particular individual.

At the office   Crime Scene Norway   Out in the field   Stairs

Figure 8.2 Images of belonging

a: At the office
This photo illustrates belonging to both my organisation and unit. These nice people are four of the 15 members of my group, but they represent the entire group. They spend much time in the districts solving cases, but they still manage to give me a sense of both professional and social belonging by being engaged, thoughtful, available, and motivated. Well done, and as you can see in the picture, there are very few people in the hallway where we are sitting.

b: *Crime Scene Norway*
The photo is from the TV programme *Åsted Norge* (*Crime Scene Norway*). Our crime prevention officer says goodbye to a young man who has had a conversation at our police station after being taken from the city on a Saturday night on suspicion of drug abuse. Before he leaves, the officer has a good chat with him, which I think was valuable for both of them. This is at the core of what we do. Prevention, being present, and communication. This is important in my job, and it also has to reflect what I do. And it doesn't matter if I'm a civilian office worker who is far from the street. I'm very proud of TV reports like these, and this was partly the reason why I chose to work for the police.

c: Out in the field
For me, the photo symbolises solidarity, belonging, and strength in the department I work at. "A single twig breaks, but the bundle of twigs is strong" (Chief Tecumseh of the Shawnee Tribe, 1812). This photo also shows pride, joy, competence, enthusiasm, and determination, as well as the sense of belonging we feel towards the organisation, work tasks, and each other.

d: Stairs
My initial thought was to take a photo of our section, but then I realised that my sense of belonging applies to the entire police station. That's why my photo had to include all the floors in the building. I couldn't take a picture from the outside because then it would look just like another building, but taken from the inside, it's more about us, the people who work here.

When police leaders reflected on their own photos and shared their thoughts on belonging with other police leaders who took part in the study, it became obvious that belonging for them is associated with being proud of working in the police force. Helping others involves a strong sense of belonging, and the social mission is perceived as meaningful. They also indicate that belonging is directly linked to the field of expertise and to physical and geographical locations. In this sense, one may feel they belong to, for example, law enforcement, investigations, intelligence, or crime prevention, and to the part of the country where they work. According to police leaders, being part of a community gives them a lot, but it also deprives them of something if they think of the police organisation as a whole. Belonging results in solidarity when everyone contributes. The sense of belonging is achieved by being there for each other, getting a pat on the back, completing work tasks together, and being equal, which is emphasised as essential. In stark contrast to most other organisations, policing work often involves tragic lives, accidents, victims, the injured and aggrieved, etc. Work tasks are often unpredictable and associated with powerful experiences. Due to emotional coping, a high workload, and

Piketten – Break room   Operations centre   Parole-briefing

Figure 8.3 Images of belonging
a: "Piketten" – break room
This is a photo of the break room at the patrol section where I work. This is where we socialise and chat. Here, everyone can talk to everyone, and for me, belonging is about being part of this.
b: Operations centre
Belonging for me is the operations room! It was obvious that I had to choose a picture of "my team", when illustrating belonging. I feel a great sense of belonging to my close colleagues, my team, at the operations centre. I want to justify this with the fact that I am part of the team, and the team members are important to me and my function. It is my task, as leader of the team, to build the team, create relationships and social support through belonging and team spirit in the group. I believe that this increases their desire to perform, and promotes individual skills as well as team skills. A well-functioning team work is crucial in an operations centre, where I as operations leader/team leader must make decisions quickly, and often based on a thin factual basis. If the team members, including myself, do not feel a sense of belonging and have a team spirit, this will have negative consequences for the team's overall competence, as we are not stronger than the weakest link.
c: "Parole" – briefing room
This photo symbolises belonging for me. When I walk into the briefing room and everyone is there, I can feel a positive atmosphere all around. There is smiling, small talk, some laughter, and great colleagues who bring about a sense of belonging. This makes me proud and happy, and the fact that they are there motivates me as a leader. We are a great team of motivated employees who are hungry for knowledge, and who help each other out. They help me do a good job as a leader. An amazing team I'm very proud of and feel I belong to. I'm lucky to have this, and I appreciate it as often as I can

tasks that require shared effort, colleagues have to trust each other when it comes to their own safety and task completion. This is why, compared to most other organisations, there is an additional dimension to the sense of belonging in the policing profession that encompasses belonging through exercising and engaging in physical activities together, through the 24/7 shifts, or through the same police education, continuing and further education/training, or duty assignment at NPUC. These factors reinforce the sense of belonging but can also be exclusionary and result in the formation of silos based on the type of police work, profession (lawyer, police officer, or civilian employee), or geography. This is the challenge of belonging. A strong sense of belonging to a leadership practice can lead to groupthink. A strong in-group and the notion of "us" are reinforced by treating those who are outside of the leadership practice as "the others", that is out-groups. Irving L. Janis's (1982) well-known groupthink theory (game theory) provides a good explanation for this phenomenon. He argues that groups which are pressed into a strong cultural community tend to protect their collective "truths" and stereotype their opponents (out-groups) as stupid because they threaten the group's existence.

Belonging influences and is influenced by who we identify with. This is why belonging and identity should be understood as integrated with the practices that police employees participate in. A practice will typically have its own identity that the members gather around. This identity has to be consistent with the members' identities in order for them to feel a sense of belonging. This membership needs to be essential for their social identity. Higher-level police leaders refer to formal practice, but belonging is also largely nurtured in informal communities of practice because these communities are chosen by the members themselves, while formal communities of practice are invariably assigned to them.

Communities of practice

The concept of communities of practice was introduced in order to demonstrate how informal groupings affect the learning process.[1] Belonging, social identity, and identification are central to the community of practice theory, and it also includes how the community wants to be perceived by others. A community of practice is defined by common interests and the value it places on the knowledge that it will represent. Communities of practice help to understand informal groups in an organisation, as according to Wenger, it is social identity that forms and develops communities of practice. He defines a community of practice as "a group of people who share a concern, a set of problems, or a passion about a topic, and who deepen their knowledge and expertise in this area by interacting on an ongoing basis" (Wenger, McDermott, & Snyder, 2002).

A community of practice connects practice and community through three features of competent membership. These three features of competence form the basis for developing a collective sense of belonging and collective sensemaking in a community of practice:

1   *Mutual engagement* – negotiations and establishment of norms and guidelines for the community of practice. To be competent means to contribute to and engage in the community of practice in a way that other members can rely on.
2   *Experience of collective activities and efforts* – being a full competent member in order to understand what the community is and should be.
3   *Shared practice through common repertoires* – common resources, language, routines, sensibility, artefacts, tools, stories, and the like. To be competent means to have access to the repertoire of the practice and be able to use it effectively. Through participation in community of practice, the members collectively define what the competence of the community is.

The competence and membership of the community of practice combines the three features as illustrated by Wenger (2003) (see Figure 8.4).

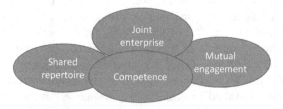

Figure 8.4 Membership and knowledge components in communities of practice

An informal community of practice can form spontaneously. For example, recent graduates can "find" each other within the police. They share the experience of being in the same situation and identify with each other as policing newcomers. Another example would be female police leaders who choose to be part of an informal group comprising other female police leaders. Among other things, they discuss possible challenges associated with being women, and they achieve a common identity both as women and as female police leaders. The third example is often visible in processes of change. Employees who represent a former department or police district that has been merged into a larger unit come together in a community of practice where they collectively identify with "the way it used to be". There are many examples of communities of practice in all organisations. In the police force, employees are members of several community of practice, where they develop a community feeling by representing something they identify with. Through mutual engagement, they all contribute to the community on equal terms and gather around a repertoire of resources and competence they identify with. The participants have chosen each other and are bound together by collectively developed competence, established norms and rules of interaction, and communal language, routines, values, artefacts, stories, and so on (Hislop, 2004; Lesser & Everest, 2001; Wenger, 1998; Wenger et al., 2002). The informal aspect does not mean that everyone agrees, or that there is no expression for power and politics in the community of practice. There will also be members who feel disconnected and isolated, lack a sense of mastery, feel tensions within the community, or lack the sense of belonging (Delahunty, Verenikina, & Jones, 2014; Filstad, 2014b). This is why negotiations will occur in a community of practice. Participants in communities of practices have different interests and want to legitimise their demand for knowledge in competition with others as part of internal negotiation processes (Contu & Willmott, 2003; Levina & Orlikowski, 2009). There will also be negotiations on what a community of practice should be and what it means to be a full member. The informal aspect allows the members to gain access to membership and, in doing so, earn it. Membership in informal communities of practice does not follow the formal structure of the police organisation. Instead, it is the result of common identification and the competence it represents. Competence here becomes essential in the same way that competence in a formal leadership practice is essential for social identity and belonging. This is why it is time to take a closer look at the notion of competence in the next chapter.

Note

1 The book on situated learning was published by Jean Lave and Étienne Wenger in 1991. They introduced the concept of learning as participation in social practices and communities. 1991 was also the year when Seely Brown and Paul Duguid published the article on communities of practice and their effect on situated learning. The concept of community of practice was later developed by Wenger in his book from 1998.

References

Bandura, A. (1986). *Social Foundations of Thoughts and Action: A Social Cognitive Theory*. Englewood Cliffs: Prentice Hall.
Bäck, T. (2020). *Från polisutbildning till polispraktik: polisstudenters och polisers värderingar av yrkesrelaterade kompetenser* [From police education to police practice: Police students' and police officers'

perceptions of professional competences] (doctoral thesis). Umeå: Umeå University, Faculty of Social Sciences, Department of Education. http://umu.diva-portal.org/smash/record.jsf?language=sv&pid=diva2%3A1387291&dswid=203.

Bradford, B., Murphy, K., & Jackson, J. (2014). Officers as mirrors: policing, procedural justice and the (re)production of social identity. *British Journal of Criminology*, 54(4), 527–550.

Caless, B. (2011). *Policing at the Top: The Roles, Values and Attitudes of Chief Police Officers*. Bristol: Policy Press.

Chan, J. (1997). *Changing Police Culture*. Cambridge: Cambridge University Press.

Charman, S. (2017). *Police Socialisation, Identity and Culture: Becoming Blue*. Portsmouth: Palgrave Macmillan.

Child, J. & Rodrigues, S. (2011). Social identity and organizational learning. In M. Easterby-Smith & M.A. Lyles (Eds.), *The Blackwell Handbook of Organizational Learning and Knowledge Management*. Malden: Blackwell.

Cockcroft, T. (2020). *Police Occupational Culture: Research and Practice*. Bristol: Policy Press.

Contu, A. & Willmott, H. (2003). Re-embedding situatedness: the importance of power relations in learning theory. *Organization Science*, 14(3), 283–296.

Delahunty, J., Verenikina, I., & Jones, P. (2014). Socio-emotional connections: identity, belonging and learning in online interactions. A literature review. *Technology, Pedagogy and Education*, 23(2), 243–265.

Ellemers, N., de Gilder, D., Haslam, S. A. (2004). Motivating individuals and groups at work: a social identity perspective on leadership and group performance. *Academy of Management Review*, 29(3), 459–478.

Filstad, C. (2014a). Learning and knowledge as interrelations between CoPs and NoPs. *The Learning Organization*, 21(2), 70–82.

Filstad, C. (2014b). The politics of sensemaking and sensegiving at work. *Journal of Workplace Learning*, 26(1), 3–21.

Filstad, C. (2017). *Nyansattes organisasjonssosialisering. Perspektiver og læringsstrategier* [New employee organisational socialisation. Perspectives and learning strategies]. Bergen: Fagbokforlaget.

Filstad, C., Traavik, L., & Gorli, M. (2019). Belonging at work: the experience, representations and meanings of belonging. *Journal of Workplace Learning*, 31(2), 116–142.

Filstad, C. (2021). "If I'm not police, then who am I?" – about belonging and identity in the police. *Police Practice and Research: An International Journal*. For review.

Gibson, D. & Cordova, D. (1990). Women's and men's role models: the importance of exemplars. In A.J. Urrell, F.J. Crosby, & R.J. Ely (Eds.), *Applied Social Research: Mentoring Dilemmas: Developmental Relationships Within Multicultural Organizations* (pp. 121–141). Mahwah: Lawrence Erbaum.

Hagerty, B. M. K., Lynch-Sauer, J., Patusky, K. L., Bouwsema, M., & Collier, P. (1992). Sense of belonging: a vital mental health concept. *Archives of Psychiatric Nursing*, 6(3), 172–177.

Haslam, S. A., Platow, M. J., Turner, J. C., Reynolds, K. J., McGarty, C., Oakes, P. J., Johnson, S., Ryan, M. K., & Veenstra, K. (2001). Social identity and the romance of leadership: the importance of being seen to be "doing it for us". *Group Process Intergroup Relations*, 4(3),191–205.

Haslam, S. A., Reicher, S. D., & Platow, M. J. (2011). *The New Psychology of Leadership: Identity, Influence and Power*. London and New York: Psychology Press.

Hislop, D. (2004). The paradox of communities of practice: knowledge sharing between communities. In P. Hildreth & C. Kimble (Eds.), *Knowledge Networks Innovation Through Communities of Practice* (pp. 36–45). London: Idea Group Publishing.

Hoggett, J., Redford, P., Toher, D., & White, P. (2014). *Challenge and Change: Police Identity, Morale and Goodwill in an Age of Austerity*. Bristol: UWE.

Hoggett, J., Redford, R., Toher, D., & White, P. (2019). Challenges for police leadership: identity, experience, legitimacy and direct entry. *Journal of Police and Criminal Psychology*, 34, 145–155.

Janis, I.L. (1982). *Groupthink: Psychological Studies of Policy Decisions and Fiascoes* (2nd edn). Boston, MA: Houghton Mifflin.

Lesser, E. & Everest, K. (2001). Using communities of practice to manage intellectual capital. *Ivey Business Journal*, 65(4), 37–41.

Levina, N. & Orlikowski, W.J. (2009). Understanding shifting power relations within and across organizations: a critical genre analysis. *Academy of Management Journal*, 52(4), 672–703.

Lockwood, P.J. & Kunda, Z. (2000). Outstanding role models: do they inspire or demoralize us? In A. Tesser, R.B. Felson & J.M. Suls (Eds.), *Psychological Perspectives on Self and Identity* (pp. 147–171). Washington, DC: American Psychological Association.

Loftus, B. (2009). *Police Culture in a Changing World*. Oxford: Oxford University Press.

Malone, G. P., Pillow, D. R., & Osman, A. (2012). The general belongingness scale (GBS): assessing achieved belongingness. *Personality and Individual Differences*, 52(3), 311–316.

May, V. (2011). Self, belonging and social change. *Sociology*, 45(3), 363–378.

Moriearty, J. & Robbins-Carter, J. (1985). Role models in library education: effect on women's careers. *Library Trends*, 34(2), 323–342.

Pickett, C.L., Silver, M.D., & Brewer, M.B. (2002). The impact of assimilation and differentiation needs on perceived group importance and judgments of ingroup size. *Personality and Social Psychology Bulletin*, 28(4), 546–558. doi:10.1177/0146167202287011.

Platow, M. J., & van Knippenberg, D. (2001). A social identity analysis of leadership endorsement: the effects of leader ingroup prototypicality and distributive intergroup fairness. *Personality and Social Psychology Bulletin*, 27(11), 1508–1519.

Platow, M. J., Haslam, S.A., Foddy, M., & Grace, D. M. (2003). Leadership as the outcome of self-categorization processes. In D.van Knippenberg & M. A. Hogg (Eds.), *Leadership and Power: Identity Processes in Groups and Organizations* (pp. 34–47). London: Sage.

Rowe, M. (2006). Following the leader: front-line narratives on police leadership. *Policing: An International Journal of Police Strategies and Management*, 29(4), 757–767.

Steffens, N. K., Haslam, S. A., & Reicher, S. D. (2014). Up close and personal: evidence that shared social identity is a basis for the 'special' relationship that binds followers to leaders. *Leadership Quarterly* 25(2), 296–313.

Van Maanen, J. (1978). *On Watching the Watchers: Policing: A View from the Street*. Santa Monica, CA: Goodyear.

Waddington, P.A.J., Kleinig, J., & Wright, M. (Eds.) (2013). *Professional Police Practice: Scenarios and Dilemmas*. Oxford: Oxford University Press.

Wenger, E. (1998). *Communities of Practice: Learning, Meaning and Identity*. New York: Cambridge University Press.

Wenger, E. (2003). Communities of practice and social learning systems. In D. Nicolini, D. Yanow, & S. Gherardi (Eds.), *Knowing in Organizations: A Practice-based Approach* (pp. 76–99). London: Routledge.

Wenger, E., McDermott, R., & Snyder, W.M. (2002). *Cultivating Communities of Practice: A Guide to Managing Knowledge*. Boston: Harvard Business School Press.

Wilson, J.A. & Elman, N.S. (1990). Organizational benefits of mentoring. *Academy of Management Executive*, 4(4), 88–94.

Chapter 9

Knowing in practice

This chapter views knowledge as action and doing, not as individual possession, and hence, as knowing in practice. Knowledge and knowing as interweaving dynamic processes are in accordance to a leadership of practice perspective, where the chapter builds up an argument of why knowing rather than knowledge is a fruitful approach. In doing so, the chapter describes and discusses tacit and explicit knowledge and the importance of distinguishing between the two for knowledge sharing purposes in leadership practices. The chapter also argues that policing needs to be acknowledge as knowledge work and the police as a knowledge organisation, and with what consequences.

Two main approaches to knowledge stand out as the epistemology of possession and the epistemology of practice (Sfard, 1998; Cook & Brown, 1999). These two approaches will be further elaborated as approaches to learning in Chapter 13. The possession approach treats knowledge as the person's property and something the individual has, while the participation approach views knowledge as something people do (Elkjaer, 2004; Newell et al., 2009). The leadership-as-practice approach rests on the critics from the epistemology of practice literature on knowledge arguing that knowledge is constructed and negotiated through social and cultural relations in different contexts – i.e. in leadership practices (Lave & Wenger, 1991; Brown & Duguid, 1991; Gherardi, 2009).

In attempting to combine the two approaches, Cook and Brown (1999) argue for talking about both knowledge used in action and knowing as part of the action. They explain that "knowledge is a tool for knowing, that knowing is an aspect of our interaction with the social and physical world, and the interplay of knowledge and knowing can generate new knowledge and new ways of knowing" (p. 381).

The social and context dependence of knowledge, as socially situated, draws attention to the active, dynamic, processual, negotiated, social, and cultural nature of knowledge (Newell et al., 2009). Accordingly, the knowledge as practice approach prefers to talk about knowing rather than knowledge to underline the interweaving of what people know and what they do and who and where they are (Newell et al., 2009). The integration between knowledge and knowing gives associations to Dewey's (1938) "thinking in action" in avoiding the two exclusive epistemologies that dominate the knowledge and learning literature (Elkjaer, 2004).

Leadership as practice acknowledges these underlying assumptions of understanding knowledge and use knowing rather than knowledge to outline the dynamic and context dependent by using a verb rather than a noun on what knowledge is in leadership practice. Knowing is an ongoing accomplishment through social and cultural relations as constructions of engagement in social practices (Orlikowski, 2002). The dynamics

DOI: 10.4324/9781003224105-13

between knowledge and knowing and distinctions between the two rely heavily on the extent to which knowledge (including educational knowledge) is used and applied in practical work and thus, how to bridge the knowledge-knowing gap in leadership practice.

Educational and professional knowledge

The Norwegian police maintains a high level of professional competence. Police employees largely rely on intrinsic motivation and engagement in accordance to the social mission by safeguarding and protecting the Norwegian public in the best way possible. There is a high level of trust in the police among the population, and since 1992 they have completed a three-year higher bachelor's degree programme at the Norwegian Police University College. Police lawyers are highly educated professionals with a law degree. The Norwegian Police University College also offers master's degree programmes and continuing and further education in policing disciplines and police leadership. Mandatory training in policing disciplines is organised in cooperation with the districts and with the assistance of police instructors and the Norwegian Police University College. There is also a significant proportion of police employees who take master's degrees at other educational institutions, with a special focus on management and administration. Last but not least, the police organisation has a long history of practical policing and having police leaders with extensive leadership experience.

Overall, this puts the Norwegian police in a unique position in terms of educational level in the fields of policing and leadership disciplines. The same is true for the level of trust among the population. The level of trust has slightly decreased from 83% in 2017 to 77% in 2018, only to increase again. In 2019, 79% of the population responded that their level of trust in the police is quite high or very high. This was in spite of the negative media coverage related to police reform. Since 2016, the police organisation has implemented very extensive changes as part of what is now referred to as the biggest police reform ever. Additionally, Norwegian criminal patterns are considered to have become increasingly more complex and challenging.

The police as a knowledge organisation

The police can be characterised as a knowledge organisation, with knowledge and knowing as its main resources for providing good police services (Gotvassli, 2020). Knowledge-organisations must communicate, coordinate, cooperate, and continuously share and develop knowledge from many professional fields. Knowledge work is often complex, and it challenges established routines and formulas. This high degree of complexity includes both tacit and explicit knowledge (Irgens & Wennes, 2012), the broader organisational context, and the entire network of more or less interconnected practices (Newell et al., 2009). Accordingly, knowledge work requires autonomy and independence, which I describe as manoeuvring space in Chapter 11. Police officers have to tackle the complexity involved in problem solving, and they have to be analytical and represent both diversity and a multitude of professional disciplines, as well as flexible specialisation (Gotvassli, 2020). Good leadership of knowledge workers therefore involves motivating them through personal conduct, decisions, goal formulation, and relational behaviour, since those who are led have strong professional competence (often greater than the leader) and a high status (Bonvik, 2014).

In the police's organisational strategy *Towards 2025* (Police Directorate, 2017: 9), the purpose of the Norwegian Community Policing Reform is defined as follows: "A police that is operational, visible, and available, and that has the capacity and competence to prevent, investigate, and prosecute criminal activity and ensure public safety." The concepts of both knowledge and competence are widely used in this document. A strategic goal is "a police with better competence and capacity that shares knowledge and learns from experience". Another strategic goal is "a more modern and competent police that focuses on strengthening competence, learning, and development based on the following":

1   Establishment of knowledge-based policing as the underlying principle.
2   Development of new learning processes and methods of evaluation and knowledge sharing as experience-based learning.
3   Facilitation for differentiated pace of education and competence development among employees.

Knowledge and knowing are not the same, as argued earlier. The challenge is when mixing the two and hence, not acknowledging knowledge as more stable and knowing as dynamic and that knowledge is integrated in knowing as context dependent. Knowledge is often attributed to education and theory as individual knowledge. I found that to a certain degree this is also the case in the police. The purpose of the reform to make the police more knowledge-based means that intelligence services are responsible for data collection and analysis, which will then govern practical policing without accounting for how intelligence material and knowledge needs to be transformed and applied as knowing in practical policing.

In a knowledge organisation such as the police, the concept of knowledge is not limited to statistics and crime analysis as knowledge-based (or evidence-based policing), which is instead a method for knowledge development in policing. The dynamics of knowing implies the way in which the police makes use of and applies the knowledge produced by, among others, intelligence services. The most important task leaders at all levels face is how to enable their employees to develop knowing by applying knowledge in practical work within a leadership practice. This knowing must meet the ever-changing requirements caused by more complex criminality patterns. To succeed in this effort, it is important to clarify what knowledge and knowing (and important competencies) are, exactly, and to understand the complexity of competent policing, tacit and explicit knowledge must also be defined.

Knowledge and knowing

Knowledge refers to making sense of what, for instance, distinguishes good leadership. Knowledge about leadership enables an individual to nuance, interpret, and identify patterns of, for example, the leader's behaviour (Tsoukas & Vladimirou, 2001). The main difference between knowledge and knowing is, however, that knowledge focuses on the *what* and knowing on the *how*. Knowledge is a prerequisite of knowing, but as a rule, knowledge cannot be applied directly – it has to be adapted to the situation (what should be done) and the context (the relationships to those involved). These requirements need to be met in order for knowledge to find its way into practice in the form of know-how.

A leader can have much knowledge about leadership, but they need to acquire the necessary skills in order to make use of that knowledge in practice. This requires leadership training, and the development of knowledge into the leader's knowing and competencies calls for extensive leadership practice. This is obviously not a linear process. Within a leadership practice, the leader and their subordinates move back and forth between knowledge and knowing, between learning new skills and acquiring knowledge, and so on. These dynamic processes of learning, knowledge, and knowing enable knowledge sharing and knowledge development within a leadership practice, which are prerequisites for new forms of knowing and therefore for competent actions (Cook & Brown, 1999). Knowledge and knowing are integrated into a leadership practice and exist in the form of both tacit and explicit knowledge (Newell et al., 2009).

Tacit and explicit knowledge

The difference between tacit knowledge and explicit knowledge is important, not least for knowledge sharing within leadership practices, which is the topic of the next section. Science theorist and philosopher Michael Polányi (1966) was the first to assert that "we can know more than we can tell". This is how he defined tacit knowledge, which is the knowledge that cannot be articulated by means of words and language and can therefore not be expressed explicitly (Polányi, 1966). Explicit knowledge is the knowledge that can be expressed in the words, numbers, and symbols of a language. It can be conveyed within an intranet, through guidelines, and in strategy documents, books, and the like. Explicit knowledge, however, requires processing and sensemaking, as described above. This is what differentiates knowledge from information.

There are many examples of tacit knowledge in the police. Knowledge of arrest techniques is not the same as being competent and thus, knowing how to conduct arrests, and the same applies to investigations. An arrest technique applied in practice involves attempting to predict the next move and react to the unforeseeable. Police officers must be able to adapt to whatever happens in practice. In retrospect, it may be hard to explicitly explain why the arrest went the way it did without being able to show it in practice. However, practice will not demonstrate all the tacit knowledge in play either. Competent policing in conducting the arrest is grounded in long experience and, not least, training, which are both necessary for developing tacit knowledge.

Competence in investigations may focus on what is good enough. This means knowing when the investigation is completed and when there is enough evidence for prosecution. Understanding what is good enough is also based on experience and training in solving similar cases and bringing investigations to a conviction. What is good enough can hardly be articulated explicitly because it is not about the number of pieces of evidence to collect, but rather about assessing the kind of evidence required for this particular investigation. It is similar to the importance of exercising discretion within the police and "the police gaze", which are largely based on tacit knowledge.

Polányi (1966) distinguishes between tacit and explicit knowledge. He argues that tacit and explicit knowledge are two modes of a person's overall knowing. This is the approach I support myself, not least because separating the two concepts can easily create a gap between theoretical and practical knowledge (Tsoukas, 1996). But the distinction between tacit and explicit knowledge is still useful for analytical purposes. It can make sense to distinguish between primarily tacit and primarily explicit knowledge in an organisation. If it is primarily tacit knowledge that will be developed into competence within a leadership practice, then learning arenas for knowledge sharing will be completely different than in the case of primarily explicit knowledge. This is due to the fact that tacit knowledge is embedded in practice, in the action itself, in the particular context and situation. Tacit knowledge can only be expressed through body language, actions, collective practice, and/or observing others in practice and applying other non-verbal communication forms.

A situation in which it is possible to combine explicit explanation with practical execution provides good conditions for sharing of tacit knowledge. Within a leadership practice, mutual engagement is necessary to understand and share tacit knowledge. Tacit knowledge can be acquired relatively automatically through experience without thinking or reflecting over it, but instead only acting in accordance with it. This is why it helps to be aware of one's own tacit knowledge and reflect on it. In an organisation such as the police, many situations that require employees with special competence are associated with a great deal of tacit knowledge. Sharing tacit knowledge about what happens in practice is extremely difficult if the knowledge involved must only be made explicit. If a leader who is known for being good at conflict resolution is asked how they resolved a particular work-related conflict, they would probably answer that they figured out which of the employees were involved, discerned how the conversation with a particular individual developed, adapted their "style" so that it was possible to reach an agreement, picked their battles wisely, etc. That leader would hardly be able to explicitly convey what happened and articulate what exactly they discerned.

Tacit knowledge is based on experience and rooted in an understanding of interrelations. Colleagues need to have the opportunity to observe and practise together in order to collectively achieve the development of competence based on sharing tacit knowledge. It is therefore the leader's responsibility to facilitate this development. Tacit knowledge is developed through skilful effort and performance that lead to new activities and thus new knowing (Demetris & Tsoukas, 2019). This is why tacit knowledge constitutes a practice in which the development of such knowledge includes both physical and mental aspects, as well as actions, interactions, and reflection. Tacit knowledge as knowing also implies some unconscious actions that help place focus on the goal. Which actions will be unconscious and which will require focused awareness depend on the context and the particular situation. If all the attention is placed on the arrest technique, it would affect the arrest if the police officer has not mastered and automated this technique. The same applies to shooting technique. If the focus is on the technical aspects of weapon and shooting technique, there is not much room for analysing the situation and evaluating the course of events. The police deals with all kinds of people in all stages of life, including both major and minor crises. Dealing with other people involves a lot of tacit knowledge: what does it take to overcome a crisis situation? What is likely to happen if the situation escalates? How should an interrogation evolve to obtain as much information as possible? What are the hypotheses for what could have happened? This is why the importance of professional discretion and "the police perspective" are discussed in connection with competent policing.

Within a leadership practice, employees' knowledge is primarily valued when it is applied in practical policing and thus contributes to developing competence. Maximising knowledge mobilisation is necessary for making the greatest possible use of the knowledge and knowing the community possesses. I therefore define knowing as "the dynamic processes where the choice of most suitable knowledge, attitudes, and skills are constructed and applied in accordance with the requirements and expectations of a particular situation" (Filstad, 2017: 76).

Knowing is, as described in this section, more comprehensive than technical and professional knowledge. When professional knowledge is applied, various other components such as values and ethics, capabilities in the form of what is possible to achieve, and skills that are learnt through experience all come into play. Knowing is, and must be, complex within a leadership practice – only then will it represent much tacit and experience-based knowledge. To enable the development of knowing and competencies and help it become embedded in a leadership practice as much as possible, knowledge sharing, including sharing of tacit knowledge, is required. This is the topic of the next section.

Knowledge sharing

Knowledge sharing refers to combinations of obtaining, receiving, reflecting, and providing feedback on knowledge and competence in a leadership practice (Hansen, 2002). Knowledge sharing requires learning through participation and practice within a leadership practice, where it is integrated into collective processes of exercising the most competent practice possible. In accordance with a practice perspective on leadership, knowledge sharing should be understood as situation-dependent, negotiated, and distributed among the members within a leadership practice (Raelin, 2016; Filstad, 2020). It should not be limited to individual relations but instead be integrated and involve all participants in the community (Østerlund & Carlile, 2005).

Knowledge sharing transforms knowledge into the knowing and competencies of the leadership practice, as opposed to individual knowledge and knowing, which disappears as soon as the employees quit. This way, new members cannot access that either (I will come back to learning and knowledge sharing through participation and practice in Chapter 13).

From a practice-based perspective on learning, it is due to reflection that participation in a practice results in learning and development. Knowledge sharing also facilitates reflection over the established practice. Colleagues share their knowledge and experience of what went well and why, or what the potential for improvement is if things did not go well. What kind of new knowledge do they need to develop leadership practice? Who needs to learn what, and from whom? Opportunities to reflect before, during, and after doing something provide good learning points for development of a leadership practice.

The following factors are important for knowledge sharing (Mooradian, Renzel, & Matzler, 2006):

1   What kind of knowledge and competencies are to be shared, and is the knowledge primarily explicit or tacit? These questions are important because sharing tacit knowledge requires observation and opportunities to practise together. Explicit knowledge can be shared at meetings or in written form.

2   How can the leader's actions be characterised, and what does management consider important? Does the leader facilitate knowledge sharing, and is it encouraged? Is it possible to share knowledge as desired? What kind of incentives are there for knowledge sharing? Here, it is important to consider whether goals and "rewards" promote or inhibit knowledge sharing.

3   What are the characteristic features of the environment and the interpersonal rela-
     tionships? Is there a common language, and do the members collectively make sense
     of why knowledge sharing is important?
4   How do members relate to the leadership practice? What is their relationship to
     their leader, and what are their attitudes and motives? The degree of commitment to
     the leadership practice is going to influence the desire and opportunity for knowl-
     edge sharing.

Knowledge sharing is influenced by the combination of these four factors. Since leaders,
environment, interpersonal relationships, and other employees have an influence on
knowledge sharing, it is not enough to focus only on the knowledge that is to be shared.
After all, it is up to an individual employee to want to share knowledge and to make the
daily choices that would enable such sharing. It is necessary to evaluate to what extent
one wants to share, allocates time for sharing, or recognises the need for sharing their
knowledge. Additionally, there are such factors as the employee's own assessment of their
knowledge and whether it is valuable, and hence whether it should be shared with colleagues. The characteristics of the knowledge itself are also relevant to how it can and
should be shared. The type of knowledge involved must therefore be the starting point
for the leader who facilitates knowledge sharing.

The purpose of knowledge sharing is, on the one hand, to utilise the knowledge that
resides in a leadership practice, and on the other hand, to mutually improve performance
by providing opportunities for reflection and further competence development. To succeed in this, a common leadership practice needs to be established that would positively
influence and motivate the interpersonal relationships necessary for knowledge sharing.
Knowledge sharing is an effective way to make use of the employees' knowledge and
experience (Hinds, Patterson, & Pfeffer, 2001). It can also help to reduce costs and provide more effective policing services. Several research projects demonstrate that knowledge sharing increases the productivity of teams, departments, and projects, as well as
better equips the organisation for changes and innovative solutions (Wang & Noe, 2010).

A police leadership practice depends on other actors both within and outside the
police. It is therefore not enough if leadership practice only provides for inward-oriented
knowledge sharing. Identifying external sources of important knowledge is key to the
development of leadership practices. These sources could be other areas of expertise
within one police unit, in other police units or districts, or in the police as a whole. They
can also be within the same areas of expertise between groups of employees who work
in different units. They can involve cooperation between joint function agencies and
local police services. There may be expectations of interdisciplinary cooperation at many
levels of the police organisation. In policing, various professional groups are interdependent. This awareness of the need for close connections between different leadership practices is the strength of the leadership-as-practice perspective (Carlile, 2004;
Levina & Orlikowski, 2009; Pyrko, Dörfler, & Eden, 2019). Investigators depend on the
job that patrol officers do on-site for presentation of evidence and interrogations. Prosecution depends on the work of both the patrol officers and the investigators. Whether
or not crime prevention officers manage to establish trust relationships with young
people depends on how other patrols behave upon meeting them. The intelligence service depends on the information it gets from all other professional groups within the
police to be able to do an analysis and define the priorities that others are going to be

guided by in their work, and so on. Who and what becomes good sources of knowledge for sharing with other departments, and how this is facilitated is crucial to the knowing of the leadership practice. Additionally, there are other actors who will typically act as sources of knowledge. The emergency response service relies on the competence of many other public agencies. Patrolling involves everyday cooperation with, among others, emergency care, ambulance, and child welfare services.

Knowledge sharing and trust

The sense of trust between the participants is a prerequisite of knowledge sharing. Trust is often emotional and subjective, which makes it hard to explain why people sometimes feel trust and other times do not. Informal communities of practice are characterised by a high degree of trust between the participants. This can be explained by the fact that people are more likely to trust those they identify with and recognise themselves in because these were the defining factors for choosing to be part of the community in the first place.

Interpersonal trust is defined as "the willingness of a party to be vulnerable" (Abrams et al., 2003). It means relying on the competence of others, knowing what they stand for, and trusting that they know what they are doing and have experience, legitimate authority, and so on. Trust involves expecting a colleague or a leader to act or communicate in a way one could vouch for. Trust also means having faith in the colleague's actions and not needing to control them. Accordingly, a leader who trusts their team will count on them to do a good job without having to control how they perform the tasks. Trust is therefore the willingness to rely on a person, a group of people, or a thing.

Trust is based on the expectation that colleagues have sufficient knowledge, abilities, and benevolence, and that they act in the best interests of their colleagues and have integrity that is consistent with the values of the organisation (Mayer, Davis, & Schoorman 1995). Trust poses the risk of obtaining incorrect information and knowledge or following bad advice. The vulnerability associated with trust therefore resides in relying on people who should not be relied on. Trust is a psychological state defined by the intention to accept vulnerability based upon one's positive expectations of the intentions or behaviour of another (Lines, Stensaker, & Langley, 2006). Having trust in colleagues and leaders is based on the belief and confidence that they have the knowledge they give the impression of having and that they will act in the best interests of the leadership practice and the police.

A leadership practice has to be based on mutual trust between the subordinates and the leader but must also include systemic trust. A leadership practice must have trust in the system, for example, the police organisation. There are two factors that are central to developing that mutual trust. The first one is that trust involves dealing with risk and uncertainty. The second is that trust means accepting vulnerability. Overall, various forms of trust focus around: (1) companion trust, (2) competence trust, and (3) commitment trust (Newell et al., 2009). Companion trust means that people within, for example, a leadership practice believe that everyone is open, honest, and morally upright. This type of trust develops over time as the participants get to know each other. Competence trust involves relying on others' competence and believing that this competence is used as expected. Commitment trust is believing that others do what is necessary to complete common tasks.

Combined, these are the forms of trust that should be developed within leadership practices. For example, a leader has to let go of control over subordinates and give them the necessary room to manoeuvre so that they can sort out something that does not function perfectly by themselves. Another example is when an employee shares their expert knowledge and trusts (without having to control it) that colleagues will properly apply this knowledge in relation to the public. The examples show that both the leaders and the other employees become vulnerable in the sense that colleagues may fail to do things properly. At the same time, other employees develop a sense of mastery and a more proactive approach to problem solving when the leaders and colleagues rely on and have trust in them. They are also motivated by being trusted that they have the necessary competence (and by the opportunities to develop it) and integrity to find the right solutions.

It can be challenging to share knowledge with colleagues because it can also reveal a lack of knowledge. Some people will also typically estimate what they will get in return. It becomes a kind of a mental account where one wants to balance the knowledge one "gives away" to others and the new knowledge one receives in return. Opportunities to reflect on new solutions with colleagues and get feedback on one's own actions create knowledge sharing. Trust in knowledge sharing involves a subjective assessment of whether possible disadvantages (for example, openness about a lack of knowledge) can be out-weighed by the benefits (learning from colleagues' experience). Within a leadership prac- tice, we can therefore distinguish between, for example, trust in leaders, trust in colleagues, trust in oneself, trust in the system, trust in the organisation, or trust in the technology.

The literature suggests that the key to knowledge sharing lies in the interpersonal rela- tionships, in the established leadership practice, and in colleagues and leaders who are motivated and willing to share and access each other's competence (Feldman & Orli- kowski, 2011). The literature distinguishes between many forms of trust. However, trust in the competence of a person or a leader and trust in the benevolence and integrity of a person or a leader are highlighted as the two main forms of trust within interpersonal relationships (Abrams et al., 2003). Trust in a leadership practice and trust in the police are based on the confidence that police leaders at all levels have the necessary competence and exercise leadership in the best interests of the police. Criticism of the police reform within the police may originate from the police officers' lack of trust in government authorities, the Police Directorate, and/or police management. The following quotes from a sub- ordinate and two police leaders express the recurring viewpoints shared by several infor- mants. They are evidence of a culture of blame that can be explained by a lack of trust but also by performance management in the police, which I will come back to later:

A major challenge is that police leaders hide problems and blame them on the chief of police and so on. It creates a culture of cowardice and fear by first doing what you can and then having someone else to take the responsibility.

There is no room for giving real feedback. Instead, we hear that leaders are fighting the battles, everything will be all right, we have to be patient. We need to avoid rocking the boat.

We need a strong feedback culture, otherwise we will just follow along the estab- lished path. This is a big challenge for the professional aspects that are out of line.

In this part of the book, I have focused on culture, identity, belonging, knowing, and trust as the characteristic features of leadership practices. These features have an effect on participation, strategies, and activities, which are considered in the following chapters. In the next part, I will therefore focus on participation in leadership practices with a special emphasis on sensemaking and manoeuvring space.

References

Abrams, L.C., Cross, R., Lesser, E., & Levin, D.Z. (2003). Nurturing interpersonal trust in knowledge-sharing networks. *Academy of Management Executive*, 17(4), 64–77.

Bonvik, Ø. (2014). *Frist meg ikke inn i ledelse* [Do not tempt me into leadership]. Bergen: Fagbokforlaget.

Brown, J.S. & Duguid, P. (1991). Organizational learning and communities of practice. Towards a unified view of working, learning and innovating. *Organizational Science: A Journal of the Institute of Management Science*, 2(1), 40–57.

Carlile, P.R. (2004). Transferring, translation and transforming: an integrative framework for managing knowledge across boundaries. *Organizational Science*, 15(5), 555–568.

Cook, S.D.N & Brown, J.S. (1999). Bridging epistemologies: the generative dance between organizational knowledge and organizational knowing. *Organization Science*, 10, 381–400.

Demetris, H. & Tsoukas, H. (2019). Toward a better understanding of tacit knowledge in organizations: taking stock and moving forward. *Academy of Management Annals*, 13(2), 1941–6067.

Dewey, J. (1938). Experience and education. In J.A. Boydston (Ed.) (1988), *John Dewey: The Later Works*. Vol. 13. Carbondale, IL: Southern Illinois University Press.

Elkjaer, B. (2004). Organizational learning the "third way". *Management Learning*, 35(4), 419–434.

Feldman, M. & Orlikowski, W. (2011). Theorizing practice and practicing theory. *Organization Science*, 22(5), 1240–1253.

Filstad, C. (2017). *Nyansattes organisasjonssosialisering. Perspektiver og læringsstrategier* [New employee organisational socialisation. Perspectives and learning strategies]. Bergen: Fagbokforlaget.

Filstad, C. (2020). *Politiledelse som praksis*. Bergen: Fagbokforlaget.

Gherardi, S. (2009). Knowing and learning in practice-based studies: an introduction. *The Learning Organization*, 16(5), 352–359.

Gotvassli, K.-Å. (2020). *Kunnskap, kunnskapsutvikling og kunnskapsledelse i organisasjoner* [Knowledge, knowledge development, and knowledge-oriented leadership in organisations] (2nd edn). Bergen: Fagbokforlaget.

Hansen, M.T. (2002). Knowledge networks: explaining effective knowledge sharing in multiunit companies. *Organization Science*, 13, 232–248.

Hinds, P.J., Patterson, M., & Pfeffer, J. (2001). Bothered by abstraction: the effect of expertise on knowledge transfer and subsequent novice performance. *Journal of Applied Psychology*, 86, 1232–1243.

Irgens, E. & Wennes, G. (2012). *Kunnskapsarbeid. Om kunnskap, læring og ledelse i organisasjoner* [Knowledge work. On knowledge, learning, and leadership]. Bergen: Fagbokforlaget.

Lave, J. & Wenger, E. (1991). *Situated Learning. Legitimate Peripheral Participation*. New York: Cambridge University Press.

Levina, N. & Orlikowski, W.J. (2009). Understanding shifting power relations within and across organizations: a critical genre analysis. *Academy of Management Journal*, 52(4), 672–703.

Lines, R., Stensaker, I.G., & Langley, A. (2006). *New Perspectives on Organizational Change and Learning*. Bergen: Fagbokforlaget.

Mayer, R.C., Davis, J.H., & Schoorman, F.D. (1995). An integrative model of organizational Trust. *Academy of Management Review*, 20(3), 709–734.

Mooradian, T., Renzel, B., & Matzler, K. (2006). Who trusts? Personality, trust and knowledge sharing. *Management Learning*, 37(4), 523–540.

Newell, S., Robertson, M., Scarbrough, H., & Swan, J. (2009). *Managing Knowledge Work and Innovation*. New York: Palgrave Macmillan.

Orlikowski, W.J. (2002). Knowing in practice: enacting a collective capability in distributed organizing. *Organization Science*, 13(3), 249–273.

Polányi, M. (1966). *The Tacit Dimension*. London: Routledge & Kegan Paul.

Politidirektoratet [Police Directorate] (2017). *Politiet mot 2025. Politiets virksomhetsstrategi. POD-publikasjon 2017/08* [Towards 2025 – the police's organisational strategy. The National Police Directorate's publication 2017/08]. www.politiet.no/globalassets/05-om-oss/03-strategier-og-p laner/politiet-mot-2025—politiets-virksomhetsstrategi.pdf.

Pyrko, I., Dörfler, V., & Eden, C. (2019). Communities of practice in landscapes of practice. *Management Learning*, 50(4), 482–499.

Raelin, J.A. (Ed.) (2016). *Leadership-as-Practice: Theory and Application*. New York: Routledge.

Sfard, A. (1998). On two metaphors for learning and the dangers of choosing just one. *Educational Researcher*, 27(2), 4–13.

Tsoukas, H. (1996). The firm as a distributed knowledge system: a constructionist approach. *Strategic Management Journal*, 17, 11–25.

Tsoukas, H. & Vladimirou, E. (2001). What is organizational knowledge? *Journal of Management Studies*, 38(7), 973–993.

Wang, S. & Noe. R.A. (2010). Knowledge sharing: a review for future research. *Human Resource Management Review*, 20, 115–131.

Østerlund, C. & Carlile, P.R. (2005). Relations in practice: sorting through practice theories on knowledge sharing in complex organizations. *Information Society*, 21(2), 91–107.

Part 4

Participation

Lave and Wenger's situated learning model (1991) is based on learning through participation in social practices, as described previously. This approach has also been termed the "participation metaphor of learning" (Sfard, 1998). The participation metaphor focuses on learning through becoming a new member of a community of practice and moving towards full membership. Situated learning therefore includes legitimate peripheral participation to make sure that participation leads to becoming a competent practitioner (Lave & Wenger, 1991). Legitimate peripheral participation is the ability of potential new participants to act in order to move from the periphery of the community to full membership. This involves access to practices that make full membership possible. Through participation in these activities, the peripheral member learns the culture in the form of language, perception of reality, basic assumptions, etc., as well as

Figure P4.1 Police leadership as practice model: participation

DOI: 10.4324/9781003224105-14

the norms of interaction, the values that are important for performing work tasks, and the unique and "accepted" truths within that culture. Participation, however, is not only about membership in a practice. To demonstrate the importance of participation in various social practices, the literature refers to the concept of trajectories, and accordingly, how trajectories can be disrupted by knowledge boundaries between practices (Carlile, 2004).

It is the participation of the leaders and their subordinates that establishes and develops leadership practices. Participation refers to how a community creates a common meaning relating to, for example, what a leadership practice should constitute. Practices change when new participants replace the ones who leave. The experienced ones often appear to be experts on practice. They have long participated in a practice that consists of social, informal, relational, cultural, formal, and practical components. Competence that is most relevant for police services develops through participation and practice. Participation also indicates the close connection between identity, competence, culture, and trust, and how these factors continuously evolve through participation. Work tasks are defined and meaning is created together with the leader and colleagues. Established participants are often carriers of the culture and competence that are passed on to new participants. Participation includes such activities as learning and change (which will be described later) and characteristic features of the culture in the form of norms, sanctions, negotiations, values, and interests (described earlier). In this part of the book, which focuses on participation, the topics are sensemaking in leadership practices (Chapter 10), manoeuvring space (Chapter 11), and power and politics (Chapter 12).

References

Carlile, P.R. (2004). Transferring, translation and transforming: an integrative framework for managing knowledge across boundaries. *Organizational Science*, 15(5), 555–568.

Lave, J. & Wenger, E. (1991). *Situated Learning: Legitimate Peripheral Participation*. New York: Cambridge University Press.

Sfard, A. (1998). On two metaphors for learning and the dangers of choosing just one. *Educational Researcher*, 27(2), 4–13.

Chapter 10

Sensemaking

This chapter provides a brief literature review on the sensemaking concept and the importance of leaders influencing the sensemaking of leadership practices through sensegiving activities. Sensemaking processes are divided into stages of identifying something, interpreting what that something is, and engaging in activities in accordance with what was identified and how it was interpreted. Sensegiving was introduced in order to study the leaders' responsibility for influencing the sensemaking of their subordinates, especially during change processes. Hence, the chapter focuses on police leaders' sensemaking (or the lack of such) in police reform and how sensemaking influences their sensegiving activities.

Sensemaking refers to processes, often in collaboration with others, where people attempt to understand ambiguous and confusing circumstances and events. In these processes, people construct their own subjective perception of reality in order to achieve a form of balance and certainty. Sensemaking for certainty involves a degree of foresight. Sensemaking processes are crucial when new factors disrupt the established practices and thus require new processes of sensemaking.

Sensemaking is how one acts in a particular situation based on what one finds to be the best solution at the time, and how one looks back at that situation retrospectively so that the action makes sense. Therefore, sensemaking involves both reducing ambiguity and discovering novelty. Since sensemaking disturbs a former perception of reality, one has to reconstruct it. This is crucial to reducing ambiguity and ensuring a form of stability, certainty, and predictability. Sensemaking can therefore be described as learning processes in the form of interpreting novelty, where meaning is constructed and reconstructed to create a new understanding of reality. New meaning is developed on the basis of one's own experiences and everything that is perceived as new, which therefore does not make sense yet. Change processes provide many examples of how new meaning is created (Weick, Sutcliffe, & Obstfeld, 2005; Dewey, 1938).

Changes have to make sense for those involved, for example, how the work of the patrols will change when the operations centres introduce vehicle fleet management. The new system ensures a more centralised way to practise operational work, and the former autonomy and independence have to be exercised differently. This may change the employee identity associated with what patrolling police officers will represent and what kind of responsibility they will have in terms of the social mission. Their sensemaking involves how they create meaning out of vehicle fleet management and what they feel and experience as consequences. This sensemaking process will result in a new understanding of reality which can create new and modified ways of thinking and acting (Karp & Helgø, 2008). The literature on change suggests that many changes do not make sense and therefore do not change the established practice.

DOI: 10.4324/9781003224105-15

Sensemaking processes can be divided into three integrated stages: (1) identifying and noticing something, (2) interpreting what that is, and (3) engaging in activities in accordance with what was identified and how it was interpreted. In a leadership practice, the leader influences the subordinates' sensemaking, and the subordinates influence the leader's sensemaking (Maitlis & Christianson, 2014). The subordinates also influence each other's sensemaking. The leader is responsible for influencing the sensemaking of their subordinates. Influencing the sensemaking of subordinates occurs when the leader actively engages in the sensegiving processes. Sensegiving was introduced in order to study the leader's responsibility for influencing the sensemaking of their subordinates, especially during change processes. The studies suggest that leaders who make sense of the changes themselves also positively engage in sensegiving activities in order to influence the sensemaking processes of their subordinates. This applies both when leaders facilitate and participate in change activities and when they provide guidance on how to change an established practice in accordance with the change initiative (Filstad, 2014b).

People who have a profound effect on the sensemaking of others can help to extend our knowledge of power and politics within leadership practices. This process can also be understood as meaning power, which can be both formal and informal. Influencing one's own sensemaking and the sensemaking of others is often more important in informal communities of practice, where there are no formal leaders. Instead, there are people who have informal and legitimate power and authority (Filstad, 2014a). Police leaders have a formal-meaning power by virtue of their leadership position, but formal power does not automatically result in legitimate power or lead to influencing the subordinates' sensemaking. Other people and groupings can often be the most important influencers. Research also shows that colleagues in leadership practices have a strong influence on each other's sensemaking.

A leader has a special responsibility for influencing subordinates and setting the direction in accordance with the organisation's goals and strategies. This implies that the leader must have established legitimate power and authority. Police leaders are also responsible for facilitating and taking part in sensegiving activities, which can be in the form of day-to-day management, workshops, meetings, and other learning and knowledge-sharing activities, to name a few. An obvious challenge is when a police leader does not make sense of something themselves, which is the case for many leaders in the course of the Norwegian Community Policing Reform. I would like to consider sensemaking in the context of police reform in more detail by first presenting how police employees evaluate the consequences of the reform on policing services (Figure 10.1).

The police employee survey (2020) addresses several main goals of the police reform. The figures (Likert scale 1–5) demonstrate a high degree of negativity among the 83% of the employees who were asked how the changes introduced by the police reform contributed to policing (Figure 10.2).

Figures 10.1 and 10.2 are indicative of both a lack of sensemaking and a lack of beliefs. Police employees still have not made sense of how the police reform results in better policing, so this is why they do not believe in reforming police services. This can mean that the police reform has been given a chance, but it is still not working as intended. This lack of belief could also be due to the fact that the sensemaking of the change initiatives was not active enough and that leaders have not been actively influencing the sensemaking of their subordinates. This may have been reinforced by the fact that just under 10% of the informants report that they have been involved in the New Police District Project, and even fewer (just over 6%) have been involved in pilot projects.

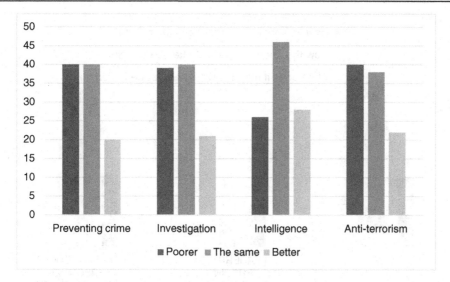

Figure 10.1 Consequences of the police services in police reform

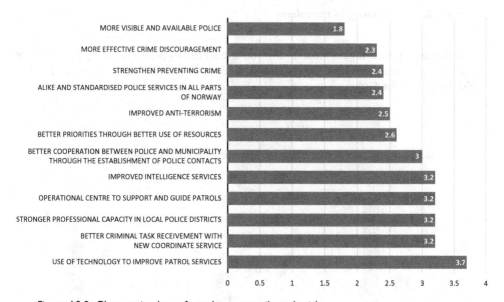

Figure 10.2 Changes in the reform have contributed with...

The extent to which some other factors make sense show correspondingly low results (Figure 10.3).

The figures refer to those who disagree or completely disagree that the way they are going to perform their duties as part of the reform makes sense. Not surprisingly, leaders with personnel responsibility are somewhat more positive towards how the reform will affect their work and change their leadership. Leaders without personnel responsibility show uncertainty at a level comparable to all employees. What I would like to emphasise

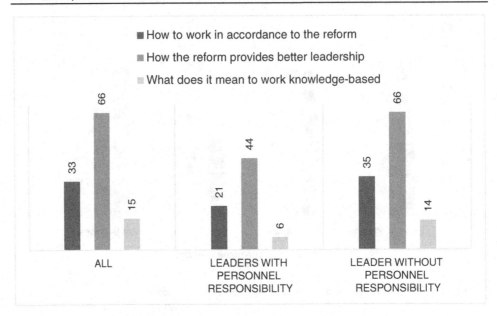

Figure 10.3 Sensemaking of the reform

here is that although it makes sense to introduce changes to police services, this does not necessarily mean that everyone agrees that it results in better policing. This can be illustrated by Figure 10.4 (the answers are rounded up to the nearest whole number).

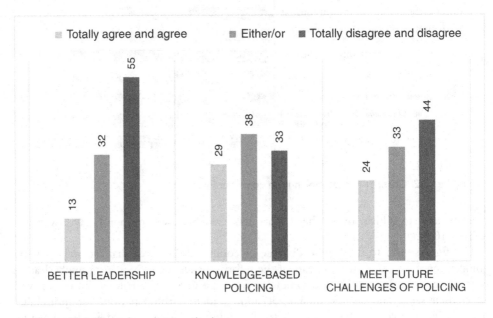

Figure 10.4 The reform has resulted in...

Sensemaking does not necessarily mean that everyone agrees, but it is crucial to understanding (1) from what initial state one needs to change, (2) how one should change, and (3) to what resulting state one needs to change.

Possible reasons for the lack of sensemaking regarding police reform are further elaborated in my field studies. The police competence that already exists within the established practice is not utilised enough, and little time is spent finding a balance between the exploitation of that competence and the exploration of new knowledge. (This is the topic of Chapter 14, which is about change management as practice.) This balance becomes especially important during change processes because the established practice, which already makes sense, has to be challenged and developed into a new practice. The balance is not set in stone, and it may sometimes be more important to exploit the existing knowledge and other times to explore new knowledge. The lack of exploitation will, however, result in a sense of powerlessness and inability to utilise one's influence since competent policing and previous efforts are left behind after the reform. This sentiment is clearly expressed by many informants, and, according to my findings, it is the main explanation of the lack of sensemaking. It is also connected with the fact that the police reform has largely relied on controlling rather than leading, and that police leaders and other employees have been involved in reform projects and pilots only to a limited extent.

It is important to repeat that police leaders' sensemaking should not be narrowed down to agreeing or disagreeing only. The problem is that a police leader does not see how the established practice that they are responsible for is going to be changed and developed in accordance with the guidelines that have been decided on. I observed that when something is decided, police leaders say they "have to be loyal to it". In this way, loyalty can come at the expense of sensegiving activities and, in the worst-case scenario, result in a leadership practice where the leader only communicates what is decided and their subordinates do as they are told. In that case, the leadership practice does not own and create common meaning within itself, which, according to my studies, is absolutely necessary for achieving the goals and strategies of the police force.

Loyalty can also be a conscious way of retaining the power of definition within the police force in terms of what is good policing, and what is the majority's opinion.

Two police leaders explain:

Internally, there is not much respect for regulations, or more precisely, for the bureaucratic rules and regulations. There is also little respect for another's opinion if it does not support the majority's opinion. A lot of renegotiations and rematches take place, and so there is a lack of respect for the established routines for cooperation.

In my experience, you face suppression techniques if you are not critical of the reform. We can be openly critical here, but you have to follow the majority's opinion. I experience suppression techniques when the people in question say they have had typical jobs that give a status in the police, or that they have a long history of experience in the organisation. This is more important than your opinion, and this is why it is difficult for the newcomers to suggest that there are, for example, many positive aspects to the police reform because I think the reform has received much undeserved criticism.

There is room for openness and the opportunity to criticise the police reform internally, but preferably in informal arenas. Criticism can also be expressed at management meetings and other formal arenas. However, externally and when facing other units, the Police Directorate, and the like, things that are reported are usually what the Police Directorate expects to hear. I will return to this topic in the chapter on power and politics.

To conclude this chapter, it can be relevant to talk about distributed sensemaking. As the name suggests, distributed sensemaking refers to shared understanding, and therefore distributed meaning, within a leadership practice. It refers to how the leader and other employees share information and knowledge as sources for the creation of a new collective meaning. Distributed leadership is a new concept that is adapted to a practice-based approach with the main focus on the relational and collective aspects of sensemaking. Distributed sensemaking takes time and requires, among other things, discussion, communication, evaluation, and reflection. This is why it is important that a dominating opinion does not get all the support, and that critics experience common sensemaking as suppression techniques. After all, sensemaking is all about how leadership practices at all levels of the police organisation are going to utilise the competence they have within their areas of responsibility. Sensemaking and competence are also essential for the development of manoeuvring space, which is the topic of the next chapter.

References

Dewey, J. (1938). Experience and education. In J.A. Boydston (Ed.) (1988), *John Dewey: The Later Works*. Vol. 13. Carbondale, IL: Southern Illinois University Press.

Filstad, C. (2014a). Learning and knowledge as interrelations between CoPs and NoPs. *The Learning Organization*, 21(2), 70–82.

Filstad, C. (2014b). The politics of sensemaking and sensegiving at work. *Journal of Workplace Learning*, 26(1), 3–21.

Karp, T. & Helgø, T.I.T. (2008). From change management to change leadership: embracing chaotic change in public service organizations. *Journal of Change Management*, 8(1), 85–96.

Maitlis, S. & Christianson, M. (2014). Sensemaking in organizations: taking stock and moving forward. *Academy of Management Annals*, 8(1), 57–125.

Weick, K.E., Sutcliffe, K.M., & Obstfeld, D. (2005). Organizing and the process of sensemaking. *Organization Science*, 16, 409–421.

Chapter 11

Manoeuvring space

This chapter introduces the concept of manoeuvring space to acknowledge the dynamics of discretion and autonomy that need to be constructed in leadership practices, rather than formally "given" or not "given" as the leaders' property. The importance of police leaders socially constructing manoeuvring space to ensure employees' constructions of their collective manoeuvring space are demonstrated. So are the challenges of how to create manoeuvring space in balancing the structural, bureaucratic, and the cultural, practical logics in the police. Through empirical studies of Norwegian police leaders, the chapter also adds what constitutes and what their perceptions are of the content of manoeuvring space.

The notions of discretion and autonomy are widely used in leadership, but without precise definitions (Yukl, 2013; Tengblad, 2012). These concepts are often associated with the leader's ability to make independent choices and "local decisions" within the requirements, constraints, and resources available. Discretion typically refers to the choices a leader has and the process whereby a leader consciously uses the opportunities available in order to create room for manoeuvre within a leadership practice. This is referred to as the leader's set of behavioural alternatives in the literature (Hambrick & Finkelstein, 1987; Stewart, 1989; Espedal, 2009).

Manoeuvring space is a term that is strongly associated with discretion and a term widely used and discussed within the Norwegian police. Many police leaders, for instance, think manoeuvring space has shrunk as a consequence of the reform. Others claim that there are still opportunities to create manoeuvring space. Yet others find that police leaders do not have a culture of creating manoeuvring space, that is using opportunities to develop the necessary room for manoeuvring. Police leaders at higher levels report on larger manoeuvring space than leaders further down the hierarchy (Filstad, Karp, & Glomseth, 2018).

In the contexts of leadership, which are complex, evolving, and dynamic, Filstad, Olsen, and Karp (2020) argue for the use of manoeuvring that will include discretion and autonomy but as socially constructed and dynamic in leadership practices. Leadership is about influence and mastery, where a leader has a specific responsibility for deciding which actions will be performed and how in developing leadership practices (Yukl, 2013). Accordingly, the police leader's opportunities to influence requirements, constraints, and choices are, I would argue, preferably referred to as manoeuvring space. At the same time, the literature suggests that the prerequisite for allowing a leader to create manoeuvring space is that constraints be reduced in favour of providing more alternatives and choices (Stewart, 1982, 1989; Espedal & Lange, 2005). There is a distinction

DOI: 10.4324/9781003224105-16

between formal manoeuvring space and subjectively defined manoeuvring space (Hambrick, 2007; Hambrick & Finkelstein, 1987; Stewart, 1989). The formal manoeuvring space is affected by requirements, expectations, goals, resources, and the like, as well as by hierarchy, structure, power, responsibility, specialisation, rules, and norms. The micromanagement of goals, structure, and resources also influences the leader's manoeuvring space. To explore major differences in manoeuvring space for police leadership, we have to consider how a particular police leader interprets manoeuvring space (Filstad et al., 2018). In this case, we are looking at subjective manoeuvring space. The subjective manoeuvring space is affected by the mindset, motivation, competence, and experiences of a leader. Expectations, requirements, goal achievement, and structural aspects can be interpreted, perceived, defined, and shaped, and they can therefore create different meanings and constructions of manoeuvring space for leadership, including within seemingly the same framework conditions. The sensemaking perspective (Weick, 1995; Weick, Sutcliffe, & Obstfeld, 2005) provides meaningful concepts to understand how this active construction of manoeuvring space occurs through noticing and attending to cues, making interpretations, engaging in action and learning (Maitlis & Christianson, 2014; Weick, 2009).

Subjective manoeuvring space is socially constructed within a leadership practice, which is why it is subjective rather than objective. Manoeuvring space for leadership is not something police leaders receive automatically. It has to be created through continuous processes between a leader and their subordinates within a leadership practice. It is therefore dynamic and has to be continuously developed. Developing leadership therefore requires learning to develop the necessary manoeuvring space by practising leadership (Filstad et al., 2018). This is why manoeuvring space is also affected by the leader's perceptions, reflections, and cognitive capacity, as well as by experiences and learned leadership. The theory of victim roles and actor roles is relevant for understanding manoeuvring space for leadership. Some leaders appear to be more autonomous and proactive in their leadership, while others tend to find it impossible to influence their own leadership and consider themselves victims of the circumstances (Karp, Filstad, & Glomseth, 2019). Correspondingly, this affects whether and how they create the necessary manoeuvring space in their relationships with subordinates as part of a leadership practice.

Manoeuvring space highlights the importance of how leaders understand formal requirements and contradictions in the choices they are presented with. Anything that creates meaning affects leaders' choices and actions the most (Espedal, 2009, 2015, 2017), and by making active choices, leaders influence framework conditions more than by simply adapting themselves (Perrow, 1986; Weick, 1995).

Leadership often involves facing dilemmas. Dilemmas mean that it is difficult to choose one thing at the expense of the other. Manoeuvring space is affected by conflicting demands which leaders cannot always fulfil, and which they instead have to deal with as part of their leadership. Dilemmas can also be associated with different types of logic within an organisation. In the police, the logic of hierarchy and bureaucracy often contradicts the operational and cultural logic. An example would be when the bureaucratic logic aims to standardise, centralise, and ensure enough resources, while the operational logic is concerned with the complexity of police services (Johannessen, 2015). Manoeuvring space for leadership has to accommodate contradicting types of logic and the dilemmas they represent.

Manoeuvring space in practice

The literature on manoeuvring space is dominated by studies where leaders report on what they can do rather than studies of the leaders' manoeuvring space in practice (Key, 2002). The research also places a one-sided focus on manoeuvring space as something a leader is assigned, and thus something a leader has, instead of something that needs to be created. Manoeuvring space is not fixed. It depends on the situation and context where it is implemented. Manoeuvring space is therefore dynamic and evolving in relationships, which means it is developed collectively within leadership practices. There are only a few studies that highlight the dynamic nature of manoeuvring space and the fact that it changes over time (Finkelstein & Peteraf, 2007; Wangrow, Schepker, & Barker, 2015; Hutzschenreuter & Kleindienst, 2013) and across various contexts (Peteraf & Reed, 2007).

Understanding manoeuvring space should be based on studying leadership practices and the idea that new opportunities for creating manoeuvring space occur through ongoing and dynamic processes in practice (Cunliffe, 2001). Given its dynamic nature, the concept of manoeuvring space can be understood as a verb that describes the process of continuously manoeuvring between dilemmas and challenges in order to create a space for action. The room for manoeuvring is sometimes big, and other times small or non-existent, and is therefore affected by the complex, changing, and dynamic factors of a leadership practice. Since leadership involves tackling numerous dilemmas, the concepts of manoeuvring and space for manoeuvring are a good illustration of the idea that leadership is about making the right manoeuvres. The English notion of *manoeuvring space* highlights its dynamic nature and the idea that the room for manoeuvring has to be created. Our introduction of the concept of *manoeuvring space* is based on the studies of Norwegian police leaders in 2016 (Filstad, 2014). In these studies, we argue that leadership is largely learned through developing manoeuvring space, where learning occurs through the process of participation in practice and leadership and requires experiences and reflections within a leadership practice. Police leadership, at least at the senior level, involves facing the dilemmas that different types of logic represent. This is illustrated by Figure 11.1.

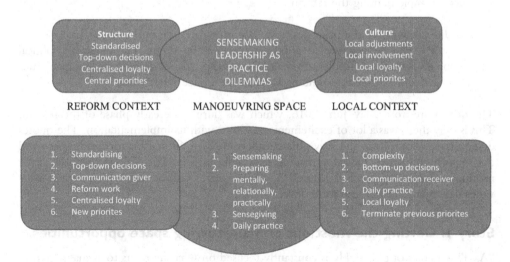

Figure 11.1 Police leaders' manoeuvring space

The model demonstrates the dilemmas of practical police leadership. Centralised political decisions are made by senior leadership/the Police Directorate, and police leaders are expected to perform according to those priorities. We have found that police leaders are very loyal to central decision-making authorities, but they also have to find meaning in practising at the local level. In order to change the established practice, centralised decisions on structures, services, and deliverables have to be "translated" into leadership practice. Manoeuvring space refers to the process by which police leaders are mastering leadership by avoiding choosing one thing at the expense of another. This is challenging because the leader is expected to be loyal to their team, the social mission, and senior leadership/central decision-making authorities. The following selected quotes from police leaders can be useful to reflect on:

> You must have the ability to create a manoeuvring space, and you have to be a bit strategic, I think. I have to try to take on necessary manoeuvring space for us to succeed with the police reform and make it ours.

> Is the manoeuvring space perhaps too large? But many find it too small. It is very limited when it comes to budgets, but concerning everything else it is wide open. As a police leader, you have wide authority to change both culture and structure.

> We are managed quite strongly within some areas, so then I feel that I don't have any other manoeuvring space than to just obey. But I still don't understand why police leaders talk about having such a limited manoeuvring space, that is not my experience.

> When I look at the plans we are presented with, I find that my room for manoeuvring becomes even smaller. You just have to do the job, and others will make the decisions. I've been thinking a lot about why it is like that.

> I have to be loyal to the decisions that have been made, and that's easy for me. I also think I have to try and get the necessary manoeuvring space to ensure that we succeed in implementing the reform.

> It's difficult with all the priorities now. We must set aside our own priorities, and as a result it will be too late to continue working on them. This ongoing political jumping around is a problem. My task is now to balance everything we have built up so far, and at the same time be loyal to the Police Directorate.

The quotes are from May–June 2016, which was during the early phase of the reform. This is why there was a lot of excitement associated with its implementation. The quotes demonstrate variations in the way police leaders interpret formal manoeuvring space and the opportunities they have for making local adjustments. The following stories, each relating to leadership levels 1, 2, and 3, respectively, confirm that manoeuvring space varies depending on the leadership level.

Story 1: Getting the most out of manoeuvring space opportunities

"Axel" is a chief of police. He is constantly focused on what he refers to as manoeuvring space for himself as a leader and for his team. He spends much time every day interacting with his team, both formally and informally. He chairs meetings but also stops by other meetings to get a brief overview of important information and to discuss the positive and negative aspects of various services and areas of responsibility. He is very clear in terms of the responsibility of his police district and the Police Directorate. He also has a very clear understanding of what they can and cannot influence, so he spends much time encouraging loyalty for both central and local decisions. He explains that a lot of his time is spent motivating and encouraging his team to keep going, without overlooking their frustration over the lack of resources and the constant pressure to deliver results as part of the reform. He is also worried that as a result of him being too proactive in ensuring manoeuvring space at the local level, his team can seize too many opportunities and commit to too many projects. He emphasises that leadership is about creating manoeuvring space, and that it is therefore important to be strategic.

Story 2: Recognising the potential for larger manoeuvring space

"Anne" is a level 2 police leader. She is worried that she has missed the opportunity to ensure herself more room for manoeuvring. She has primarily focused on following orders and being best in class in terms of delivering results to the Police Directorate. She has therefore used much of her time focusing on the day-to-day deliverables. She admits that from now on it is important that she create her own manoeuvring space in order to help her subordinates construct theirs. She finds it difficult to facilitate too much – her subordinates need to be able to take that responsibility themselves. She says that she is very detail oriented. She wants to help her teams but realises that she actually ends up controlling them. This strategy can be reflected in her own actions and relationships with her leaders and the Police Directorate. She is therefore concerned with becoming tough and confident enough to be able to create a larger manoeuvring space for herself.

Story 3: Is the culture to blame for the lack of manoeuvring space?

"Alex" is a level 3 police leader. His concern is that police leaders do not develop their own manoeuvring space, and that there is no culture of taking advantage of the manoeuvring space opportunities that exist. He proves this by his own example. He has the potential for developing his own manoeuvring space but instead focuses on meetings, primarily due to lack of resources. At the same time, he argues that the manoeuvring space for anything other than resources is wide open in the police. He thinks that leadership training is key and that it should set clear expectations for the leaders to construct their own manoeuvring space. This becomes even more important during police reform, he believes. He finds it too easy to just sit still and wait for things to happen.

It is not surprising that higher leadership levels provide for a larger manoeuvring space. Senior management responsibility influences, among other things, budgeting and allocation of resources. At the same time, expectations for a larger manoeuvring space locally can give leaders at a lower level (and their subordinates) correspondingly larger space for manoeuvring.

These three stories show that the ability to create manoeuvring space has to be learned and that it requires experience in leadership practices to acquire the necessary knowledge for creating it. I would like to look more closely at how police leaders learn to lead. First, I would like to share the results of a survey from the autumn of 2018. The purpose was to investigate manoeuvring space as something more than just a question of resources and political decisions, to attempt to get to the core of the organisational culture.

Manoeuvring space and workload

Our findings confirm the connection between the employees' manoeuvring space and positivity regarding their own work performance. At the same time, the manoeuvring space of the employees is negatively related to the ability to reduce work overload. In cases of high work overload, it is therefore not enough to increase the employees' manoeuvring space. When employees experience work overload or struggle to complete the required work tasks, it is the leader's manoeuvring space that can reduce the work overload (Filstad et al., 2021). Such issues as, for example, ineffective or challenging work requirements have to be addressed via the leader's manoeuvring space.

We asked police employees how they think certain factors affect their manoeuvring space. The results are shown in Figure 11.2. (The numbers demonstrate what, in the employees' opinions, influences their manoeuvring space, not how the manoeuvring space is practised.)

Figure 11.2 shows that trust from the immediate manager is key. Leaders with personnel responsibility express this idea more clearly than those without personnel responsibility and other employees. Influencing decisions or having decision-making authority are further emphasised as absolutely essential, and the field studies confirm these numbers. In the employees' experience, their immediate manager does bring up their concerns at higher levels of the system but does not get enough support. The research also shows that manoeuvring space has shrunk during the reform, which has led to an increase in micromanagement and the number of requirements for efficiency and reporting. Many police leaders have responsibility but not the necessary authority for developing the required manoeuvring space to be able to fulfil this responsibility for their own unit. Figure 11.3 shows to what extent police leaders develop their manoeuvring space, and to what extent they think it is affected by various factors.

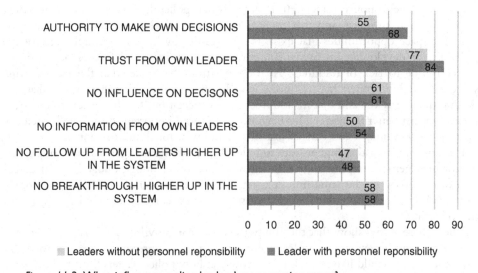

Figure 11.2 What influences police leaders' manoeuvring space?

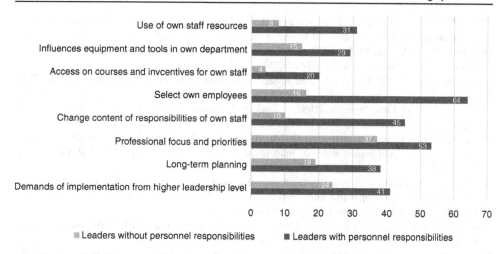

Figure 11.3 Police leaders' manoeuvring space and personnel responsibility

Figure 11.3 shows that a leader with personnel responsibility has very limited influence on the use of resources, employee development, professional focus and priorities, and long-term planning. Leaders without personnel responsibility have significantly fewer opportunities to exert influence than those with personnel responsibility. There is a need for more studies to explore manoeuvring space in leadership practices. One of the important considerations is how power and politics affect the learning and development of manoeuvring space in leadership practices. Power and politics are therefore addressed in the next chapter.

References

Cunliffe, A.L. (2001). Managers as practical authors: reconstructing our understanding of management practice. *Journal of Management Studies*, 38(3), 351–371.

Espedal, B. (2009). Maneuvering space for leadership. *Journal of Leadership & Organizational Studies*, 16, 197–212.

Espedal, B. (2015). Is managerial discretion good or bad for organizational adaptiveness? *Leadership*, 11, 142–157. doi:10.1177/1742715013514879.

Espedal, B. (2017). Understanding how balancing autonomy and power might occur in leading organizational change. *European Management Journal*, 35, 155–163.

Espedal, B., & Lange, B.K. (2005). *Handlingsrom for ledelse: I hvilken grad og på hvilken måte har ledere valg- og handlefrihet?* [Manoeuvring space for leadership: How and to what extent do leaders have freedom of choice and discretion?] SNF Working paper 35/05. Bergen: Samfunns- og næringslivsforskning.

Filstad, C. (2014). Learning and knowledge as interrelations between CoPs and NoPs. *The Learning Organization*, 21(2), 70–82.

Filstad, C., Karp, T., & Glomseth, R. (2018). How police leaders learn to lead. *Policing: A Journal of Policy and Practice*. https://academic.oup.com/policing/advance-article-abstract/doi/10.1093/police/pay043/5050176.

Filstad, C., Olsen, T.H., & Karp, T. (2020). Constructing managerial manoeuvring space in contradictory contexts. *European Management Journal*, 39(4), 467–475. https://doi.org/10.1016/j.emj.2020.10.003.

Filstad, C., Solberg, E., Karp, T. & Mayiwar, L. (2021). The leader–employees co-production in organisational change. *Scandinavian Journal of Management*. In press.

Finkelstein, S. & Peteraf, M.A. (2007). Managerial activities: a missing link in managerial discretion theory. *Strategic Organization*, 5, 237–248.

Hambrick, D.C. (2007). Upper echelons theory: an update. *Academy of Management Review*, 32(2), 334–343.

Hambrick, D.C. & Finkelstein, S. (1987). Managerial discretion: a bridge between polar views of organizational outcomes. *Research in Organizational Behavior*, 9, 369–406.

Hutzschenreuter, T. & Kleindienst, I. (2013). (How) does discretion change over time? A contribution toward a dynamic view of managerial discretion. *Scandinavian Journal of Management*, 29, 264–281.

Johannessen, S.O. (2015). Å forstå politiet som organisasjons- og ledelsespraksiser [Understanding the police as organisational and leadership practices]. In S.O. Johannessen & R. Glomseth (Eds.), *Politiledelse* (pp. 22–41). Oslo: Gyldendal Akademisk.

Karp, T., Filstad, C., & Glomseth, R. (2019). 27 days of managerial work in the police service: being foremost among equals. *Police Practice and Research*, 20(5), 427–443.

Key, S. (2002). Perceived managerial discretion: an analysis of individual ethical intentions. *Journal of Managerial Issues*, 14, 218–223.

Maitlis, S. & Christianson, M. (2014). Sensemaking in organizations: taking stock and moving forward. *Academy of Management Annals*, 8(1), 57–125.

Perrow, C. (1986). *Complex Organizations: A Critical Essay* (3rd edn). New York: Random House.

Peteraf, M., & Reed, R. (2007). Managerial discretion and internal alignment under regulatory constraints and change. *Strategic Management Journal*, 28, 1089–1112.

Stewart, R. (1982). A model for understanding managerial jobs and behavior. *Academy of Management Review*, 7, 7–13.

Stewart, R. (1989). Studies of managerial jobs and behavior: the ways forward. *Journal of Management Studies*, 26(1), 1–10.

Tengblad, S. (2012). Conclusions and the way forward: towards a practice theory of management. In S. Tengblad (Ed.), *The Work of Managers: Towards a Practice Theory of Management* (pp. 337–356). Oxford: Oxford University Press.

Wangrow, D.B., Schepker, D.J., & Barker, V.L. (2015). Managerial discretion: an empirical review and focus on future research directions. *Journal of Management*, 41, 99–135. https://doi.org/10.1177/01492063145554214.

Weick, K.E. (1995). *Sensemaking in Organizations*. Thousand Oaks, CA: Sage.

Weick, K. E. (2009). *Making Sense of the Organization: The Impermanent Organization*. Chichester, UK: Wiley.

Weick, K.E., Sutcliffe, K.M., & Obstfeld, D. (2005). Organizing and the process of sensemaking. *Organization Science*, 16, 409–421.

Yukl, G. (2013). *Leadership in Organizations* (8th edn). Boston: Pearson.

Chapter 12

Power and politics

This chapter focuses on how power and politics fuel the inner life of leadership practices and need to be addressed in order to increase our knowledge of police leadership. Political struggles, due to different interests and the use of power and influence in negotiations in order to gain control over conflicts in the relationships between leaders and subordinates, needs acknowledgement as integrated in developing leadership practice. This is of particular relevance to change, where knowledge domains are challenges and power positions in the form of status and informal authorities are subject to change. The chapter outlines the power and politics literature and demonstrates the political play and use of different types of power in police reform.

Famous sociologist Max Weber (1864–1920) defined power as the ability to exercise one's will in a social relationship, even against the resistance of others and regardless of what that ability entails. For Weber, power relationships are characterised by legitimacy. This means that a situation where a leader gives orders to a subordinate is perceived as normal. Another famous sociologist, Pierre Bourdieu (1930–2002), develops Weber's ideas on legitimacy further. He believed that actors have different strategies for obtaining legitimacy for themselves at the expense of the legitimacy of others. Formal and informal power, and what is perceived as legitimate power and authority, are therefore essential for understanding power and politics in leadership practices.

Power and politics are integrated into practices, and it can be difficult to distinguish between them. Politics can refer to actions that are based on power, but at the same time, political actions also create power structures. Power is not property that someone possesses or is assigned. Foucault (1980) emphasises that power is relational and productive and thus can be described as episodic and systemic, respectively. Episodic power refers to discrete political activities initiated by, for example, self-interested employees. Voronov (2008) describes the use of episodic power as surface politics. Systemic power, on the other hand, is diffused and embedded in routines and basic established power structures. Voronov (2008) describes the use of systemic power as deep-structure politics.

Power and politics will always be present in the establishment, development, and change of communities of practice. I have previously mentioned that participants in communities of practice have different interests and often want to legitimise their demand for knowledge while competing with others through negotiations (Contu & Willmott, 2003; Levina & Orlikowski, 2009). Political struggle, and the use of power and influence in negotiations in order to gain control over conflicts in the relationships between leaders and subordinates, is integrated into the inner life of a leadership practice (Schneider 2007). This is why a leadership practice should be considered in terms of the

DOI: 10.4324/9781003224105-17

power relations within and between communities of practice. Changing leadership practices as part of police reform, for example, will entail significant changes to power relations. Some individuals and groups strengthen their positions, while other positions are weakened.

In this respect, Foucault (1980) emphasises the connection between knowledge and power and describes how individuals will guard "valid" knowledge by upholding their power to define knowledge in order to maintain their position during change processes. The same is true for the established boundaries between professions, departments, and communities of practice that are challenged by new organisational structures (Mørk et al., 2010; Nicolini et al., 2017). This is why studying political struggle for control, and thereby the active, resistant forces or passive forces at play, is crucial to understanding practices (Fox, 2000; Schneider, 2007). Power and politics, however, have received little attention in the studies of communities of practice. I will consider this in more detail in the next section.

Power and politics in communities of practice

Lave and Wenger (1991) argue that communities of practice are embedded in power relations. Wenger, McDermott, and Snyder (2002) suggest that power in the form of negotiations, or one's own competence in competition with others' competence, is an important part of practising. Power and politics are central to understanding learning, change, and innovation, as well as variations between different practices, for example, when new knowledge does not get transferred to the existing areas of expertise in connection with change processes because it threatens the existing power structures and knowledge positioning. Another example would be when knowledge boundaries between communities of practice are extremely tight, which inhibits knowledge sharing across different practices. During change processes, the knowledge boundaries between different communities of practice are challenged and must therefore be renegotiated (Robertson, 2007; Easterby-Smith et al., 2008).

There are few studies of power and politics in communities of practice.[1] The existing studies tend to suggest that power and politics are always integrated into practice and therefore greatly affect the day-to-day life of organisations, but the studies do not explore what exactly this entails. The concept of a community being purely harmonious and inclusive has also dominated the literature, which has formed an incomplete picture of communities of practice and their characteristic features. A community of practice represents various power relations between the participants and the political processes that can be an obstacle to full participation and legitimacy (Contu & Willmott, 2003; Gherardi, 2009). The question, however, is not only about exercising power over something or someone – just as important is understanding power as something productive and as having power to act in relation to something or someone (Foucault, 1980). An example could be decision-making, where having power means controlling scarce resources. The next step is processes and the expanded or limited access to decision-making, and finally, the way interest groups create meaning and form what is going to become the legitimate agenda.[2] It is, however, necessary to point out the importance of negotiations as essential political processes, regardless of whether the power is exercised over, or in relation to, something or someone and/or whether the power is part of relationships between participants within a practice-based approach and between different communities of practice. Neither internal structures nor external relationships are stable during changes. Changing formal and informal practices is a political process (Mørk et al., 2010). By way of introduction to this part of the book on participation, I have explained that employees are participants in several practices. Trajectories between these practices can be disturbed by knowledge boundaries and power relations (Carlile, 2004). Change processes require knowledge sharing across boundaries and transferring, translating, and transforming knowledge in order to reduce knowledge boundaries.[3] This relates to power and politics in and between leadership practices in the police.

Power and politics in the police

Political struggle, and the use of power and influence in negotiations in order to gain control over conflicts in the relationships between leaders and subordinates, is integrated into the inner life of a leadership practice (Schneider, 2007). People can be rational, subjective, emotional, strategic, intuitive, and evaluative. Power and politics can be manifested through recognition, empowerment, loyalty, submission, and dominance (Johannessen, 2013). Power and politics in the police can involve positioning, status, career opportunities, protecting one's own or others' interests, as well as access to resources and other benefits within the police organisation.

Formal power refers to the formal organisation of the police and describes the power one has in accordance with their position and area of responsibility. Formal power entails politics that refer to the actions a police leader can take by virtue of their formal position, followed by political actions the leader assesses as legitimate in accordance with their formal power. Formal titles formalise power structures, and the number of stars and a professional status within the police are often part of everyone's subconscious. Police leaders at lower levels, for example, say that a professional status can be earned through an impressive foreign service. According to a police leader at level 4, even after many years of police service, he will always be "the one from the emergency squad". Those with senior titles have therefore psychological and often formal advantage over those with lower titles. We have found that a status related to certain professional expertise within policing is not necessarily followed by a formal position.

This is similar to other organisations where the necessary authority and hence legitimacy are often given by informal power. Legitimacy is of great importance in all forms of power relations (Weber, 2020). People may have different strategies for establishing their own legitimacy, which can accordingly reduce the legitimacy of others (Bourdieu, 1999). The literature has particularly focused on knowledge and competence – especially a reputation of being a consummate professional – which are more important for legitimacy than formal positions (Bourdieu, 1999).

Leaders with formal power but no authority have to rely on their formal positions and can only resort to ordering their subordinates. In the police, formal exercise of power in the form of orders can also indicate loyalty to, for instance, the social mission rather than one's legitimacy as a leader. Police leaders have to build up their legitimacy and authority because these things do not automatically result from their formal position. The legitimacy of a police leader is crucial to the establishment and development of leadership practices. Police leaders are "assigned" formal power by virtue of their formal position. However, authority and hence legitimacy have to be learned and developed within a leadership practice. Some participants in leadership practices have legitimate power both as informal leaders and by virtue of their competence, including their technical expertise. A person can also have legitimate power simply due to their personal qualities and their highly valued role in social practices. Legitimate power and authority are established through social relationships with other participants and leaders. Informal legitimate power is therefore less visible to anyone other than the members of, for example, a leadership practice.

Power and politics are often viewed as negative. Employees are moved around like pawns with no purpose or meaning, other than perhaps for the leader. Employees are only concerned with their own interests and hold on to their knowledge and expertise to maintain their position within the organisation. However, power and politics also deserve a positive view. They have to be considered as a necessary means for achieving the desired goals within an organisation. Protecting someone's interests does not have to be in contradiction with protecting the interests of the police. A leader using their formal position to implement certain measures can be absolutely necessary for developing team knowledge or facilitating interdisciplinary cooperation between leadership practices. This requires legitimate power, and hence the leader has to have the necessary authority within a leadership practice. Again, this does not mean that there are conflicts within a leadership practice or that new measures are met with resistance, at least in the short term. Power and politics are therefore integrated into a leadership practice's culture, values, norms, negotiations, and conditions for participation.

In Chapter 2, I presented a table based on police leaders' descriptions of what actions characterise their everyday experience (Table 2.1). I commented on the low figures for power and politics. Only 21% agreed that dealing with power and politics was a significant part of their everyday routine as leaders. When asked about both decision-making and priorities, 86% thought each was a significant part of their daily activities. The figures indicating leaders who thought serving their department formed an essential part of their everyday were also low (21%), and the figures for solving dilemmas and conflicts were not especially high either.

It is interesting that though they work in a politically controlled organisation, police leaders are not more aware of the important role that power and politics can play in their leadership and leadership practice. Our research shows that police leadership at all levels involves power and politics, and it should. Police leaders are expected to know "the game", which is how they often describe it themselves. Here are the examples from two chiefs of police:

> A political system, a ministry, their task is to support the minister... You must know this game. You have to sort it out yourself when it is within your power. You have to be tough enough as a leader and not ask your higher-ups for permission all the time.

> We were very loyal to the intention behind the reform and the framework and guidelines for its implementation. But for the requirements, we had to find our own way. And we had to find our own way of meeting the requirements within the framework and the guidelines because initially those requirements didn't make much sense at all.

The tendency not to push the problems further up the chain to the National Police Directorate or the Ministry of Justice and Public Security indicates an understanding of the political game at all leadership levels. Many leaders explain that this helps to avoid having the problems come back in the form of more detailed control. They must be proactive and take the manoeuvring space they need, instead of being reactive and simply relying on the manoeuvring space that is "assigned" to them. Manoeuvring space involves not only utilising the existing resources, but also accessing more resources. This can result in power struggles and competition between professional groups, units, and districts. Table 12.1 demonstrates what police leaders and other employees think about competition for resources.

We can see that the higher the leadership level, the more police leadership is about competing for resources. A large proportion of the informants believe that when someone gets more resources, others lose theirs because the total amount of resources is quite stable. As many as 32% of all employees also believe that some people/professional groups advance and obtain resources at the expense of others, who have consequently lost their resources. Here, they refer to the police reform prioritising, among others, emergency response, intelligence (knowledge-based police work), and robust professional environments in common units. Accordingly, this was done at the expense of some of the earlier priorities where crime prevention, general investigations, and proximity to the public (patrolling) were the focus. The political game that, according to our findings, is the most prominent in policing, and that also relates to manoeuvring space, is silo mentality, which is also reinforced through the way the police is organised.

The characteristic feature of power and politics is the lack of explicit expression. Overall, power and politics provide the social energy that fuels learning and knowledge sharing, rather than being a dysfunctional aspect of an organisation (Lawrence et al., 2005). At the same time, the features of power and politics are embedded in organisational structure and police culture(s). This is why we need to consider dysfunctionality versus "healthy" competition and prioritising in the best interests of the police. Structures and cultures need to be changed and developed in order for power and politics to change accordingly. Power and politics are characterised by the lack of explicit expression. The two concepts are also not the same. Power is embedded in a particular leadership practice, while politics is the actual action that is embedded in power. Power can therefore be simply defined as something that *is*, and hence something that characterises practice, while politics is something that *becomes*, the very *action*. In other words, politics is power that is transformed into action.

Table 12.1 Manoeuvring space and resources

Understanding opportunities	Not leaders	Leaders without personnel responsibility	Leaders with personnel responsibility	All
Competition for resources/opportunities	47	55	58	50
Some get – others lose	37	44	58	41
More resources for some – less for others	40	50	44	43
Advancement at the expense of others	32	29	18	30

Before I focus on power and politics as part of change processes in policing in the next section, it would be relevant to consider the types of power and the differences between them. They are process power, meaning power, and resource power (Lawrence et al., 2005). Process power is expected to be exercised at leadership levels, especially the senior ones. Decisions made at different leadership levels within the police, in connection with the reform, must address the most suitable and effective change processes aimed at achieving the reform objectives.

Who is involved in what central decision-making processes within the police reform, who is given the opportunity to implement pilot projects, who are members and leaders of the New Police District Project, what kind of responsibility and authority is given to that project, to what extent are police districts and the different leadership levels involved – all of these factors distinguish the use of process power. The lack of participation, which can prevent police leaders and their subordinates from contributing to decision-making processes, can result in the lack of legitimacy and trust in decision-makers. Among other things, this may have a serious effect on change processes because what needs to be changed is the established practice, and employees and first-line managers can use their process power by choosing not to change the leadership practice in accordance with the reform.

The overall goal of police reform is to ensure the best possible use of the total resources that are allocated to the police in order for it to accomplish the social mission. Police leaders spend a lot of their time obtaining the necessary resources to enable their own leadership practice to complete the social mission in the best way possible. The political struggle for resources can be characterised by silo mentality and the expectation that police leaders are going to compete for their own leadership practices, as described above. Being proactive for the purpose of developing manoeuvring space can also be described as a political process. The same applies to strategies for cooperation, interdisciplinary work, and the like. Accordingly, resource power does not only have to be formal. Resource power involves using political processes to gain the necessary authority and legitimacy by motivating and ensuring that subordinates and other leaders believe in the desired strategies. This in its turn can involve meaning power.

Police leaders are expected to exercise meaning power and thereby influence the sensemaking of their team. I have previously referred to the use of political processes to influence the sensemaking of others as sensegiving (Chapter 10). Police leaders engage in sensegiving by, among other things, actively participating in various sensemaking learning processes, which will later result in making sense of how to change the established practice. This requires that police leaders themselves make sense of what the police reform entails and what change processes they need to introduce in their leadership practices. Therefore, meaning power presupposes relations and negotiations that extend beyond the formal power structures, where the purpose is to influence the sensemaking of others. A level 1 police leader explains these processes while talking about the early phase of the reform:

> It is also a fight for stealing interesting new tasks and resources; that is very predictable. And to prepare my staff and myself, you don't say anything explicit, but we work to get something that is stated between the lines; that's how it is. And we have to be prepared and get our views heard; now everyone works politically at all levels.

What has been considered so far demonstrates how power and politics constitute an integrated part of practice in the police generally, and within different leadership practices in particular. To understand the game of politics that, among other things, is represented by such a major change process as the Norwegian Policing Reform, we need to consider process power, resource power, and meaning power as interrelated. Understanding a leadership practice should therefore be based on power and politics which are manifested in daily practice. Power and politics will always be integrated with the reality of a leadership practice and should not be considered as negative and hence dysfunctional, unless the behaviour of the participants in a leadership practice proves to be this way. I would like to conclude this chapter with some stories from my field studies that illustrate power and political processes. The stories provide an opportunity to reflect over the role of power and politics in police reform.

Examples of power and politics within police reform

In the previous chapter, I argued that knowledge development and knowledge sharing/dissemination are crucial to the successful implementation of changes. Power and politics in change processes can therefore be linked to competences, for example those associated with leadership, professional groups, or a particular police employee. Police reform does not only change the areas of knowledge and thus the definition of good policing, it also changes knowledge processes. Additionally, it brings about significant changes to professional groups, management teams, geographical units, and so on. The established forms of power, such as expert power, model power, agenda-setting power, power of definition, experience-based power, status associated with competence and/or positioning, and not least informal power and position, are all in play. Accordingly, change processes include power and politics in the form of negotiating changes and the establishment of, among others, new leadership, management teams, management practices, and areas of expertise.

Example 1: A political game involving new leader positions

A head of section tells what happened when all leadership positions were put into play as part of the police reform. As the new positions were advertised and those who were leaders at the time were asked to apply, only those with rights and obligations for the particular jobs had the opportunity to apply. The section leader refers to the informal political game that took place in connection with this. He says that most leaders in the police know each other, and many of them have previous experience from a number of leadership jobs in different locations. In many ways, they become one big family, he explains. So they agreed in advance which jobs they would and would not apply for, so as to stay out of each other's way. This, he continues, was a way of saying that the others deserved those positions and thus should not experience competition, but it was also a way of protecting their own career interests for the future. As part of the informal relationships, some people were earmarked for certain positions, so for others there was no point in applying for them. Several other leaders tell similar stories, and some point to cases where they were asked to withdraw their applications because the position in question was earmarked for a specific person. Therefore, they say that some of these job advertisements were only mock processes because in fact decisions had already been made.

Example 2: A political game involving goal management

The game of politics associated with goal management becomes evident in discussions on reporting. Goal management is based, among other things, on red, yellow, and green target figures, which determine the allocation of resources. In Chapter 5, on goal management in the police organisation, I pointed out that many police leaders do not think their target numbers are related to quality. Accordingly, the political game here resolves around the way police leaders report on their performance to ensure they maintain the necessary resources. They are concerned with figures not being too green because that would lead to the loss of resources. They also refer to a culture of "passing the buck" because a case can have an effect on achieving green figures, and therefore it is sometimes better if another unit takes it. Sometimes police leaders choose the strategy of not reporting the whole truth for fear of being micromanaged as a result. Finally, they also refer to positions that are kept vacant in order to maintain the budget for a certain number of positions.

Example 3: A political game involving interdisciplinary cooperation

The final example I would like to share is about the political game between different units, and between units and common units. The example is mainly about the way resources are allocated, even though there is no guarantee that they will continue to come in. Because of the lack of such guarantees, and hence the lack of predictability in relation to interdisciplinary cooperation, good solutions are not being implemented. Instead, departments and units expand their areas of responsibility to secure the necessary resources, which either reduces the amount of desired interdisciplinary cooperation or makes it unclear who is responsible for what. The political game here also involves keeping close to the important decision-makers to gain support for one's own solutions. This in turn maintains and reinforces competition between units and special units instead of protecting the interests of the entire organisation, which, as the majority agree, serves the best interests of the police overall.

The political games described in these three examples are an integral part of participation in leadership practices. Politics are also manifested in the form of concrete activities aimed at achieving the desired goals, which is the topic of the next part of this book where I focus on learning activities and change management activities. The power and politics that are integrated into these activities also play an important part in learning and change management.

Notes

1 See, for instance, Contu & Willmott, 2003; Easterby-Smith et al., 2008; Mørk et al., 2012; Filstad, 2014.
2 Lukes (1974) describes this as a three-level framework, which Hardy (1996) develops further to include four levels that are integrated into the system and taken for granted.
3 Carlile (2004) argues that a direct transformation of knowledge does not reduce knowledge boundaries. The knowledge must make sense and be collectively understood through "translation". Common knowledge means having a collective sense of reality and making sure that different interests are negotiated through political processes to achieve new mutual knowledge and address ongoing issues.

References

Bourdieu, P. (1999). *Symbolsk makt. Artikler i utvalg* [Symbolic power. Selected articles]. Oslo: Pax Forlag.

Carlile, P.R. (2004). Transferring, translation and transforming: an integrative framework for managing knowledge across boundaries. *Organizational Science*, 15(5), 555–568.

Contu, A. & Willmott, H. (2003). Re-embedding situatedness: the importance of power relations in learning theory. *Organization Science*, 14(3), 283–296.

Easterby-Smith, M., Graca, M., Antonacopoulou, E., & Ferdinand, J. (2008). Absorptive capacity: a process perspective, *Management Learning*, 39(5), 483–501.

Filstad, C. (2014). The politics of sensemaking and sensegiving at work. *Journal of Workplace Learning*, 26(1), 3–21.

Foucault, M. (1980). *Power/Knowledge: Selected Interviews and Other Writings, 1972–1977*. C. Gordon (Ed.). New York: Pantheon Books.

Fox, S. (2000). Communities, Foucault and actor-network theory. *Journal of Management Studies*, 37 (6), 853–867.

Gherardi, S. (2009). Knowing and learning in practice-based studies: an introduction. *The Learning Organization*, 16(5), 352–359.

Hardy, C. (1996). Understanding power: bringing about strategic change. *British Journal of Management*, 7(special issue), 3–16.

Johannessen, S.O. (2013). *Politikultur. Identitet, makt og forandring i politiet* [Police culture. Identity, power, and change in the police]. Trondheim: Akademika Forlag.

Lave, J. & Wenger, E. (1991). *Situated Learning: Legitimate Peripheral Participation*. New York: Cambridge University Press.

Lawrence, T.B., Mauws, M.K., Dyck, B., & Kleysen, R.F. (2005), The politics of organizational learning: integrating power into the 4I framework. *Academy of Management Review*, 30(1), 180–191.

Levina, N. & Orlikowski, W.J. (2009). Understanding shifting power relations within and across organizations: a critical genre analysis. *Academy of Management Journal*, 52(4), 672–703.

Lukes, S.M. (1974). *Power: A Radical View*. London: Macmillan.

Mørk, B.E, Hoholm, T., Aanestad, M., Edwin, B., & Ellingsen, G. (2010). Challenging expertise: on power relations within and across communities of practice in medical innovation. *Management Learning*, 41(5), 575–592.

Mørk, B.E., Hoholm, T., Manninen-Olsson, E., & Aanestad, M. (2012). Changing practice through boundary organising: a case from medical R&D. *Human Relations*, 65(2), 261–286.

Newell, S., Robertson, M., Scarbrough, H., & Swan, J. (2009). *Managing Knowledge Work and Innovation*. New York: Palgrave Macmillan.

Nicolini, D., Mørk, B.E., Masovic, J., & Hanseth, O. (2017). Expertise as trans-situated: the case of TAVI. In J. Sandberg, L. Rouleau, A. Langley & H. Tsoukas (Eds.), *Skilful Performance: Enacting Expertise, Competence, and Capabilities in Organizations* (pp. 27–49). Oxford: Oxford University Press.

Robertson, M. (2007). Translating breakthroughs in genetics into biomedical innovation: the case of UK genetic knowledge parks. *Technology Analysis & Strategic Management Journal*, 19(2), 189–204.

Schneider, U. (2007). Coping with the concept of knowledge. *Management Learning*, 38(5), 613–633.

Voronov, M. (2008). Towards a practice perspective on strategic organizational learning. *The Learning Organization*, 15(2), 195–221.

Weber, M. (2020). *Makt og byråkrati. Essays om politikk og klasse, samfunnsforskning og verdier* [Power and bureaucracy. Essays in politics and class, social research and values]. E. Fivelsdal (Ed.) (3rd edn). Oslo: Gyldendal.

Wenger, E., McDermott, R., & Snyder, W.M. (2002). *Cultivating Communities of Practice: A Guide to Managing Knowledge*. Boston: Harvard Business School Press.

Part 5

Activities

In a leadership practice, a range of activities occur simultaneously, and employees are consciously engaged in particular activities to achieve their goals. Activities are an indication of a practice, but a practice is more than activities alone, which I illustrated earlier in this book. It is also impossible to distinguish between activities that are typically described as participation in a practice and activities that do not contribute to participation. An example of the latter can be activities that do not contribute to common sensemaking, identity, collective goals, or common manoeuvring space, which are some of the characteristic features of a leadership practice. The two major activities I would like to explore form the basis for the development of a leadership practice and its competence. In accordance with the leadership-as-practice perspective, this part of the book on activities within leadership practices focuses on the topics of learning as practice and change as practice.

Figure P5.1 Police leadership as practice model: activities

DOI: 10.4324/9781003224105-18

Chapter 13

Learning as practice

This chapter approaches learning as practice where learning is situated, relational, cultural and context dependent, and embedded as collective actions and reflections among the participants in leadership practices. The chapter outlines the learning as practice perspective and how this perspective adds the understanding of learning in the police. The importance of reflections is highlighted and so are the possibilities of taking advantage of important learning arenas at work, or facilitating learning arenas to provide better opportunities for learning as integrated in daily practice, which includes police leaders' learning. The chapter uses quotes from empirical studies where police leaders explain their interpretation of their own learning processes as police leaders. Finally, the chapter discusses what constitutes the police as a learning organisation.

Learning from a practice perspective

There are two main approaches to learning (Elkjaer, 2004). One is the individual cognitive perspective that views learning as the individual's personal acquisition of knowledge for future use (Filstad, 2016). In the same way as learning is primarily individual, knowledge that is learned is moreover regarded as the property of the individual,[1] where knowledge is the objective and something concrete (Hislop, 2013). This perspective is also characterised as a structure perspective (Gotvassli, 2020). The other perspective focuses on the situation-dependent nature of learning and studies learning through participation and practice. From this perspective, the social and cultural relations and context, the situation, and the kind of tasks to be performed are crucial to learning. This perspective is therefore also described as sociocultural (Gotvassli, 2020). Learning (and knowledge as knowing) is integrated into a leadership practice in the form of practising and acting, and occurs through participation, belonging, and experiences adjusted to the characteristics of the community of practice (Sfard, 1998; Elkjaer & Wahlgren, 2006).

Learning enables the development of new knowledge in a leadership practice and ensures that knowledge is applied in the form of competence, as referred to earlier in this book. It is the situation-dependent and relational aspects, the continuous dynamic processes that occur through practising, the "here and now" that can result in learning and hence new knowledge. Practising is a prerequisite for learning but practising on its own certainly does not automatically result in new knowledge or change. To develop as a leader, it is not enough to simply exercise leadership. A leader might exercise the same kind of leadership they have always used. The same can be true for other employees. They might go to work every day and perform their tasks in much the same way as

DOI: 10.4324/9781003224105-19

before, without being challenged or having to think in a new way. This would not form a basis for learning processes and knowledge development, for the leader or their subordinates. Learning presupposes that leaders and their subordinates challenge themselves and each other, or are challenged by new ways of leading or performing work tasks, finding new solutions, collaborating with other actors, developing new relationships, and so on.

The two main approaches to learning have a different focus. The individual cognitive perspective places the main attention on the individual learner, while the participation and practice perspective primarily focuses on the practice itself and the social and cultural relationships between the participants. Of course, this also implies that leaders and other employees learn individually and have knowledge and competence that can be described as personal. However, a practice perspective on learning would rather consider knowledge and knowing as something that is integrated into leadership practice as a whole than try to distinguish between the individual and collective competence.

In addition to using opportunities to learn through challenging the established practice and taking on challenges in one's daily practice, reflection is also essential for ensuring that participation and practice result in learning. Elkjaer (2004) argues for the third way where the two main perspectives to learning are integrated through reflection and "thinking in action", as pragmatic learning. Dewey (1938) views the individual and the social and cultural context as integrated. One may reflect on experiences, on the kind of situations that require a particular type of leadership, on events that happened and why, and so on. The point Dewey made is that it is the exploration in the context that leads to reflective thinking, which in turn leads to learning (Dewey, 1938).

Reflection for learning in practice

Reflection does not have to take place after an action was taken, and it should not be narrowed down to a question of evaluation in retrospect, for example, when police officers exercise or do training drills. Schön (1983: 62) refers to reflection both at the time an action occurs and in retrospect: *Reflection-in-action* allows for a critical evaluation of the situation.

Reflecting on an action at the time it happens gives opportunities to reconstruct and experiment in the moment, which in turn can lead to new discoveries and new experiments. This process involves more than just problem solving. The individuals act in evolving situations that they participate in themselves. They reach their goals, but why they do so may not always be clear in the process. It is usually something they realise only after the action is done. What distinguishes reflection is its immediate significance for an action. The re-evaluation leads to experimenting on site, as well as thinking further, which in turn affects the way an action evolves in a particular situation. To resolve conflicts, competent leaders can, for example, build upon the situation and the employee's reaction – they can improvise, vary, combine, explore, and test, all in order to find effective solutions to conflicts.

Reflection-on-action is reflecting on an action in retrospect in order to be able to describe it well and understand the reasoning behind it. Reflecting on previous actions provides for a dialogue between thinking and acting. A leader may in retrospect consider other actions to be a better alternative to what was done, identify missed opportunities, decide whether a conversation was different from other similar conversations, find possible reasons why the conversation went well, and so on.

Reflection is necessary for learning from experience (Newell et al., 2009). Reflection as a premise for assessing, evaluating, interpreting, and understanding actions and attitudes provides a basis for developing new understanding and new actions (Hetzner, Helmut, & Gruber, 2015). A practice perspective emphasises that reflection processes *are embedded* in the social context. Understanding reflection as a process that is embedded in a leadership practice involves regularly taking a step back to make sense of the events and experiences that the given situation gave rise to. This means disengaging from the established practice and considering other actions and perspectives, but not just for the purpose of solving problems. It is equally important to reflect upon one's thinking and actions even when things are going well. In this way, reflection becomes a collective ability to question the assumptions that are often taken for granted and that govern organisational processes and practices (Raelin, 2016).

Similar to knowledge sharing, facilitating for reflection is also the leader's responsibility. Reflection and knowledge sharing are not separated processes within a management practice. Both are important prerequisites for learning. In that sense, it is learning that needs to be facilitated for, which in turn creates opportunities for either reflection or knowledge sharing, or for both. Much of what happens in a leadership practice is based on informal relationships between a leader and their subordinates, and also between colleagues and leaders within the police organisation and other external actors. This is why informal learning constitutes a large part of the learning that occurs at all leadership levels in the police. Research indicates that communities of colleagues are particularly important in policing. This may take the form of partnerships, training, informal conversations and observations of, among others, leaders and colleagues, common sporting and social activities, common difficult and demanding experiences, frustration, joy, and so on. There are many opportunities for reflection on what goes well and not so well, hence the potential for learning.

A practice perspective highlights the importance of informal learning, not least for leaders. Informal learning is not formalised, and it takes place when the employee performs independent or collective work tasks, communicates, or observes and/or practises together with colleagues and other actors either in the workplace or in connection with work (Filstad, 2016). Because such a significant part of learning is informal, informal learning and participation in informal communities of practice can result in acquiring the "wrong" knowledge and competence. This may be the learning of political games that are undesirable, developing exclusionary professional environments, learning ineffective leadership methods or unwanted behaviour towards the public, and the like. Central to understanding a leadership practice is understanding how leaders and other employees learn, which includes what they learn (who the sources of knowledge are) and why (culture, identity, competence, sensemaking, structure, goals, politics).

How police leaders learn to lead

According to police leaders, learning to lead through practising as a leader is not facilitated enough in the police. At the same time, they find police leadership to be primarily practice-based, and they want to be hands-on in relation to their subordinates. For many police leaders, their previous experience as first-line managers meant hands-on involvement in operational practice, most often in the role of leaders who are out on operations. Many of them still consider this hands-on approach to subordinates important for their leader roles. The majority of police leaders have moved up the ranks internally, from being first-line managers to climbing the steps of the career ladder further up within the police organisation.

The Norwegian police maintains a high level of professional competence, and there are requirements for competence development in the form of continuing professional development and training. Training is mandatory for police officers to advance to the next professional level (and get a new star on the shoulder). Technical expertise in policing has been a more important factor of career advancement and higher salary than leadership skills. Many informants say that leadership has been prioritised more as part of police reform. Various leadership activities were organised, including leader meetings and training courses, the establishment of new management teams supported by HR, mentoring for female leaders, and so on. I have to clarify here that I do not have an overview of all local leadership measures that were implemented in different police districts. Based on my research, leadership activities are rarely focused on facilitating leadership development in the daily exercise of leadership, that is, facilitating for practice-based learning of leadership in the process of developing one's own leadership practice. I also found that not much is done to facilitate knowledge sharing between leaders at different levels and the establishment of leadership networks for supporting knowledge sharing.

It is usually up to the particular police leader to develop their own management practice. The same applies to reflection on one's own leadership practice, either alone or together with one's team or other leaders/external actors. Several police leaders have expressed their concern about the fact that they do not learn from each other enough and that there are few opportunities to discuss day-to-day practice with other leaders. They say that leadership courses provide opportunities to reflect upon their leadership together. They believe these courses help them understand their own leadership practice better and increase their confidence as leaders.

At the same time, police leaders are concerned with leadership education that can be applied in practice. Many also reflect on what good leadership is for them. They describe leadership as an ability to see their team members, be available for them, mean something to them, and influence their everyday routines and work tasks in a positive way. They also say that formal education in leadership gives them confidence and is an important foundation that ensures the legitimacy of their leader role. For many of them, legitimacy as a police leader is based on their policing education, and those who do not have it focus precisely on the lack of policing education. Leaders without leadership education find other ways of building up the necessary legitimacy (emphasising their leadership experience and sometimes downplaying leadership education because it can be somewhat theoretical) and highlight other qualities that can compensate for it (in other words, their perception of what is legitimate).

Another recurring idea is that many police leaders feel the need for upskilling in the form of leadership education after they have already been leaders for a while. Many of them did not receive any special training when they first became leaders. (There are some exceptions here such as mentoring programmes for female leaders.) Leaders underscore that they learn a lot from other leaders, and that leadership is all about proximity to practice and the people who are working in the field. In other words, they believe that just as the police profession is practice-based, so is the leadership of police work. Learning to lead through participation and practice can also account for the fact that many of them learn from other leaders.

Many have had a great leader who has encouraged them to try leadership, and this support and encouragement have made a difference for them. Others talk about having good leaders in the past who they have learned from and who have given them knowledge about leadership. They also mention leaders that they have observed and/or practised with who have been examples of how not to lead. Noticeably many leaders say they have been singled out and in this way encouraged to apply for their first leadership position.

They are concerned with finding a balance between theory and practice in leadership so that theory could at least provide them with some reference points and guidelines for practical work.

Here is a selection of quotes on how leaders themselves view their leadership development and learning (Filstad, Karp, & Glomseth, 2018; Filstad, 2020):

> You know, I've learnt from others – through others and through being managed by others. I feel that both in the military and in the police, I have been lucky to have skilled managers who I've looked up to, who I've learnt from, and I've had a formal education too… So you learn a little by yourself, a little from each other, and a little from the classroom.

> I think the education and the credits I have played an important part. They have given me an overview and a sense of confidence regarding the things I'm supposed to learn in this field. But getting to the point where I am today as a leader has involved gaining experience, and it's been experience-based. It's a matter of trial and error. It's about having confidence in your role. It's about feeling more secure. But I'm not saying that it is unnecessary to study leadership as a discipline, because this has at least given me confidence.

> Leadership is related to the practice field very much. How I lead today is based on formal leadership education, but a lot of it is also experience-based and comes from learning from other leaders, from the people who have been my role models and mentors up to this point.

> I have learned some leadership through studying… Otherwise, I have learned leadership from the leaders who I thought were good. I've learned by observing. And I've learned quite a lot about my own leadership (LOU2[2])… captured some ideas that suited me and the kind of person I am, because it has to fit in with me as a person too. I also think I have some role models in leadership. Otherwise, I think it is life that has taught me a lot, and I'm very concerned with some principles: honesty, justice, daring to come into conflicts.

> Leadership is a very practical subject… it is not something you can learn just by studying in the first place, but it is very practical to have some knowledge about it. So I think that the education programmes LOU1 and LOU2 have given me a lot. But it is also a very practical subject, because it is about treating people, talking to people, leading people and getting them to do what you want, setting a direction and establishing a culture; it's very complex and requires a very versatile range of knowledge, experiences, and qualities. So you know… you can study something, but most of it you just have to experience. And there is common sense, too, it is

very related to the subject. So it's hard to say how you learn to lead, it's very complex.

Yes, how do you master a leadership role? I have said it here, too, that there is a bit of a lack of support and guidance when you are starting out as a leader. I did get education in leadership and organisational development, but nobody said it would lead to anything special, there were no expectations. No special training in the systems. It's a bit of trial and error, I think. That's still the way it is.

I know you have to make yourself vulnerable, you have to be willing to see flaws and shortcomings, and address them. And I think you learn best when you do it based on your own practice.

We have no particular tradition of gathering leaders to let them talk about leadership, so I'm trying to do it with my leaders.

When I just started out, I was offered a training course for new leaders... and then you find the way as you walk... And you can be both inspired by good leaders you've had and demotivated by bad ones, right? You also have to pick up things you think work well for you or things that worked well in a particular situation. But then you have to make them your own. You cannot just copy someone.

I certainly know which of the leaders were good, who were good leaders in my experience, and I found the things they did important; and there is something about it, I think I'm trying to pass on some of it, because I have experienced their leadership as something good.

Sure, you feel more secure when you have these reference points (knowledge from leadership education), and perhaps you won't have such a hard time when you need to motivate people, give them responsibility, follow up on something, and so on. You've got these reference points and theoretical knowledge on these things, you can look it up afterwards, and you also get some feedback from the group you work with, and from studying as well, as part of collaboration and from the feedback you get there.

I was quite young when I became a leader (about 30 years old), and I remember I hesitated terribly... I spent so much time finding my role, and there was no one who could show me the way, so it was a bit like learning by doing really.

But what has taught me good leadership, is probably things that got me reflecting on how I want to come across as a leader. I've also observed many of the leaders I've had and picked up things that I found useful or thought that I should never behave like that... So I've tried to benefit from all the good people around me, and this helped me to find my way.

So I think leadership... it's actually quite lonely... There is no definitive answer here... From time to time, you need someone to give you nice feedback, it's not like everything you do is perfect all the time, so having a good network around you is absolutely crucial for a leader, I think.

These quotes demonstrate the main message of this book – leadership must be learned as practice. Police leaders gain knowledge about leadership from leadership education and training courses. This knowledge must be applied in exercising day-to-day work within a leadership practice. This is how they master leadership. Bridging the gap between knowledge that is taught in an explicit form and the way this knowledge is transformed into competence in how to exercise leadership in practice involves tacit knowledge and informal learning. Here, police leaders point out that they learn by trial and error and gain experiences that are essential for learning.

Mastering the leadership role, learning, and acquiring new knowledge and competence through experience all turn complex leadership tasks into something more manageable. Expectations play an important part in learning in the form of what leaders expect from themselves and their subordinates, what subordinates expect from leaders, and, last but not least, what "the system" expects. Police leaders learn leadership through relationships with other employees, fellow leaders, and other actors involved in the tasks to be completed. Additionally, training, courses, role models – all as part of the learning process – help a leader develop their leader identity. All of these factors combined give a good idea of how police leaders learn. Accordingly, this should be the starting point for facilitating learning of leadership in practice and understanding what type of form and content leadership courses should have.

It needs to be acknowledged that police leaders learn leadership through practising as leaders. To facilitate it, we need to address the challenges, dilemmas, trials and errors, vulnerabilities, and sensemaking of a situation-dependent and culturally determined environment in which leaders socially construct their leadership. Leadership theories, frameworks, or leadership training on their own are not sufficient. Learning leadership requires continuous and dynamic learning processes within a leadership practice.

Police leaders call for more time to discuss leadership and say that leadership is rarely part of the agenda at management team meetings, which mainly focus on discussing and resolving specific cases and problems. They emphasise the value of being able to discuss leadership with fellow leaders, having leadership networks, and having the opportunity to talk and reflect with other leaders. It is therefore argued that having access to other leaders as sources of knowledge to learn from is important. In Chapter 9, which was on knowledge sharing, I explored the importance of tacit knowledge for knowledge sharing. Knowledge sharing makes sure that competence in the organisation is not attributed to an individual police officer or leader, but instead constitutes an integrated part of police organisational competence overall. The same applies to learning. Organisational learning in the police requires that leaders and other employees learn from each other and thus share their knowledge. This is why organisational knowledge characterises the police as a learning organisation. This implies that learning and knowledge sharing are not reserved for a particular leadership practice. As a learning organisation, the police requires learning and knowledge sharing across leadership practices and between different leadership levels.

The police as a learning organisation

From a practice perspective, learning, knowledge, and competence must be understood as dynamic processes integrated into daily practice. The same view underlies the concept of a learning organisation. A learning organisation refers to the dynamic systems of an organisation that promote continuous learning to be able to respond to the demands and expectations of the environment. The notion of a learning organisation also includes prerequisites for individual learning, which can transform an organisation into an organisation that learns integrally and collectively.

The concept of a learning organisation is usually associated with the earlier contributions by Senge (1990) and Argyris and Schön (1978) – theories of single-loop learning, double-loop learning, and deutero-learning (learning to learn). Senge divides a learning organisation into five disciplines: (1) personal mastery, (2) the basis for new mental models, (3) shared vision, (4) team learning, and (5) system thinking or culture. Argyris and Schön (1978) suggest that a learning organisation implies double-loop learning. Double-loop learning occurs when basic values and assumptions are continuously evaluated and modified. To develop a learning organisation, it is necessary to reflect on the guiding values, structures, and the established truths in a culture. Single-loop learning only refers to reactive actions that are taken to avoid facing the same problems in the future, so it does not provide for the necessary learning and knowledge development in learning organisations.

Recent contributions refer to the following factors as crucial for the development of a learning organisation (Örtenblad, 2013):

1   Learning at work is based on continuous learning through practice, which means learning outside of formal courses and training. Learning is embedded in social practice and is largely dependent on knowledge sharing between employees. The focus is on informal learning, change, being direct, taking responsibility for one's actions, and integrity.
2   Organisational learning requires knowledge sharing and hence moving from the individual to the collective and the organisational. This implies that learning is embedded in an organisation's routines, common perceptions, and organisational knowledge and memory.
3   Learning climate relies on leaders who facilitate learning activities and depends on how they facilitate the development of a positive working climate that encourages and stimulates learning.
4   Learning structure refers to an organisational structure and organisational culture that makes learning possible.

A number of surveys have focused on the extent to which an organisation can be described as a learning organisation. The results of these surveys show that the higher the level of leadership, the more the leaders perceive their organisation to be a learning organisation (Borge et al., 2018).

A widely used survey that was developed by Marsick and Watkins (2003) highlights the following features of a learning organisation:

1   Creates continuous learning opportunities
2   Promotes inquiry and dialogue
3   Encourages collaboration and team learning
4   Establishes systems to capture and share learning
5   Empowers employees towards a collective learning vision
6   Connects the organisation to its environment
7   Provides strategic leadership for learning

These features formed the basis of our survey among all police employees in the autumn of 2018 (Filstad & Karp, 2018). We have also considered the differences between police districts, but there were no significant deviations. Figure 13.1 presents the responses from all employees in the police districts:

There are many employees who neither agree nor disagree, especially with "openness to the opinions of others" and "open and honest feedback". Only 26% and 35%, respectively, agree that these two statements characterise the police organisation. There is also a large proportion of employees who answer neither/nor to whether leaders facilitate learning. Only 19% agree that leaders do this, and almost half of the informants believe both that leaders do not facilitate learning and that leaders are not perceived as coaches or mentors. Many report on little time for learning and few opportunities for experiential learning. "Helping each other with learning" is the statement that scores highest in the survey. Only 7% disagree, and as many as 65% agree that this characterises the police organisation.

It is interesting to see whether the results would be different if we ask police leaders. In Figure 13.2, I have divided police leaders into those with and without personnel responsibility.

According to police leaders, they facilitate learning to a greater extent than what is signalled by the employees. However, the figures are still low for both facilitation and coaching/mentoring (about 26% agree). Leaders without personnel responsibility are more positive about time for learning than those with personnel responsibility (47% and 36%, respectively). The numbers here are considerably higher than the 27% among all employees. Police leaders agree even more than other employees that helping each other with learning characterises the police organisation. This is confirmed by 74% of police leaders without personnel responsibility and by 78% with personnel responsibility.

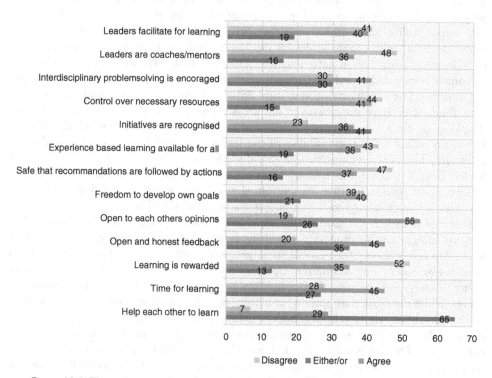

Figure 13.1 The police as a learning organisation (N=4450)

Figure 13.2 Police leaders' views about the police as a learning organisation (N=2678)

A learning organisation is premised on the concept of leadership for development. It should identify important learning opportunities for the employees and facilitate and direct the efforts for learning at all levels in the organisation. Developing a learning organisation is a demanding task that requires hard work and a common learning vision. It implies a common understanding of learning and learning processes in practical work (Filstad, 2016). The idea needs to be anchored at the senior leadership level. Senior leaders must not only make the decision to develop a learning organisation, but also give the necessary responsibility and authority to the different leadership levels. These responsibilities and authority enable leaders at the lower levels to transfer their understanding of a learning organisation into practice. The fact that 64% of police leaders with personnel responsibility believe that initiative is recognised is positive for a learning organisation, but it is worrying that only 25% think their initiatives find support, and 25% think they have control over resources. Senior leaders are not the ones who should guide their subordinates towards and facilitate learning and knowledge sharing in practice. This is the responsibility of the leadership levels below. Higher leadership levels are, however, responsible for interdisciplinary problem solving. Only 42% of leaders believe that interdisciplinary problem solving is encouraged, and only 30% of all employees agree with that. As a result, the silo mentality that was described earlier becomes a real challenge to developing a learning organisation.

First-line managers are particularly important for developing a learning organisation and for integrating learning into the daily practice of completing work tasks.[3] The leadership levels above must enable these processes, and the entire police organisation needs to be more open to different opinions and to providing feedback. Only 35% of police leaders with personnel responsibility experience openness to the opinions of others, while the figures are somewhat better (47%) for open and honest feedback. The results for these two topics are higher than among all employees (26% and 28%, respectively), but there is still significant potential in terms of developing a learning organisation. On the positive side, helping each other with learning scores high here too. The survey, however, does not take into account how the concept of learning is understood. In my field studies, I usually do not find a mutual understanding of *what learning is*. For many informants, learning is associated with training, education, courses, and experiential learning. In the police, experiential learning primarily refers to learning points resulting from specific events or training. I will take a closer look at experiential learning in the next section.

Experiential learning in the police organisation

The Finstad report refers to the concepts of experiential learning, knowledge-based experiential learning, and knowledge-based police work.[4] The report primarily focuses on special cases processed by the Norwegian Bureau for the Investigation of Police Affairs and points to the potential for learning from the assessment of possible failures in policing practice. The Finstad report suggests a new phrasing of the Bureau's mission:

> The Bureau shall pass on the experiential knowledge it acquires through the processing of individual cases that may be of interest to other divisions of the police organisation apart from the districts or special agencies that are directly affected. The Bureau shall primarily pass on the experiential knowledge to the National Police Directorate, which will decide on further actions in each individual case.

Relevant research shows that the question of values and norms associated with such cases is rarely raised, and that the established practice lacks a strategy for collective learning from these cases (Wathne, 2012).

It was largely up to an individual police leader to decide on how to follow up (or not to follow up) on the cases in their own units. As a result, instead of assessing the importance of the cases for learning within the established practice, the administrative processing and reporting on the measures was taken back to the Police Directorate. The report concluded that the experience gained from the Bureau's cases provides for a small degree of collective and organisational learning (Hoel & Bjørkelo, 2017).

Experiential learning must involve more than learning through one's own and others' experiences. It should not be narrowed down to adopting a direct solution to a problem. This would only result in a short-term solution at best — that is, single-loop learning — instead of reflecting on the basic values and perceptions of reality that underlie practice in order to find the cause of the problem, which thereby provides for double-loop learning (Argyris & Schön, 1978). In single-loop learning, the problem will repeat itself, and the organisation will only be good at solving this particular problem at the expense of other tasks, because the focus has only been placed on the actions aimed at a certain type of problem. Cautious reflection may show, for instance, that the deficient emergency response on 22 July resulted in single-loop learning in that measures and priorities, and hence the actions of the police, were unanimously directed at solving a similar problem — a new terrorist attack — and no sufficient analysis was made of what caused the problems, or most importantly, why. Within the police organisation, there is a general concern about the one-sided focus on emergency response at the expense of other important police work. The COVID-19 crisis became another major challenge for the emergency response system in Norway. This invisible enemy gives the police completely different emergency response tasks than those associated with terrorism. The two events both refer to emergency preparedness in Norway and the danger of learning by having a one-sided focus on solving the same problem as last time instead of developing an emergency response system that can tackle several unforeseen scenarios.

This does not mean that an organisation should not learn from experience. The process of establishing routines for learning through experiences is described as "systematic experiential learning". Systematic experiential learning does not only involve learning from particular incidents – it is instead about seeing the incidents in context, which means evaluating practice, systems, and cultures to reflect upon the unintentionality, prerequisites, and common perception of reality that dominate, for instance, a leadership practice. This is why experiential learning involves much more than "learning the lesson". Learning through experience, as opposed to reactive control, requires a proactive approach to identifying the problem. The Finstad report suggests that the police develops into a learning organisation where learning is embedded in the "employees' knowledge tradition and that it focuses on daily practice in the communities of colleagues". Another relevant report is the Hove report on knowledge-based experiential learning related to emergency response in the police organisation. This report uses the definition of knowledge-based police work from the Finstad report (Hove, 2014):

> Knowledge-based work in the Norwegian police is described as the systematic and methodical obtaining of relevant information and knowledge, which are analysed with the purpose of making strategic and operational decisions in relation to preventive and combative measures. Knowledge-based policing expects the police to actively relate to and apply types of knowledge other than its own experience-based knowledge.[5]

The purpose of knowledge-based policing is to combine practical experience with analytical and science-based knowledge (Gundhus, 2013). Experiential learning relies on the connections between experiences and theoretical knowledge and hence on knowledge-based experiential learning (Hove, 2014). In order for experiential learning to not be random, these connections require reflection and systematic evaluation.[6] Knowledge-based practice relies on three sources of knowledge: experience-based knowledge, research-based knowledge, and knowledge about policing from the public and from cooperation partners (Hove, 2014: 20):

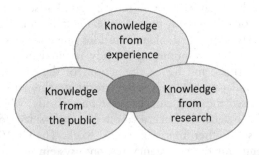

Figure 13.3 Knowledge foundation in knowledge-based experience learning (KEL)

The purpose of knowledge-based experiential learning is to develop a knowledge-based practice that relies on a systematic approach to learning through (1) planning, (2) acting, (3) reflecting, and (4) improving to apply the knowledge foundation. Furthermore, a knowledge-based practice presupposes the following:

1   Ability to transform *lessons identified* to *lessons learned*
2   Ability to use oral and written sharing platforms across organisational boundaries
3   Leaders and other employees who are able and willing to continuously improve
4   Leaders at all levels who facilitate the integration of formal and informal learning and who set clear goals, take action, and follow up on the outcome
5   An open learning culture that promotes experience and knowledge sharing, documented results, and contextual focus

The key factors of a knowledge-based practice highlighted in the Hove report refer to a strong learning culture, which is the term I use to illustrate the idea that learning must be embedded in the culture of an organisation. To sum up, I find the following factors to be central to the development of a strong learning culture (Filstad, 2016):

• Common understanding of learning, knowledge, and competence
• Continuous focus on learning, knowledge development, and knowledge sharing in practice
• Support by senior leadership
• Middle managers as facilitators and instructors
• Identification and improvement of effective learning arenas
• Differentiation between knowledge and competence
• Identification of tacit and explicit knowledge
• Facilitation of formal learning, education, and training
• Trust in and focus on knowledge development among colleagues and shared responsibility for learning and knowledge development
• Awareness of informal learning
• Infrastructure and arrangements that facilitate learning; roles: mentors, coaches, consultants
• Knowledge and learning goals that are embedded in the overall strategic goals
• REFLECTION in and upon practice

The Hove report takes a thorough look at what is important for developing a knowledge-based practice with a focus on emergency response in the police. Similar to a practice perspective on learning, a knowledge-based practice refers to how various types of knowledge find their application in practical work. However, the report emphasises the systematic aspects of learning step by step rather than acknowledging the dynamic nature of the learning processes that are integrated into daily practice. It also emphasises that informal learning is organised into a system, which, according to my findings, is not the case. Instead, it is about being aware of informal learning, facilitating for it, and encouraging it as a positive contribution to a leadership practice. I find that police reports tend to limit experiential learning to technical expertise and do not account for competence the way I described it earlier. The same also applies to police leadership. These reports largely focus on what police leadership should be and what police leaders should do, and they place less attention on how they should exercise police leadership and thereby learn leadership for the development of their leadership practices. Knowledge-based experiential learning should be more concerned with how leaders learn and how they develop knowledge-based leadership practices. Thus, knowledge-based experiential learning is an important starting point for understanding what police leaders learn, while understanding how they learn refers to the way in which they apply the knowledge-based experiences. Learning as practice refers precisely to how police leaders learn in the same way that change as practice, which is the topic of the next chapter, refers to how they learn to lead change processes in order to develop and modify leadership practices.

Notes

1 For more information on an individual cognitive approach to learning, please see Filstad (2016), Chapter 2.
2 *Translator's note*: Leadership and Organisational Development Programme.
3 For more knowledge on learning organisations, see Filstad (2016), Chapter 12 (on how to develop a strong learning culture).
4 Official Norwegian Report NOU 2009: 12. A responsible police force: openness, control and learning.
5 Official Norwegian Report NOU 2009:12. A responsible police force: openness, control and learning.
6 Official Norwegian Report NOU 2009:12. A responsible police force: openness, control and learning.

References

Argyris, C. & Schön, D.A. (Eds.) (1978). *Organizational Learning: A Theory of Action Perspective*. Reading: Addison-Wesley.
Borge, B.H., Filstad, C., Olsen, T.H., & Skogmo, P.Ø. (2018). Diverging views of the Norwegian police services as a learning organization. *The Learning Organization*, 25(6), 399–409. doi:10.1108/TLO-02-2018-0024.
Dewey, J. (1938). Experience and education. In J.A. Boydston (Ed.) (1988), *John Dewey: The Later Works*. Vol. 13. Carbondale, IL: Southern Illinois University Press.
Elkjaer, B. (2004). Organizational learning: the "third way". *Management Learning*, 35(4), 419–434.
Elkjær, B. & Wahlgren, B. (2006). Organizational learning and workplace learning: similarities and differences. In E. Antonacopoulou, P.V. Jarvis, V. Andersen, B. Elkjaer, & S. Høyrup, S. (Eds.), *Learning, Working and Living. Mapping the Terrain of Working LifeLearning* (pp. 15–32). New York: Palgrave MacMillan.
Filstad, C. (2016). *Organisasjonslæring – fra kunnskap til kompetanse* [Organisational learning – From knowledge to competence] (2nd edn). Bergen: Fagbokforlaget.
Filstad, C. (2020). *Politiledelse som praksis* [Police leadership as practice]. Bergen: Fagbokforlaget.
Filstad. C. & Karp, T. (2018). *Ledelsesimplementering, effekter og resultater av nærpolitireformen* [Leadership implementation, outcomes and results of the Norwegian Community Policing Reform]. Oslo: Politihøgskolen.
Filstad, C., Karp, T., & Glomseth, R. (2018). How police leaders learn to lead. *Policing: A Journal of Policy and Practice*. https://academic.oup.com/policing/advance-article-abstract/doi/10.1093/police/pay043/5050176.

Gotvassli, K.-Å. (2020). *Kunnskap, kunnskapsutvikling og kunnskapsledelse i organisasjoner* [Knowledge, knowledge development, and knowledge-oriented leadership in organisations]. (2nd edn). Bergen: Fagbokforlaget.

Gundhus, H.O.I. (2013). Experience or knowledge? Perspectives on new knowledge regimes and control of police professionalism. *Policing: A Journal of Policy and Practice*, 7(2), 178–194.

Hetzner, S., Helmut, H., & Gruber, H. (2015). Using workplace changes as learning opportunities: antecedents to reflection in professional work. *Journal of Workplace Learning*, 27(1), 34–50.

Hislop, D. (2013). *Knowledge Management in Organizations* (3rd edn). Oxford: Oxford University Press.

Hoel, L. & Bjørkelo, B. (2017). Kan det være godt politiarbeid? En undersøkelse av erfaringslæring av gråsonesaker [Is that good enough policing? An investigation of learning from experience of grey area cases]. *Nordisk Politiforskning*, 4(2), 187–210.

Hove, K. (2014). *Kunnskapsbasert erfaringslæring* [Knowledge-based experiential learning]. PHS Rapport. Oslo: Politihøgskolen.

Marsick, V. & Watkins, K.E. (2003). Demonstrating the value of an organization's learning culture: the dimensions of the learning organization questionnaire. *Advances in Developing Human Resources*, 5(2), 132–151.

Newell, S., Robertson, M., Scarbrough, H., & Swan, J. (2009). *Managing Knowledge Work and Innovation*. New York: Palgrave Macmillan.

NOU 2009: 12 (2009). *Et ansvarlig politi. Åpenhet, kontroll, læring* [A responsible police. Transparency, control, and training]. www.regjeringen.no/no/dokumenter/nou-2009-12/id560793.

Raelin, J.A. (Ed.) (2016). *Leadership-as-Practice: Theory and Application*. New York: Routledge.

Schön, D.A. (1983). *The Reflective Practitioner: Toward a New Design for Teaching and Learning in Professions*. New York: Basic Books.

Senge, P.M. (1990). *The Fifth Dicipline: The Art and Practice of the Learning Organisation*. Melbourne: Random House Australia.

Sfard, A. (1998). On two metaphors for learning and the dangers of choosing just one. *Educational Researcher*, 27(2), 4–13.

Wathne, C.T. (2012). The Norwegian police force: a learning organization? *Policing* 35(4), 704–722.

Örtenblad, A. (Ed.) (2013). *The Oxford Handbook of The Learning Organization*. Oxford: Oxford University Press.

Chapter 14

Change management as practice

This chapter challenges the change management literature relying on top-down control, structure and linear processes rather than acknowledging the complexity, unpredictability, and uncertainty of change. The chapter describes the change as practice perspective and outlines how this approach to change enables us to better understand the substantial resistance to police reform. The police reform represents substantial amounts of new tasks, new competence requirements, new relationships and locations, new technology, new structures, new strategies, a new identity, new power relations, and new culture(s). The main argument is that change processes are about balancing top-down and bottom-up in processes of exploration and exploitation of knowledge. And about sensemaking how to change established practice and for what reason, using all leadership levels as change agents.

Change management is demanding, complex, and requires alternative ways of leading (Kotter, 1996; Karp & Helgø, 2008; Stensaker & Haueng, 2016; Michel, By, & Burnes, 2013). It is often impossible to predict employees' reactions to changes that involve identity change and sensemaking in order to develop and transform established areas of knowledge and practice. Some consequences of changing the established leadership practices are changes to cultures, identities, belonging, competence, and manoeuvring space that must be re-established in the form of new leadership practices (By, 2005; Karp & Helgø, 2008; Vaara & Whittington, 2012).

According to change literature, around 70% of change initiatives do not deliver the expected results (Balogun & Hailey, 2004; By, 2005; Karp, 2014). Changes do take place and reforms are implemented, but because many changes "live their own lives", they often lead to something other than the initial purpose.

Change failures commonly occur in top-down structural change initiatives that do not take into account the complexity the changes entail for the people involved. This involves change control rather than change management (Mintzberg, 2009; Yukl, 2013). This process does not leave much room for viewpoints, alternative solutions, direction adjustments along the way, or taking account of any unforeseen circumstances. Because major changes are associated with uncertainty, the unforeseen will always occur. Change literature indicates that many change processes in practice are unstructured, random, and not engaging enough, and that employees are not given sufficient time to change. Additionally, the necessary space, budgets, and/or resources to implement the changes are often not provided either. Many initiatives are therefore met with more resistance than expected. The following quote illustrates this idea (Niccolò Machiavelli from *The Prince*):

DOI: 10.4324/9781003224105-20

There is nothing more difficult to carry out, nor more doubtful of success, nor more dangerous to handle, than to initiate a new order of things. For the reformer has enemies in all who profit by the old order, and only lukewarm defenders in all those who would profit by the new order.

Much attention in this chapter on change management as practice is naturally devoted to the Norwegian Community Policing Reform. It is a comprehensive and ambitious police reform that entails both structural and qualitative changes. For the vast majority of police leaders, the last 4.5 years have involved leading the reform implementation in parallel with leading daily practice. The reform has therefore taken up a significant amount of time and resources for the police leaders and their subordinates during this period, and it is still not finalised. The reform implementation involved preparing, clarifying, mobilising, caring, motivating, sensemaking, discussing, communicating, comforting, encouraging, facilitating, decision-making, and changing.

Police reform is not unique to Norway. Police reform researchers point out that more than 70% of change initiatives in policing fail (Fyfe, Terpstra, & Tops, 2013). Since a police reform occurs as a political response to a crisis of confidence, there is usually a lack of support within the police organisation. This may be the case in Norway, where the efforts of the police on 22 July 2011 have received significant criticism. The Gjørv Report emphasised that the distribution of resources was not properly coordinated that day. To some extent, the police can refute some of this criticism by saying that it did not have sufficient resources in the first place. The need for change in the police organisation was, however, nothing new. In this respect, the police reform has had a positive impact in terms of upgrading equipment and technologies, establishing the new National Police Emergency Response Centre and new operations centres, and so on. The need for change was also argued for in the Finstad report, referred to in the previous chapter. But above all, the need for change has been associated with the ever-changing criminal landscape involving an increased scale of globalisation and new forms of crime and threats.

Police leadership in the future will involve continuous change management, even without new police reforms in place. In a society that is developing and changing at an increasingly rapid rate, change management will be part of the everyday lives of all organisations. Accordingly, the police will be constantly challenged, so it needs to adapt to the ever-increasing pace of change in society. These rapid changes will challenge police leadership in new ways. They will call for police leaders who are willing to learn and good at changing their leadership practices.

International police researchers argue that future police leadership will combine administration, change, organisation, budgeting, and human resources management. Police leaders need to be able to motivate and communicate with their teams, and police leadership must be strategic, analytical, and reflective all at the same time (Flynn & Herrington, 2015; Herrington & Colvin, 2015; Martin & Mazerolle, 2015; McLeod & Herrington, 2016; Roberts et al., 2016).

As mentioned earlier, several countries have implemented police reforms. Denmark, Sweden, the Netherlands, Scotland, and England are perhaps the most natural reference points for comparison. Common traits of the police reforms include centralisation of the police and economisation of police services. An increasing political pressure is put on the effectiveness of police services, including opportunities for other actors to perform tasks that were previously reserved for the police, for example, in the field of security (Punch, 2016; Warwick et al., 2015). Police leaders must therefore undertake both operational and administrative commitments parallel with leading change in a situation where senior police leadership primarily become public guarantors of a safe and sustainable society (White & Robinson, 2014). This can also be seen in the Norwegian police service in the form of greater interdisciplinary collaboration with other important social actors. At the same time, this development leads to rather increased expectations from the police mission.

Guidelines for change?

Change processes are accompanied by a willingness to change and/or a resistance to change. The literature on organisational change focuses on resistance to change and how it can be reduced. It also suggests that change generally increases stress levels, disrupts or reduces the value of established competence, and thus challenges the leaders' and other employees' status and positioning. Since the result is often different from what was planned, major changes can also be regarded as "gambling" with the future of the organisation (Jansson, 2013). A characteristic feature of major change processes is precisely the unpredictability of the future and the way the change will be implemented. Consequently, several models of change phases and step-by-step recommendations have been developed to outline what an organisation must focus on during change processes.

The early contribution of John P. Kotter (1996) has received much attention in combination with Kotter's later contribution. The same applies to Yukl, another recognised figure in leadership research. Kotter's contribution to change management research has perhaps traditionally been the most used one. He has developed the following guidelines:

1   Create a strong idea of a change as necessary and critical.
2   Build a guiding coalition that has implementation power and the support of others.
3   Form and communicate a clear vision of the desired outcome and a flexible strategy to achieve it.
4   Communicate the vision, goals, and strategies in many ways and through multiple communication channels.
5   Empower employees to act in accordance with the change vision and remove such barriers as structures, politics, and established procedures to enable implementation, including through education and training.
6   Plan for, identify, and highlight early results, as well as short and long-term wins, and build on those in further implementation.
7   Cement the change by making new adaptations to structures, systems, and changes of practice that do not agree with the vision, in order to sustain the change process.
8   Anchor the changes in the organisation by institutionalising new attitudes and actions, and point to the connection between the change and the improvements in the new organisation.

The Norwegian Police Directorate (2017) refers to Kotter in its own guidelines for the reform process:

1   Create an understanding of the reform.
2   Establish change agent networks.

3   Develop a vision for the reform.
4   Promote commitment to change and involvement.
5   Create vigour, provide a framework, and involve the participants.
6   Do not give up.
7   Ensure that the change lasts.

However, the practice perspective on change that this book relies on does not agree with these guidelines becoming universal, that is, suitable for everyone regardless of profession, practice, culture, structure, leadership, competence, and so on. Pointing to the lasting effect of changes is problematic in the same way as desiring stability in an organisation, given that continuous change and development are going to constitute the new normal, as argued earlier.

Change management as practice

Changes involve shifting from something known to something unknown. The extent of change and the size of the unknown territory one wants to step into often depend on the understanding of reality, that is, to what degree one recognises the need for change to meet future challenges. In addition, different people in various leadership practices perceive the extent of changes differently.

A reform, however, implies large-scale changes. It involves developing new cultures in new leadership practices, which will, among other things, result in new forms of communication, power relations, identity, and values. An individual's willingness to change depends on whether the change solves a problem, and for whom. The individual must also be able to somehow envision the future situation, and it has to make sense and motivate change. Major changes must also be linked to ambitions, i.e. how hard one is willing to work for changes, and one must find support among leaders and colleagues.

The importance of sensemaking is often underestimated in change processes. Change literature has paid little attention to human processes and has largely linked change to products or services that will yield results for professional competence (Hernes & Koefoed, 2007). Changes within the reform are new tasks, new competence requirements, new relationships and locations, new technology, new structures, new strategies, a new identity, new power relations, and a new culture. Different cultures meet and begin working together, forming new management teams and new leadership practices, removing former leaders, and so on. Change processes are about giving meaning to the change itself and are therefore influenced by the individual's subjective perception of reality, and thus by the way in which employees sense/know/feel and act. These are the changes a practice perspective is concerned with, and they must be the leader's domain in a change process. Leaders and other employees have their own agenda, and change is most likely to happen when there is an overlap between the employees' agenda and the organisation's programme for change. This overlap is easier to achieve by balancing between the exploitation of the existing knowledge and the exploration of new knowledge in accordance with the reform. This balance is crucial in order for learning to occur within organisations, and hence for successful change (March, 1991).

Change literature widely agrees that the prerequisites for successful change are recognising the need for change and acknowledging that change is necessary or critical (Kotter, 1996; Stensaker & Haueng, 2016; Hennestad & Revang, 2017).

The need for change in the police

I have yet to meet police leaders who believe there is no need for change in the police. Everyone rather agrees that it is high time for changes and for the authorities to prioritise the police. Some leaders also think the police organisation should have taken action to implement the necessary changes itself, instead of waiting for a major reform to be imposed upon it. The need for change was also among the questions in the survey carried out in the autumn of 2018 (Figure 14.1).

According to the survey results, the majority of informants agree that the police should be developed into a more knowledge-driven organisation and make better use of resources. Many informants express the need for changing leadership culture and reducing the number of leaders. Leaders with personnel responsibility are the ones who, to the greatest extent, express the need for developing a more knowledge-based organisation and better utilising resources. Leaders with personnel responsibility believe to a lesser extent that there is a need to reduce the number of leaders (50%). These leaders see the need to change police leadership culture to a somewhat lesser extent, compared with the total, but their proportion is still as high as 72%. In interviews and conversations, police leaders are more nuanced in talking about changing leadership culture. Many of them are somewhat puzzled by the definitive conclusion of the Gjørv Report that there is something wrong with the leadership culture. They ask what is wrong, what exactly they, as police leaders, should change, and what the result of the changes should be. The survey confirms this sentiment in that 66% of police leaders without personnel responsibility (to the same degree as all employees) cannot make sense of how the police reform will provide for better leadership, as discussed in Chapter 10 (which was about sensemaking). Leaders with personnel responsibility are more positive, but there are still only 44% who can make sense of how to develop a new leadership culture as part of the reform.

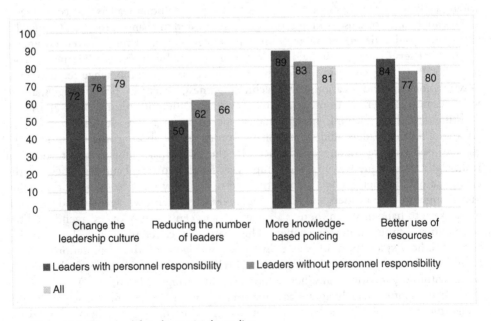

Figure 14.1 The need for change in the police

The police has extensive experience and competence in providing police services in accordance with the social mission. The reform must therefore make use of the competence that already resides in the police and balance it so as to create, construct, establish, and lead new areas of knowledge as part of organisational change processes. These processes must address the development of new ways of working and changes to be made in the established practice. These changes are not as explicit as those concerning emergency response time, unresolved cases, arrests, two police officers per 1,000 inhabitants, and the like. Instead, they are complex learning and change processes that consist of developing new competence and hence improving police services.

As mentioned earlier in this chapter, the characteristic features of change processes are, according to the Police Directorate's reform guidelines, power coalitions, empowerment of employees, and change agent networks. Leadership, however, has received little attention, and the need for changing leadership is greatly underestimated. The involvement of police leaders is crucial because they are the ones who can address the employees' established practice, identity, competencies, relationships, sensemaking, and the negotiations that are part of communication, culture, and what becomes motivation for change. It will therefore be problematic if leaders are not given the responsibility and the necessary authority in accordance with their leadership level during change processes. Figure 14.2 is based on the survey carried out 2.5 years after the beginning of the reform and shows that police leaders do not feel like they participate in decision-making processes enough.

Figure 14.2 shows that police leaders agree or strongly agree that decisions are made without them being able to influence the outcome. Many of them also believe they do not get the necessary information from the leadership level above them. Accordingly, a major challenge is the fact that they experience having broad decision-making authority. Later in this chapter, I will describe change processes in the police based on our analyses,

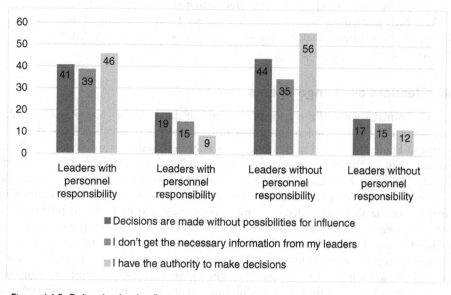

Figure 14.2 Police leaders' influence on decisions

but I will first focus a little more on the importance of competency management for the purpose of change, what police leaders think about their own role in an early phase of the reform, and why change management is so demanding.

Competent management for change

The police reform implies complex rather than linear processes where (1) knowledge is created, (2) knowledge is disseminated, (3) knowledge is implemented, and (4) knowledge is applied (Newell et al., 2009). This means that knowledge must be disseminated in order to create new knowledge, and that knowledge that is applied in turn needs to be disseminated. The dynamic aspect of these processes is crucial for successful change. For example, in order to introduce the on-site policing method, the knowledge that must be created based on the overall goals of the reform must first undergo processing, changing, adaptation, sensemaking, etc., before it can be concluded that the on-site policing method has been established. Another example is the introduction of vehicle fleet management at the operations centres. To a greater extent than on-site policing, vehicle fleet management represents new ways of working and collaborating and therefore requires the development of effective work processes and common goals and meaning. This must be anchored at all levels, and joint decision-making, common understanding, and local adaptations must be introduced in order to succeed with the new vehicle fleet management system.

These examples show why the literature on change management and innovation now places more attention on change processes than on new products and services in an organisation. The kind of processes needed for the implementation and management of these change processes are now in focus. Change processes are characterised by whether leaders and other employees "deliver results" in accordance with the reform. The dynamics of moving back and forth between creating, disseminating, implementing, and applying new knowledge in continuation of exploiting the existing knowledge has another element to it. Much of the knowledge that resides in an organisation is tacit, as described earlier. Sharing tacit knowledge occurs through common practice and/or observations. In addition, change processes are largely characterised by informal processes and involve informal groupings.

Police leaders as change agents

Leaders who make sense of the reform are aware of the need for change and are willing to do what it takes to implement the reform. Innovation, which is how the police reform can be described, can take the form of either gradual improvements and changes or radical changes that dissolve or significantly modify the established ways of working (Blackler, 2004). In both cases, knowledge sharing across different areas of professional expertise and leadership practice is necessary. Leaders must have a specific responsibility to manage and facilitate knowledge sharing. They must also prepare and motivate their subordinates, ensure they make sense of how established practices are going to be changed and developed, and overcome barriers in the form of resistance to change (which is part of all change processes). Innovation management must therefore engage all leadership levels. Leadership responsibilities across the different levels vary, but first-line managers are the most critical to the successful implementation of innovation (Newell et al., 2009; Filstad, 2016).

Police leaders' readiness for change refers to beliefs, attitudes, and intentions relating to whether reforming the police is necessary. Leaders must actively use their time, authority, and responsibility to deal with various types of resistance and encourage the willingness to change rather than just get involved when the decisions have already been made (Cinite, Duxbury, & Higgins, 2009). To function as strategic change agents, police leaders must therefore both deliver the change message and negotiate the change in relation to their own leadership practice. Change management has often been reserved for senior leadership, and middle managers have largely been reduced to change recipients instead of being intermediaries of change.

Haake and colleagues (2015) studied the implementation of the Swedish police reform and concluded that Swedish police leaders are bad change agents. Whether they can act as agents of change depends on sensemaking at the leadership levels. It also depends on the relationship between daily practice and change work, which is more challenging for police leaders the closer their leadership level is to the established practice. Another important factor is how ready for change the different leadership levels are.

Readiness for and involvement in police reform

In the early phase of the reform, police leaders said they spent much time preparing themselves and their teams for what will come (usually from the Police Directorate). They also reported having little time between the moment when decisions were made centrally and when they had to implement measures locally. Here is a selection of quotes from the police leaders in 2016 (Filstad, Karp, & Glomseth, 2018):

A success factor for implementing changes is training leaders, making sure they understand that this will be done, it will be difficult... It is difficult to change, it's very difficult. There are an incredible amount of processes involved, and with all the resistance, why people are against this, you must have strong arguments for why... the police must necessarily change as society changes. I think perhaps that's a bit of a problem with the police, that we are not good enough to evaluate... and to evolve as a result. And this is why we get these reforms forced on us.

I choose to believe that there are some opportunities in this structural reform to free up the resources so... it is possible to utilise those resources in a much better way by reducing the number of offices, getting more people doing operational work for ensuring public safety. If we believe we can solve all the problems through structural changes only, we are completely wrong.

I strongly believe in the idea of on-site policing, I believe in new technological solutions, I believe in establishing units at a functional level so that we set some standards on how to provide police services. So I do believe that this reform will help us achieve something better. And this, I think, will change my leadership, too, although I don't fully understand in what way.

I have decided to be as good a change agent as I can. I know there are many things that are problematic, it's both the goals... and the implementation that are difficult, and controlling everything I do, everything I say. I know in some forums, I can sometimes allow myself to share problems and try to find solutions, but if we want this to be a success, we must give it a chance to succeed.

I've been incredibly lucky to have been part of the reference group in the directorate for a year... I have been able to influence... We have had the opportunity, very early in the process, to start our activities before everyone else, because this was important for the district... The first challenge is that many leaders will become redundant... We will be merged with another operations centre with a completely different culture... It will be challenging for the leader... I am a little unsure on which level they believe we don't have a good leadership culture. We need leadership that dares to prioritise, dares to say what we can and cannot do.

In the reform work, I don't think we have done a good job of communicating what was so bad. There is no crisis atmosphere, no sense of urgency for change. We hear a lot about culture, a lack of leadership, a lack of control. I think it's a very general criticism of the entire police, and I don't think that everyone has taken it all in and felt it the right way, so – call it maximising the sense of crisis, which is needed to bring about a change – it is not accepted everywhere. Many say that we are ready for change... to an extent, it has been imposed on us, and I'm now very excited to see whether community policing is going to be reformed.

The challenges arise when I then go "home" and have to sell this. Everyone understands that we can not work for this money, right? I am very much in favour of the reform. What I'm afraid of is that it's too big, that it will be too much; and we already see it now: one work package comes after another, and they are now setting up working groups while the piles of cases are growing, and the situation is getting more and more serious. People who will be part of these working groups are the people who are responsible for production. And what happens then with these working groups? They won't produce results because nobody is taking over. As a result, it's going to affect the productivity, and not everyone realises that when we take something away from a place, it negatively affects everything that's left.

Some police leaders, or the districts they represent, have been involved in project pilots. According to police leaders, the New Police District Project (NPDP) and project groups at the National Police Directorate "steal" from their daily practice with all the challenges it represents. We have previously criticised the fact that such an extensive reform is implemented without supplying the police with additional resources and instead takes police employees out of their daily operations (Filstad & Karp, 2018). This is perhaps the best explanation for the low figures indicating the level of involvement in the reform, where only about 6% of all employees say they have been involved in the NPDP, project pilots, or reform planning. The figures are somewhat higher among police leaders. Almost 29% of police leaders with personnel responsibility have been involved in NPDP, and 34% have been involved in planning/project pilots. The involvement figures for police leaders without personnel responsibility are just over 19% and just under 18%, respectively.

The role of middle managers in police reform can be assessed based on whether they act as recipients or intermediaries of change. Change recipients are typically recipients of the decisions made higher up in the system. When the different leadership levels are not engaged, middle managers cannot act as agents of change. Change intermediaries, on the contrary, actively make sense of the change and influence and/or initiate a dialogue with decision-makers further up in the system, so they are therefore able to actively communicate the change to their teams and to a large extent be "carriers" of what it takes to succeed in the reform. There may be a need for a balance between the two roles – it is often not a question of either/or, but instead the balance must be created through the police leaders' sensemaking processes. They must be given the opportunity to develop sufficient manoeuvring space to ensure that other employees are adequately prepared for the reform and to prioritise the tasks that are necessary to succeed in its implementation. This is something several of the police leaders quoted above are very clear about.

At the same time, they are aware of the difficulties, not least due to the time pressure, the extent of the changes, and concerns about previous priorities because the purpose of the police reform is to equalise police services throughout the country. As a result, police leaders express several dilemmas, of which the three most prominent are: (1) the need for change versus how they should change; (2) finding a balance between tackling the reform work and daily policing when no extra resources are supplied for the reform work; and (3) following orders versus making sense of the reform and its implementation and hence changing the established practice. These dilemmas are, however, rarely addressed. This may explain the results of the survey (Figure 14.3).

Figure 14.3 (autumn 2018) shows that some of the concerns expressed by the police leaders in 2016 were justified. The figures are undoubtedly negative. The lower the leadership level, and thus the closer leaders are to the established practice, the more their negativity increases. In fact, the survey shows that leaders without personnel responsibility are somewhat more negative to the reform than the other police employees. This can quickly pose a problem to the development of new leadership practices at the level of first-line managers.

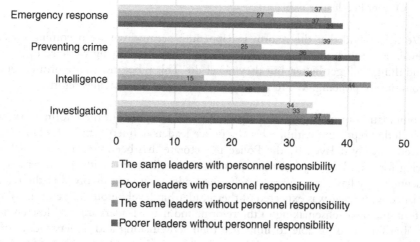

Figure 14.3 Police leaders' views about the police reform

As police leaders explain in the quotes above, certain expectations are attached to leadership during and as a result of the reform. At the same time, several leaders are concerned that they will be told what to do and will have to be loyal to the decisions made at the highest level. This effect can be quickly amplified by the fact that just over 60% of all police leaders believe they cannot influence the decisions that are made. Reference is often made to the National Police Directorate that relies on the political decisions and the overall responsibility of the Police Commissioner for the implementation of the police reform. In the police employee survey (2020), police employees were asked if they felt that the management team of the chief of police/police commissioner/ special agency/director leads the organisation in a good way. On a Likert scale from 1 to 5, the result was 3.2. This can partly be attributed to the leader-blaming culture described earlier, but the problem is perhaps more nuanced. The low level of trust in the police senior leadership can also be reinforced by the high level of trust the employees experience for their immediate manager (4.6), the immediate manager's availability (4.4), and the immediate manager's openness to input (4.3).

In 2016, only chiefs of police who led the 12 police districts were in place. The rest of the leadership positions were put into play, and the principle of rights and obligations was the basis for filling the vacancies in accordance with the new organisational chart introduced by the reform. The number of leaders was significantly reduced in most police districts, and all districts were subject to a common organisational structure based on four leadership levels.

Using the leadership levels and leaders as agents of change was therefore particularly challenging given that it was unclear who would fill the available leadership positions. Balancing between daily operations and reform work in a situation where one's own leadership position is not clarified can be particularly demanding. The reform work has also relied on limited funding, so both the reform work and daily operations had to be done within the confines of the resources and employees that the police organisation had (at least this is how the situation appeared to many police employees). Those who are involved in operational work in particular often refer to the police reform as a savings reform. One police leader explains:

> We understand that the reform is happening because we are becoming fewer and fewer, and those who quit are not replaced. They keep saying we need to be patient and things will get better, but they never do. This is because the reform is not about community policing. We're not stupid. We know it's a savings reform.

The combination of managing daily operations and carrying out the reform work, which often included reporting within what the police leaders defined as tight deadlines because they were already delayed by the Police Directorate, has been enormously challenging. Applying for a leadership job based on rights and obligations, with the uncertainty that represented, may have been a reason why the leaders were not involved in the reform in accordance with what was expected of their leadership level before the reform. All of this leads to insufficient sensemaking of the reform, and many leaders are not close enough to their subordinates to be able to influence their sensemaking and understanding of how leadership practice should be developed. The survey shows that police leaders without personnel responsibility make the least sense of the *how*, even when compared to police employees in general. They are the ones who answered that they strongly disagree or

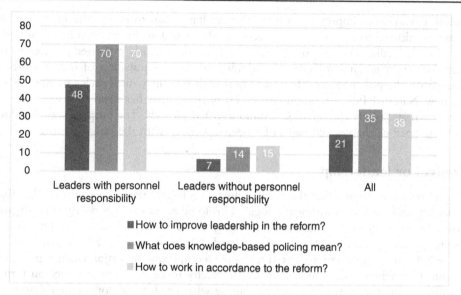

Figure 14.4 Change initiatives in the reform

disagree with the statement that it makes sense to them how the reform will provide for better leadership and how they should change their practice in accordance with the reform (Figure 14.4).

We are particularly concerned by the gap between the what and the how. If we look at the *what*, the results are somewhat more positive, but 36% of the leaders still disagree that the reform provides for better leadership, and the number is almost 56% among leaders without personnel responsibility. Leaders without personnel responsibility are also the most negative in terms of whether the reform addresses the future challenges of the police (almost 44%), compared with 25% of leaders with personnel responsibility. This negative feedback may partly be explained by the fact that first-line managers have, to a lesser extent than leaders with personnel responsibility, been counted on in the implementation of the reform. There was not much space for discussing the *how* in relation to police leadership at different levels. The how relates to leadership, and hence the expectations for each leadership level, as well as to the way leadership is learned and developed within various leadership practices. Instead, the reform implementation relied on a number of strategy and goal-setting documents stating what leadership in the police should be. Additionally, the characteristic features of the processes within the reform also have consequences for its implementation. I will focus more on these processes in the next section.

Change processes within police reform

As early as 2016, our studies of police leaders already indicated that the various measures and reports to be delivered had tight deadlines. This is why many police leaders were concerned by the fast pace of the reform, as mentioned earlier.

The time pressure limited the sensemaking of the reform implementation, as well as constructive and effective work processes. There are indications that for many police leaders, it was more important to meet the deadlines than to ensure the quality of the measures initiated to accomplish the necessary changes. This has resulted in much nega-tivity in the media, including the trade unions that have clearly expressed great concerns over both the pace and resources, in addition to the dissemination of our and others' research on the police reform. In connection with her entry into service in April 2019, the new National Police Commissioner clearly stated that her main task would be to slow down and pacify the agitation around initiated projects. The purpose was to reduce the rapid pace of change that had so far been associated with the police reform.

Control or leadership

I have previously argued that the police reform has largely relied on control rather than leadership and used an instrumental logic. This logic refers to Taylorism in that organi-sation becomes an instrument for achieving goals based on the rational approach that change processes can be planned and managed (Christensen et al., 2009). The way the police reform is governed underestimates the complexity of major change processes. "Control" is when leaders higher up the hierarchy make decisions and rely on formal instruments and top-down processes to manage what needs to be done, rather than using all leadership levels to anchor the changes. I am wary of claiming that this has solely been the case in the police.

However, I have found many examples of this approach, and it is a common percep-tion among many of the informants. NPDP has been anchored through the participants in the districts and can therefore add nuance to the overall picture. The same applies to projects and pilots that have been implemented in the districts. In the survey, just over 9% say that they have participated in the NPDP, and 6% that they have participated in planning of the reform and project pilots. Many informants come up with statements similar to that of this level 3 leader: "This reform has been dumped on our heads." At the same time, he and other leaders add that they have "been subjected to a reform because we have not been able to change ourselves". A level 2 leader puts it this way: "It is a bit embarrassing that a reform was needed, we should have addressed this a long time ago ourselves. Then we would not find ourselves in a situation where we are micro-managed and have almost no room for manoeuvre any longer."

New leadership positions

All change processes also revolve around an individual. Several leaders in the police lost their positions, were demoted, relocated, moved, etc. Others have been promoted, given greater leadership responsibilities, received new challenging tasks, or become new leaders. Behind the scenes and in informal settings, there are talks about winners and losers, and many express a sense of injustice (which is often the case in any change processes), the idea that the wrong people have been hired at the expense of others, and the like. Those who are satisfied with their new positions, work tasks, or police districts are naturally more motivated and even impatient to get started. At the same time, they have to rely on employees who might be less happy about the changes.

There might be a mixture of enjoyment and dissatisfaction, as well as a feeling of frustration at not being taken seriously. The employees might experience a lack of sui-table means to vent their frustration within the work processes or feel that they are not taken seriously. Those who came out worse off are often more sceptical and less moti-vated. They struggle to find their place, move around, and/or apply for other positions. These trade-offs are also an essential part of change processes. Such major changes come at a price, which makes it all the more important that the processes be perceived as fair, even though not everyone will be able to benefit from them. It is often reported that the staffing process, in which people with rights and obligations for particular positions were prioritised over others, has been orderly and fair, in addition to being absolutely neces-sary when changes of this scale happen in such a short time. However, there are several examples of people who benefited from the changes while others did not agree that the principle of rights and obligations had been applied correctly. There are also examples of errors in the processes that the leader failed to address before the deadline, documents that did not reach the right people, and situations when it was impossible to correct errors due to tight deadlines, so the process is not perceived as completely orderly and fair within the police. Many informants also point out that the principle of rights and obligations resulted in, as many put it, "some strange constellations". In other words, positions were not necessarily filled based on competence generally and on which parti-cular competence was needed in a particular place with the entire police organisation in mind, or what kind of competence was, for example, missing in a particular management team. A head of a unit, among other things, explains:

> I have not been given the opportunity to recruit the leaders I need based on what competence our management team is lacking as a whole. I have many leaders with the same strengths as mine, but nobody who can compensate for the weaknesses I myself have as a leader. It will therefore take time before things will straighten out.

Another factor that drew strong criticism is that leaders were the last ones to be appointed. We found this to be largely the case in the Oslo Police District (I have not investigated whether this also applies to other districts), where the leaders at different levels were appointed only after the departments had been staffed. This was the case at the operational level, so heads of departments were put in place only after the depart-ments had been formed. The same was done at the section leadership level, and finally heads of units were placed.

The criticism from many of those involved is therefore that police leaders at all levels did not have the opportunity to influence and staff their own departments and sections. Thus, leadership during the formation of sections and departments was unresolved. As a result, leadership positions at the highest level were also unresolved for a long time, and police leaders had to manage daily operations while being, as some of them say, put on pause. At the same time, they were supposed to influence the implementation of the reform in a situation where it was unclear whether they would be appointed to the leadership positions or not.

Justice

Justice and addressing ongoing issues are crucial to the success of all change processes, as research shows that the way change processes are implemented affects the motivation to do what it takes to achieve the change goals. Change processes affect everyone, including those who benefited from them, because they see that their competent colleagues are not treated with the respect they think they deserve. What prevents successful change is, as shown earlier, insufficient time, space, budget, and resources, and the fact that the needs, identity, and power that are being challenged are not adequately addressed. The latter is not talked about much, and there are complex structures and contexts in play that result in uncertainty, unexpected turns of events, and initiatives taking alternative directions. This can be illustrated by local adaptations when police leaders create manoeuvring space to develop their own practice and set priorities of their own that might be at variance with the reform. The extreme consequence could be that this behaviour becomes a way of opposing oneself to a police reform that one does not agree with.

Major change processes are often characterised by the experience of grief and loss, even among those who benefited from the changes. A large proportion of districts and units are now consolidated, which results in new geographical units, new colleagues, new working environments, and in many cases larger geographical units and fewer leaders; the police reform has also increased the extent of remote management. This has mainly resulted in a larger number of subordinates per police leader overall. Since the structural reform has been given the most attention, staffing the police in accordance with organisational charts has come at the expense of the people involved. This means that the informants are unable to identify any work processes or arenas for allowing people to get to know each other, developing new working environments or new management teams, participating in relocation processes, establishing new sections and departments at new duty stations, and so on. Although leadership meetings and training courses have made a positive contribution, they were primarily reserved for level 2 and level 3 leaders. It is also important to ensure that different cultures from former police stations meet and develop a new culture together, instead of allowing the previous cultures to strengthen by turning into typical subcultures within the new organisation. It has largely been up to the individual police leader to address these issues, which is complicated by the busyness of daily work life and balancing between daily practice and reform work. This is perhaps where the challenge of carrying out reform work while simultaneously tackling daily operations is most visible.

The lack of time and resources meant that not much could be done to facilitate the development of new working environments, so the people who had previously worked together quickly formed subcultures within the new organisation. This may be the reason why the employees of patrol sections do not want to move elsewhere, and their leader promises to fight for this at the higher levels of the system. This also explains why employees of former units are referred to as cowboys, and a geographical area is referred to as "bestfold", as mentioned earlier. In his book, Økland (2017) writes about the situation in the Norwegian police service and emphasises that there is much competition. This competition can often be expressed in a friendly way, but we also find that the districts that are now consolidated have previously competed for resources, ways to solve work tasks, and so on.

The need to find ways of working together and make use of the previous working methods to provide even better police services deserves special attention as an essential step in the development of the police. If this is not properly done, which is the case in many change processes, former cultures will be reinforced, previous practices romanticised, and the differences will become even greater and will complicate the development of new working communities as a result.

Consolidation and joint decision-making

Benefiting from consolidation processes is largely based on sharing knowledge and experience. Many people are surprised at how differently they have worked while performing the same tasks. The different geographical areas have largely found their way of working, and with a greater degree of openness, trust, and not least, time, they should be able to benefit from each other's differences while pursuing the common goal of exercising good policing. Instead, we find that many informants find that their voices are not being heard and that they are not involved in projects and special units that are set up in areas where they have a great deal of expertise. As a result, the new organisation does not necessarily benefit from the competence developed over a long time, which is obviously demotivating for those who possess that competence.

A recurring idea expressed by many informants is that they are not being heard and that decisions are made "behind the closed doors of the Police Directorate offices". We believe this is partly due to a lack of knowledge about how the National Police Directorate works. The lack of knowledge can quickly result in what professor of criminology Nils Christie describes as "the good enemy". Everything that goes wrong is attributed to the Police Directorate and the reform instead of distinguishing between the results of the reform and things that have nothing to do with it, which, according to our studies, many chiefs of police and police leaders pay particular attention to. Again, we believe that this is a matter of participation but also that police employees must take part of the responsibility.

The fact that many people are getting involved, writing posts, coming up with counter-arguments, and engaging in discussions is absolutely crucial for the reform to succeed. Such a major reform will undoubtedly include many opinions and disagreements on how to tackle various challenges. There will never be one perfect formula, but when the parties are strongly opposed to each other, which we find some examples of, it is important to find a way around protecting one's territory and to try to look at the situation from different perspectives. We see some examples of protecting one's own role, including in the actual implementation. Many are dissatisfied with the fact that those who participated in the NPDP are now fighting too much for the solutions they have developed rather than being responsive to adjustments, adaptations, and new solution proposals. In our experience, this dissatisfaction is in many ways justified as such leaders say that other employees need to stop complaining, try to see the big picture, and stop thinking only about themselves. The fact that there are conflicting voices within the reform can create an unnecessary gap between the people who were more in the position to influence decision-making and those who were not, now that they have to work side by side. Being heard or not being heard, which many believe is the case for them, also results in insufficient sensemaking of how decisions and measures can be translated into daily practice.

Those who are closest to or directly involved in practice strongly believe that the reform was initiated only to save money, as mentioned earlier in this chapter. They are often very critical of the fact that decision-makers do not know what practical policing really is or what police officers encounter in their daily work. They do not feel that the headlines stating there are now more people in the police reflect the reality. Quite the opposite – several patrol sections, among others, are struggling to get more staff. They call for minimum staffing standards similar to the Norwegian Armed Forces. They also say that on top of everything many of the resources are supplied "if it gets out of control". They explain that no one does ordinary police work anymore – everyone is getting specialised and taking courses for that, which means many people are off duty and too few cases are completed out in the field. They are immediately released to stand ready if "it gets out of control".

Structure and quality

Dividing the Norwegian Community Policing Reform into a structural reform and a qualitative reform may have been unfortunate because the structural part is concrete and explicit. It can operate with concrete actions, with the number of things that are in place, with what has been done, and with what remains, especially in view of reporting progress to political authorities. However, it is the qualitative reform that focuses on the *how* and thus on the quality of the police services in the implementation of the reform. It focuses attention on how the new and robust professional environments are to be developed and how to cultivate effective interdisciplinary forms of collaboration to address the six prioritised target areas and develop a more knowledge-based, learning police organisation.

The structural part has focused on organising generally and on ensuring the new joint organisation of police districts – filling in the new "boxes" with employees and leaders, in addition to equipment and technology. An almost identical organisational chart was drafted for each police district with sections and departments in accordance with the four main areas of expertise: patrolling, intelligence, investigation, and crime prevention. Police stations and sheriffs' offices were closed down or merged into larger geographical operating units (GDEs) and police contact personnel were appointed. The common priorities for the four main areas of expertise are: establishing a common intake office for criminal cases, strengthening the operations centres, and establishing and developing a shared services centre. A number of joint function agencies were maintained or established to ensure centralised coordination and technical expertise at the level of the entire police district, such as FOT (Common Unit for Operational Service), FEE (Common Unit for Intelligence and Investigation), FKE (Common Criminal Unit), FUF (Common Unit for Immigration and Administration), FNB (Common Unit for National Aid Resources), FF (Common Unit for Crime Prevention), FP (Common Unit for Prosecution), and FSR (Common Unit for Civil Justice).

The number of leaders was reduced in accordance with the common organisational chart based on four leadership levels: chiefs of police, heads of geographical operating units, heads of sections, and heads of departments. All of the above can be considered part of the structural reform, and the police clearly signalled, especially in the autumn of 2018, that it was high time to prioritise putting the new organisational structure into operation. If the qualitative reform had happened in parallel with the structural changes, instead of largely following them, it would have allowed for greater opportunities to make quality adjustments and ensure effective work processes in the new organisation. The focus might have been placed on delivering the best possible interdisciplinary and knowledge-based police services and, to a greater extent, involving the employees in the implementation of the structural reform. It could have also provided opportunities for greater adjustments that we are observing a need for in retrospect, and, as we can see, the idea of a unified police and almost identical organisational structure has proved to be challenging. It has now become more obvious that the "one size fits all" approach does not result in optimal solutions. It may also be reasonable to think that parallel reform would have opened more opportunities for exploiting the competence that the police already had, in the light of developing new competence as required by the reform. It would have taken more time, and not all of the changes would have been possible to implement simultaneously. At the same time, the very concerns that many of the measures and changes occurred simultaneously, and related concerns about having enough time to develop good solutions, would have been addressed. In other words, it seems that the pace and the focus on structural changes rather than quality deprived the police organisation of the opportunity to make greater use of the competence it already possessed. Three informants explain:

> Why reinvent the wheel? Nobody is interested in what we have achieved before. Instead, we have to shelve all of it, and then it's too late, or there is an increase in crime in the area.

> The entire management team has run a police district before, and we were good at it. It's as if our competence does not matter. Now we just have to adapt to the way it's done here.

> There was no point in protesting. We were told that everything had to be tested first. There was no room for us to use our knowledge. It felt like being strangers in our own home. It was very unclear what we were going to achieve – only empty rhetoric – nothing concrete. It feels so good that we finally have a say in the matter!

Resistance?

Major change processes are driven by subjectivity and people with different perceptions of reality, so they are neither rational nor objective (Jacobsen, 2018). Changes therefore involve resistance, including the kind of resistance that is positive because change initiatives can rely on limited knowledge, can be poorly justified, or can be difficult to implement. Resistance enables discussion and input. A reform that relies on loyalty to the decisions made and limited opportunities for adjustments along the way, which is the case of the structural reform, among other things, results in the following:

> I think we have got an organisation that in many ways is similar to what they have in Oslo, but we do not have enough resources to fulfil all the functions. To do that, we need to relocate the resources from other parts of the organisation. As a result, the resources are thinly spread everywhere.

> The challenge now, when we have become a larger organisation, is that many of the joint functions are consolidated with other districts… So if I want a more cost-effective system, I need a centralised decision to be made at a higher level in the organisation.

A project manager in the NPDP explains:

> The leaders were strongly affected by the changes, but they continued to take care of and reassure their teams. Other leaders, who were not as affected by the changes themselves, did their best to make their teams aware of how badly they had been treated.

Either acceptance or resistance can be based on professional agreement or disagreement, where it is argued that the new way of organising has not been adequately adjusted to all districts or geographical units to ensure effective police services. Fear of the unknown and dramatic changes for an individual in the form of a possible job loss, stress over the significant amount of extra work involved in all change processes, and loss of identity, position, social relationships, psychological contracts, and so on, are all essential aspects of all change processes (Jacobsen, 2018). Essentially, it has only been a year and a half since the structural reform was established, and the majority of the available leadership positions were filled only a year before that. When the structural reform was considered to be complete, the people involved in NPDP were largely placed back in service. Accordingly, the qualitative reform is still in its early phase, and the idea of giving the police reform a chance to prove itself, which was especially persistent among police leaders in autumn 2018, is still argued for today.

It appears that the time prior to 2018 was marked by fairly chaotic manifestations involving grief, anger, counteraction, and frustration among those who felt left behind and unappreciated, as well as professional disagreements, etc., while also involving motivation, engagement, and determination among those who were given desired positions as part of the reform. The autumn 2019 study provides an even more honest representation of how tough it was the year before, with the reactions ranging from grief and resignation among leaders to loud arguments and turning professional disagreements into personal attacks within new management teams, and so on. The last year involved getting to know new colleagues, establishing new management teams and units, and developing effective work processes and forms of collaboration. Many informants say that the situation has improved, but there is still a lot of hard work ahead. The improvements are also visible in practice: there are more discussions about interdisciplinary collaboration, and more attention is paid to the entire organisation by highlighting professional areas that were harmed by having lost a disproportionate amount of resources and by overcoming the boundaries not only between professional areas, but also between units and joint function agencies within those areas.

Informants express positivity, the desire to make use of everything that has been achieved through this tough process, and the optimism that the police themselves now "own" the reform and accordingly have more opportunities to influence quality in the future. They point out that the six prioritised functions have now been established and given time to start working, and that the focus on the target areas, and the resources that have been supplied accordingly, have resulted in many positive experiences. (I will return to this topic later in the discussion.) According to my findings, however, the important clarifications and decisions in the future are going to be made in relation to the interdisciplinary work and collaboration, to a plan for utilising resources in the police organisation as a whole, and, not least, to how the police can take the required manoeuvring space for making the necessary priorities for the future. This will be the responsibility of the police leaders and should involve all leadership levels, since many informants express an idea similar to this police employee:

> It still feels like we are waiting for something. We are waiting for someone to say something, for someone to do something... I hope there will be more action and that the necessary decisions will be made.

I have explored many issues in this chapter on change as practice based on the Norwegian Community Policing Reform, and I would like to briefly summarise the points that (according to my research) have been critical to leadership of the reform and the features that distinguish the change processes. The reform implementation is dominated by control rather than leadership, which has led to much negativity and a lack of sensemaking. Police leaders at all levels have hardly acted as change agents and thus have not been able to address the other employees' reactions to the changes and motivate them. Among other things, this has led many police employees and leaders to believe that their competence has not been used or appreciated in the development of new police services, which is absolutely essential for effective change processes.

The structural reform was more extensive than expected, according to the people responsible, so it took significantly longer than planned. As a result, it was the structural reform that brought about the major changes until the autumn of 2019. A better balance between the structural reform and the qualitative reform could have resulted in a greater sense of belonging, ownership, and sensemaking, because the focus of the qualitative reform is on work processes, forms of collaboration, the provision of police services, resource utilisation, competence, and changes in accordance with the six prioritised professional areas. In many ways, the qualitative reform was in the background until 2018. This is why the entire police reform is not yet completed. Many informants also point out that there is still a lot of hard work ahead. There is a great potential for developing effective forms of interdisciplinary collaboration between units and special units, overcoming boundaries between professional domains, further enhancing management teams and management forms, and developing leadership levels, new common cultures, and so on. This is a very demanding task for police leaders going forward, not least in terms of resources, since on the one hand, it is considered the leader's responsibility to make better use of resources, but on the other hand, the police is said to have never had so few resources.

The fact that the police reform has relied on leadership only to a limited extent makes it hard to use the leadership of the reform as an example of what is expected from police leaders in the future, especially with regard to their responsibility for change management. Accordingly, we found three main constraints to the reform's aim to change the leadership culture in the police. One is the poor balance between the exploitation of the leadership competence acquired by police leaders through practice and experience and the exploration of what competent and "good-enough" leadership means for the police in the future. The second constraint is facilitating learning to lead in the process of practising leadership and understanding that leadership is about developing leadership practices. The third constraint is the insufficient focus on barriers and motivators for good leadership practice in the police.

References

Balogun, J. & Hailey, V.H. (2004). *Exploring Strategic Change* (2nd edn). London: Prentice Hall.

Blackler, F. (2004). Knowledge, knowledge work and organizations: an overview and interpretation. In K. Starkey, S. Tempest, & A. McKinlay (Eds.), *How Organizations Learn: Managing the Search for Knowledge* (pp. 339–362) (2nd edn). Hampshire: Cengage Learning.

By, R.T. (2005). Organisational change management: a critical review. *Journal of Change Management*, 5(4), 369–380.

Christensen, T., Lægreid, P., Roness, P., & Røvik, K. (2009). *Organisasjonsteori for offentlig sektor* [Organisation theory for public sector]. Oslo: Universitetsforlaget.

Cinite, I., Duxbury, L.E., & Higgins, C. (2009). Measurement of perceived organizational readiness for change in the public sector. *British Journal of Management*, 20(2), 265–277.

Filstad, C. (2016). *Organisasjonslæring – fra kunnskap til kompetanse* [Organisational learning – From knowledge to competence] (2nd edn). Bergen: Fagbokforlaget.

Filstad. C. & Karp, T. (2018). *Ledelsesimplementering, effekter og resultater av nærpolitireformen* [Leadership implementation, outcomes and results of the Norwegian Community Policing Reform]. Oslo: Politihøgskolen.

Filstad, C., Karp, T., & Glomseth, R. (2018). How police leaders learn to lead. *Policing: A Journal of Policy and Practice*. https://academic.oup.com/policing/advance-article-abstract/doi/10.1093/police/pay043/5050176.

Flynn, E.A. & Herrington, V. (2015). *Towards a Profession of Police Leadership: New Perspectives in Policing Bulletin*. Washington: Department of Justice, National Institute of Justice (pp. 1–18).

Fyfe, N.R., Terpstra, J., & Tops, P. (2013). *Centralizing Forces? Comparative Perspectives on Contemporary Police Reform in Northern and Western Europe*. Haag: Eleven International Publishing.

Haake, U., Rantatalo, O., & Lindberg, O. (2015). Police leaders make poor change agents: leadership practice in the face of a major organisational reform. *Policing and Society: An International Journal of Research and Policy*, 27(7), 764–778.

Hennestad, B.W. & Revang, Ø. (2017). *Endringsledelse og ledelsesendring – fra plan til praksis* [Managing change and changing management – from plan to practice] (3rd edn). Oslo: Universitetsforlaget.

Hernes, T. & Koefoed, A.L. (Eds.) (2007) *Innovasjonsprosesser: Om innovasjonens odyssé* [Innovation processes: about the odyssey of innovations]. Bergen: Fagbokforlaget.

Herrington, V. & Colvin, A. (2015). Police leadership for complex times. *Policing*, 10(1), 7–16.

Jacobsen, D.I. (2018). *Organisasjonsendringer og endringsledelse* [Organisational change and change management] (3rd edn). Bergen: Fagbokforlaget.

Jansson, N. (2013). Organizational change as practice: a critical analysis. *Journal of Organizational Change Management*, 26(6), 1003–1019.

Karp, T. (2014). *Endringer i organisasjoner. Ideologi, teori og praksis* [Changes in organisations. Ideology, theory, and practice]. Oslo: Cappelen Damm.

Karp, T. & Helgø, T.I.T. (2008). From change management to change leadership: embracing chaotic change in public service organizations. *Journal of Change Management*, 8(1), 85–96.

Kotter, J.P. (1996). *Leading Change*. Boston: Harvard Business School Press.

March, J.G. (1991). Exploration and exploitation in organizational learning. *Organizational Science*, 2(1), 71–87.

Martin, P. & Mazerolle, L. (2015). Police leadership in fostering evidence-based agency reform. *Policing*, 10(1), 34–43.

McLeod, A. & Herrington, V. (2016). Fostering police leadership capacity in Solomon Islands: understanding the challenges to organizational reform. *Policing*, 10(1), 44–54.

Michel, A., By, R.T., & Burnes, B. (2013). The limitations of dispositional resistance in relation to organizational change. *Management Decision*, 51(4), 761–780.

Mintzberg, H. (2009). *Managing*. San Francisco: Berrett-Koehler Publishers.

Newell, S., Robertson, M., Scarbrough, H., & Swan, J. (2009). *Managing Knowledge Work and Innovation*. New York: Palgrave Macmillan.

Police Directorate [Politidirektoratet] (2017). *Politiet mot 2025. Politiets virksomhetsstrategi. POD-publikasjon 2017/18* [Towards 2025 – the police's organisational strategy. The National Police Directorate's publication 2017/18]. www.politiet.no/globalassets/05-om-oss/03-strategier-og-p laner/politiet-mot-2025—politiets-virksomhetsstrategi.pdf.

Punch, M. (2016). *Challenges for Police Leadership*, Presentation at Police Researchers Meet Practitioners: Leadership within the Police. Conference 10–12 May 2016. Linnaeus University, Sweden.

Roberts, K., Herrington, V., Warwick, J., White, J., & Day, D. (2016). Police leadership in 2045: the value of education in developing leadership. *Policing*, 10(1), 26–33.

Stensaker, I. & Haueng, A.C. (2016). *Omstilling – Den uforutsigbare gjennomføringsfasen* [Reorganisation – the unpredictable implementation phase]. Bergen: Fagbokforlaget.

Vaara, E. & Whittington, R. (2012). Strategy-as-practice: taking social practices seriously. *The Academy of Management Annals*, 6(1), 285–336. doi:10.1080/19416520.2012.672039.

Warwick, J; van Dijk, A., Hoogewoning, F., & Punch, M. (2015). What matters in policing? Change, values and leadership in turbulent times. *Policing: A Journal of Policy and Practice*, 10(1), 56–57.

White, V. & Robinson, S. (2014). Leading change in policing: police culture and the psychological contract. *The Police Journal*, 87, 258–269. doi:10.1350/pojo.2014.87.4.675.

Yukl, G. (2013). *Leadership in Organizations* (8th edn). Boston: Pearson.

Økland, S. (2017). *Norske tilstander. Bak frontlinjen i Norges tøffeste politidistrikt* [The Norwegian situation. Behind the frontline of the toughest police district in Norway]. Oslo: Gyldendal.

Chapter 15

Summary

In my view, a leadership-as-practice perspective contributes to better understanding of and gaining more knowledge on police leadership. This perspective addresses the complexity of leadership and multiple factors that influence it. This holistic understanding is key to gaining knowledge on what promotes and inhibits police leadership, that is, the characteristic features of structural and cultural conditions, strategies and performance management, competence, power relations, and manoeuvring space. Police leaders develop their leadership practices within these dynamics, which is why this approach does not focus exclusively on an individual leader. Instead, a leadership-as-practice perspective on police leadership challenges the established leadership literature by shifting the attention to the dynamic, relational, situation- and context-dependent nature of leadership practices, and to identity formation, development of manoeuvring space, and sensemaking within those practices.

Accordingly, leadership practices refer to collectivity, common work tasks and attitudes, and common competence, since the focus is on collective participation rather than on an individual police leader or other employee. The concept also refers to the interdependency between different leadership practices in the police, and what should be done to reduce the knowledge barriers between them. The dynamic and evolving nature of leadership practices is also evident from the continuous learning and change processes that occur in daily practice and consist of producing, practising, relating, identifying, sensemaking, and negotiating, which are understood as verbs rather than as static concepts. The strength of this perspective is that it broadens our horizons in terms of understanding strategy as practice. For example, it explains how goals and strategies are enabled or constrained by a network of leadership practices in the police.

Another strength is the awareness of the need for a close connection between different leadership practices to enable learning and change. Approaching learning as practice, change as practice, and change management as practice contributes to this awareness.

I believe that my overview model, which I consistently use throughout this book, does a fair job of visualising what needs to be studied to increase our knowledge on police leadership as practice. The structure of the model demonstrates how integrated various conditions and concepts are with one another. In accordance with a leadership-as-practice perspective, the model also highlights the importance of informal relationships and informal communities of practice to understanding police leadership as practice.

DOI: 10.4324/9781003224105-21

Figure 15.1 Police leadership as practice model

The model serves its purpose by emphasising the four main processes that are essential to understanding leadership as practice in general and police leadership in particular: strategies, community, participation, and activities. Strategic processes refer to profession-specific features – that is, what distinguishes the police and its social mission. To accomplish the social mission, the police relies on an organisation and structure that are in place to achieve the strategic goals which are appropriate at any given moment in view of an increasingly complex criminal landscape. Strategic leadership is affected by this process and hence by the opportunities that exist for its development within the police at different leadership levels. It is therefore important to identify possible barriers to strategic leadership in order to strengthen its contributing factors. This is absolutely crucial to the development of good leadership practices in the police and of the community they represent. Community in leadership practices largely involves developing a positive culture, identity, sense of belonging, and competence that promote good policing in the best way possible. Participation within the community that leadership practices represent therefore depends on sensemaking, manoeuvring space, and on being active participants, not passive recipients, in the game of politics that is inherent to all leadership practices.

Sensemaking is important in order for leadership practices to be proactive in the continuous development of the required manoeuvring space, which in turn leads to participation in negotiations and positioning for the most competent police services. This proactivity enables learning and change, which are essential for a leadership practice, not least in the form of interdisciplinary collaboration, and thus knowledge sharing, across different practices. Therefore, police leadership as practice must focus on the interconnectedness of these four main processes, where the complexity lies in the factors that affect, and become crucial for, the development of police leadership as practice.

I will not repeat the points that have already been thoroughly explored in the parts of the book on community, participation, strategy, and activities. Instead, since this is a research-based book, I would like to conclude by reflecting on possible barriers and motivators for the development of good police leadership – that is, the factors that influence and either promote or inhibit leadership development the most – and the ways in which police leaders learn to lead by practising.

The Norwegian Policing Reform emphasises leadership courses and training as a means of changing leadership culture in the police. These measures have played an important part in placing leadership as a discipline on the agenda and bringing attention to the fact that the processes of leadership development and learning are not up to an individual leader. There are three constraints when it comes to the increased focus on police leadership. One is that the leadership competence acquired by police leaders through practice and experience is not exploited enough in the process of exploring what competent and "good-enough" leadership means for the police in the future. The second constraint is that learning to lead through the practical exercise of leadership is poorly facilitated, and there is a lack of understanding that leadership is more about developing leadership practices than it is about an individual leader. The third constraint is the insufficient focus on barriers and motivators for good police leadership and on the extent of the changes that are made by removing or reducing barriers and encouraging and further developing motivators. In short, it is worth reflecting on the following:

Leadership culture. Police leaders are loyal and, as with the rest of the police, good at adapting when "things get tough". They are capable of doing their best based on "the tools they've got" which is an expression I have heard from many informants. Police leaders lead primarily because they are skilful, they master leadership tasks, and they are good at organising the day-to-day business of policing. There are many examples of good leadership in the police organisation, and many leaders are concerned with attending to and being available for their team. They would rather engage in leadership training and learn through the experience of leading than follow some leadership formulas. They call for greater facilitation of such learning in daily practice. Leadership is rarely in focus at management meetings or in similar arenas, so police leadership becomes something an individual has to figure out for themselves, including by being singled out within informal networks.

Performance management. Performance management in the police organisation does not line up with police reform well enough. Many police leaders believe that the objectives set by performance management have little to do with quality and good policing. This is why they rarely attempt to break it down to what we find should be competence objectives, which an individual leader is responsible for anchoring in their leadership practice. Accordingly, there is potential in exploring the balance between performance management and competence objectives, and the way in which performance management can be integrated as part of the adaptable competence objectives, both quantitative and qualitative.

Manoeuvring space. Manoeuvring space is important for police leadership and constitutes its most essential part. Manoeuvring space must be created within a leadership practice and is more than a question of money and resources. Room for manoeuvre is created through continuous, locally adapted, and dynamic processes. Police leadership requires manoeuvring space, and there is potential for making it part of the agenda instead of attributing it exclusively to power and politics, where it is rather concealed. The potential here is large, not least because there are indications that manoeuvring space has significantly shrunk during the police reform.

Competence. The level of professional competence in the Norwegian police service is very high. The police is also characterised by intrinsically motivated employees who are willing to do their best to accomplish the social mission. It is therefore important to exploit this competence in the best way possible and create a space for enabling this process. Police officers must have trust in the competence they possess when facing changes, and it should be clear to them what good change initiatives are. As the police reform primarily focuses on specialisation and emergency response, it is the leader's responsibility to attend to generalists and their role in the police in the future.

Leadership contexts. Police leaders balance between an instrumental logic that mostly takes the form of control, and a cultural logic that is typically applied locally, and thus they also balance between different expectations for leadership. These are often conflicting dilemmas, and police leadership mostly involves balancing the two types of logic rather than choosing one at the expense of the other. Being adaptable and loyal can result in police leaders who largely rely on the instrumental logic, which can also lead to them taking on a victim role. Police leaders who balance the two types of logic and tailor them to the development of their leadership practices are to a greater extent actors in their own leadership. We want to avoid speculating on the extent to which one logic dominates over the other, but because the reform heavily relies on control, especially in its structural aspects, there is the potential for an expansion of leadership's role in developing the police according to the qualitative reform.

Leadership of police services. Here, according to our findings, the future challenge lies in both interdisciplinary collaboration and control over and utilisation of resources with the entire organisation in mind. There are many constraining factors in that respect. For example, work processes for better use of resources must be developed. In addition, the police reform provides fewer resources than before, although some might disagree. The Norwegian police service is also part of the reform aimed at reducing the bureaucratisation that is implemented in all public sector organisations. We have observed a greater degree of silo mentality during the police reform; many informants point out that they were better at collaborating and helping each other before. Another factor to consider is an increase in work pressure, standardisation processes, and reporting. Accordingly, potential lies in the qualitative reform, where we observe active work processes that address these issues at all leadership levels and in management dialogues.

Leadership levels. Finally, the discussion revolves around exploiting the competence that police leaders have and identifying the forms of police leadership that are demanded of the police in the future. The greatest potential we see in the qualitative reform is including level 4 leaders in the process and ensuring that they largely identify themselves as part of leadership. They lead at the operational level, which is different from the forms of leadership exercised at other leadership levels. We believe that important discussions in the future will focus on the role of level 4 leaders. The same applies to remote management. It will also be important to discuss which leadership levels should be strategic and tactical, as we now observe that a large part of police leadership is exercised at a tactical level. What constitutes strategic leadership, and thus what the expectations for strategic decisions are, cannot be expressed in a formula, and police leaders will need to address several leadership levels. At the same time, it is important to clarify expectations for the different levels of leadership and for understanding strategic leadership in a politically controlled organisation like the police.

Index

Page numbers in *italic* refer to figures, page numbers in **bold** refer to tables.

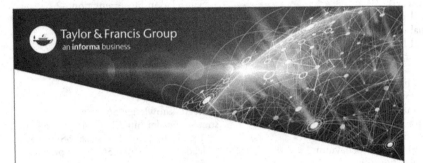

Printed in the United States
by Baker & Taylor Publisher Services